WORK PLACEMENTS, INTERNSHIPS & APPLIED SOCIAL RESEARCH

Sara Miller McCune founded SAGE Publishing in 1965 to support the dissemination of usable knowledge and educate a global community. SAGE publishes more than 1000 journals and over 800 new books each year, spanning a wide range of subject areas. Our growing selection of library products includes archives, data, case studies and video. SAGE remains majority owned by our founder and after her lifetime will become owned by a charitable trust that secures the company's continued independence.

Los Angeles | London | New Delhi | Singapore | Washington DC | Melbourne

JACKIE CARTER

WORK PLACEMENTS, INTERNSHIPS & APPLIED SOCIAL RESEARCH

⑤SAGE

Los Angeles | London | New Delhi
Singapore | Washington DC | Melbourne

Los Angeles | London | New Delhi
Singapore | Washington DC | Melbourne

SAGE Publications Ltd
1 Oliver's Yard
55 City Road
London EC1Y 1SP

SAGE Publications Inc.
2455 Teller Road
Thousand Oaks, California 91320

SAGE Publications India Pvt Ltd
B 1/I 1 Mohan Cooperative Industrial Area
Mathura Road
New Delhi 110 044

SAGE Publications Asia-Pacific Pte Ltd
3 Church Street
#10-04 Samsung Hub
Singapore 049483

First published 2021

Editor: Jai Seaman
Assistant editor: Charlotte Bush
Production editor: Victoria Nicholas
Marketing manager: Ben Sherwood
Cover design: Shaun Mercier
Typeset by: C&M Digitals (P) Ltd, Chennai, India
Printed in the UK

Library of Congress Control Number: 2020945728

British Library Cataloguing in Publication data

A catalogue record for this book is available from the British Library

ISBN 978-1-4739-8231-4
ISBN 978-1-4739-8232-1 (pbk)

At SAGE we take sustainability seriously. Most of our products are printed in the UK using responsibly sourced papers and boards. When we print overseas we ensure sustainable papers are used as measured by the PREPS grading system. We undertake an annual audit to monitor our sustainability.

For Huw and Isla – my firstborn child and grandchild

CONTENTS

LIST OF CASE STUDIES

LIST OF TABLES

LIST OF FIGURES

ABOUT THE AUTHOR

Jackie Carter is a Professor of Statistical Literacy at the University of Manchester. She co-directs the Q-Step Centre at the University of Manchester and leads the programme of paid internships which she established in 2013. In 2020 she was awarded a National Teaching Fellowship by Advance HE, the UK professional body that oversees teaching and learning in Higher Education, for her work on making an outstanding impact on student outcomes and the teaching profession in Higher Education. In the same year, Jackie was also conferred as a Fellow of the Academy of Social Sciences (FAcSS). She is a Senior Fellow of Advance HE. She sits on the University of Glasgow's Urban Big Data Centre's Advisory Committee, the ESRC's Strategic Advisory Network, and has previously held positions on various committees including with the Royal Statistical Society (RSS) and SEDA (Staff Educational Development Association).

Jackie is passionate about giving students opportunities to develop their skills in the workplace. She draws on pedagogic research and was inspired by the work of Paulo Freire, author of *Pedagogy of the Oppressed*. Her work in the UK is now being developed in Latin America through the EmpoderaData projects, working with universities in Colombia and Brazil to develop immersion activities for undergraduates to acquire research and analytical and professional skills in social research careers, whilst studying.

Jackie has won numerous research and teaching grants in her career and focuses on bringing data into the classroom, and on helping students acquire research and professional skills in the workplace.

ACKNOWLEDGEMENTS

The author would like to thank the following organisations and people.

First, this book could not have been written without the investment in the Q-Step Programme. Three funders contributed to the initiative that enabled the University of Manchester's Q-Step Centre to be set up, and the internship programme to be established: the Nuffield Foundation, the Economic and Social Research Council (ESRC) and the Higher Education Funding Agency for England (HEFCE). The latter is no longer an entity. The University of Manchester contributed to the funding for the internships and enabled us to pay a living-wage to all those who undertook work placements. Together these funding streams enabled this book to be written.

A huge debt of gratitude is owed to all the former students who generously provided their stories for the case studies in this book. They are all named in the Introduction: Alice, Anna, Ella, Julija, Marcus, Mia, Ryan, Sarah, Victoria and Zvi. In addition, I extend my thanks to those who provided the vignettes, short and longer. Without their voices throughout it would be a very different book. They all gave so willingly in order to share their lessons learned with others, and I am tremendously grateful to them for doing so, and happy that they were such a responsive bunch.

Although most host organisations are not named throughout, I want to thank each and every one who has hosted a student intern. They range from small not-for-profits, through to local and national government departments, to data consultancies and polling and market research companies, to media organisations and the World Bank. Without their willingness to take students on work placement experiences this book would be less rich.

Thank you to Jai Seaman and Charlotte Bush at Sage. Their immense encouragement, belief, advice and tremendous support were instrumental in my starting and finishing this book.

A number of colleagues warrant a mention. Steve Jones encouraged me to start the book proposal whilst undertaking my Advance HE Senior Fellowship application. Chris Orme deserves a special thankyou as he believed in me and my vision to develop the internships, and supported me in becoming a chair. Mark Brown, Lisa Williams, Dharmi Kapadia, Marta Cantioch, Patrycja Strycharczuk, Tarani Chandola and Nasira Asghar have been fantastic colleagues helping me with the internship programme. And John MacInnes, Simon Gallacher and Steve Grundy have been champions extraordinaire for developing STEM skills in the social sciences, but also hugely personally supportive of my work. There are many other Q-Step colleagues across the UK who have been wonderful sounding boards and confidence boosters – thanks to all of you. I hope this book is useful to you and your students.

Finally, friends and family deserve a special mention. I thank my sister Jean for sharing her house so I could write the book proposal, my husband and children and daughters-in-law (and especially Laura for designing Figure 4.1), and father-in-law, for just keeping me going even through two house floods, a serious illness and then the COVID-19 pandemic and all that brought with it. My female networks have been especially helpful in the final stages and a special mention to Marie Hall, Margaret Bell and all my empowerment sisters who got me over the finishing line. We all need support and networks and I thank each and every one of you for getting me to the stage where I can write this acknowledgements section.

INTRODUCTION

'A year from now you may wish you had started today.'

Karen Lamb, various work, 1990–present

Overview

Hopefully you are reading this introduction as someone interested in discovering how you can apply your learning, specifically to applied social research in the workplace. This book sets out to help you. It came about as a result of my own experience, working over a number of years with students and employers to provide real-world workplace opportunities of social research in practice. I have drawn enormous satisfaction from enabling novice and emerging researchers to understand that the knowledge and skills they acquire in their university methods and substantive courses can be applied to complex social and policy matters in a whole range of organisations, locally, regionally, nationally and globally. When I reflected on the unique combination of experiences that these students were given, it made sense to write about it so that others can learn from this, and we can collectively contribute to the global knowledge economy.

This book brings together a set of lived experiences of social science and humanities students who have undertaken a research-focused work placement or internship, paid or unpaid, formally assessed or not. It does so in the context of a framework of experiential learning developed from and applied to social research. The aim of the book is simple – to enable you to understand how to find, do, reflect on and use in your future career or study a workplace experience. You will see how the analytical, research and professional skills that you can develop through putting your learning into practice in the workplace, and reflecting on these skills, can be used to help you find a career or continue to further study.

Whilst the book is framed around social research it has far wider relevance and anyone interested in undertaking a work placement or internship will be able to benefit from it.

Let's get started.

Introducing the students

This book would not exist without the generous contribution of all the students whose voices are captured in these pages. Each of them has undertaken a work placement or internship. Each of them has been in the position of needing to start somewhere. And each of them has come out the other side and used the learning they acquired to advance their own careers, which may have involved further study. They all have a before, during and after tale to tell. This book is their story, and my job is to extract meaning from their experiences so that others can benefit from this. I wanted the collection of experiences to resonate with you. I hope therefore that you find at least one, and hopefully more, of the student voices that are included aligns with your hopes and wishes, and with your worries and concerns.

I have primarily drawn from the experiences of ten students who reflect a range of social science subjects, and who had a work placement with a diverse selection of organisations across different sectors, and in different countries. They do not all appear in each chapter; rather I have been selective in choosing the most relevant extracts to illustrate key points within the chapters. This book recounts their work placement and internship experiences, with my narrative intended to support you to follow in their footsteps and learn from their reflections. I believe that finding success, sharing and emulating it can be helpful. This is why I wrote this book.

I introduce you now to the ten former interns whose words and experiences will be used throughout the chapters. They provide the main student case studies and are, if you like, the main characters in the book. They are drawn though from a much larger pool of former interns, and so I include nuggets from other students too, often in the form of short vignettes, although these become longer in the penultimate chapter. Collectively, all these former students have generously provided feedback through testimonials, reflections or interviews, and sharing their wisdom will help you see that they are people like you, at the start of their professional lives, exploring whether a career in applied social research is feasible, desirable and achievable.

Alice, Anna, Ella and Sarah, Julija, Marcus, Mia, Ryan, Victoria and Zvi are your main guides, with supplementary material provided by others. The gender split in these ten case studies is 70/30 with women in the majority, which reflects the gender split on my own programme of work placements and I'm lucky to have such a vast pool to draw on. In seven years, I have facilitated 250 student work placements in around 60 organisations, and among all of these is a shared experience. The voices chosen for this book reflect that experience. My aim is to help you tap into that to set you on your way.

Here are the ten former interns, the case study students.

Alice

Alice graduated in **Sociology and Politics** and progressed to do a Master's degree in Social Research Methods and Statistics. Alice was one of the most enthusiastic students across all the cohorts, especially embracing reflection as a practice and so she features large in Chapter 6 on reflection. She also provides good material in how she applied the learning she undertook on her internship – which she did in London for a charity called Respect UK – to her postgraduate study, and then what she did next. Alice has been a champion at staying in touch to support cohorts that followed her, regularly speaking at events I have arranged and generally paying it forward.

Anna

Anna's story is one of immense success. She studied **Politics and International Relations** at undergraduate level, and then a Master's in Politics and Communication. Although she did not get the first internship she applied for she has gone on to become a Senior Research Consultant in industry, has achieved a Rising Star accolade, and presented her work to world leaders. Her passion for applied social research (both qualitative and quantitative) is what drives her, and the internship helped her acquire the knowledge, skills and experience to put this into practice in a way that makes a difference to society. Upon graduating Anna was offered a job for the organisation she interned at and has since mentored other interns from various universities.

Ella and Sarah

Ella and Sarah are PhD students studying in Australia. They are both **sociologists** and specialise in qualitative research. Sarah has previously worked in industry, in the public sector, and consequently already had considerable experience of applied research. She undertook an unpaid month-long internship for a think-tank during her PhD. Her experiences helped her appreciate the research skills she already had and could apply, as well as identify areas where she could learn from her internship to fill some of the gaps in her own prior experiences. Ella was lucky enough to travel abroad, to Canada, to do her internship, during which she worked three days a week for a month with a campaign organisation closely aligned to her PhD research interests. Ella's internship helped her think about what she wants to do next, in combining applied research with policy organisations. Ella and Sarah's experiences contribute significantly to Chapter 9, on how an internship can benefit you during further study.

Julija

Like Anna, Julija studied **Politics and International Relations**, and was also an international student doing her degree in the UK. She did her work placement in the BBC, in a regional news team. Julija is the only one of the ten who went straight on to do a PhD after graduating and illustrates how you can use your learning to progress your research skills and education. Her reflections were incredibly rich, and her placement shows how the world of journalism is changing rapidly. Her role was to assist journalists in getting to grips with quantitative research, including sourcing data from Freedom of Information requests. She also featured in a short film exploring the value of undertaking quantitative research in the workplace, and her story will resonate with those who may be interested in careers in the media, particularly in data journalism.

Marcus

Marcus studied **Politics, Philosophy and Economics (PPE)** at university. His internship, at the end of his second year of study, took place at a highly reputable think-tank in Manchester, UK. He was named as a co-author on the research report he worked on, and uncovered a 'killer statistic', which resulted in press coverage for the organisation. Marcus has used his work-placed experience broadly and is still involved with the organisation where he was placed.

Mia

Mia studied **Politics and International Relations** and like Julija did her work placement in the BBC with journalists and producers who were not trained in data analysis. Mia features in Chapter 6 talking about how she had to develop resilience to work under pressure in the news team. Her internship was spent uncovering stories informed by data, and although they were regional two of these stories made it into the national news. Mia went on to use her newly acquired skills in her graduate career.

Ryan

Ryan has had quite a meteoric rise in his career since graduating from his **PPE (Politics, Philosophy and Economics)** degree. Prior to taking up a position in Toronto as a Technology Policy Expert, he held, a variety of other roles, all involving applied research. Ryan did his placement at the General Medical Council in London, and predominantly had to crunch huge amounts of data on medical students' progression routes in UK Higher Education. The fact that he had conducted very little practical research prior to his internship did not thwart Ryan, and during his work placement he immersed himself in learning software and methods to tackle the research challenge he was set.

Victoria

Victoria is a **Criminology** graduate. She used her internship in a UK government department – at the end of the second year of her undergraduate degree – to help her decide what she would do next. Victoria has a very successful track record, having won a national prize for her research based on her third-year dissertation and securing a position with the government department she interned at. She is now mentoring interns and able to help them get the most out of the experience that she herself had and knows full well how important being a role model is.

Zvi

Zvi studied **Sociology** and added **Quantitative Methods** to his specialisation in his final year, having become interested in quantitative research methods throughout his degree and then during his internship. He undertook an internship with a data consultancy, in London, and used the research he did whilst on placement (on sleep patterns of young people) to develop his final-year dissertation. He has since worked for the organisation where he interned, used the opportunity to develop his CV and begin his career, and moved on to undertake social research for a police and crime department. His story is inspiring, illustrating the importance of reflecting on your experience, and how you can use this to explore your career options.

Introducing the hosts

In addition to the student voices the book also provides commentary from some of the organisations that have hosted interns. Although not the main purpose of the book, I do think it is important to include their perspective too. How else will you know what the organisations that take placement students expect from you? The organisations that provide placement opportunities have their own reasons for, and ways of, doing this and so I have tried to capture some of the useful aspects that will help you think about these from their point of view. The host organisations' voices provide extra context, rather than drive the narrative of the chapters. Therefore rather than single out named individuals or organisations here, I introduce these in the main body of the book. Consider these organisations as providing the backdrop to our ten case study students and the others; they are the stage on which our characters perform.

How the book is structured

The book has a clear structure. Some chapters will forward and backward reference each other, but in the main you can read this book chapter by chapter, sequentially, or dip in and out as you choose.

The first two chapters set the context for the book, outlining what experiential learning and applied social research are in Chapter 1, and then focusing on the benefits of doing an internship or work placement in Chapter 2. These two chapters are more academic in style, but important to include so that you can appreciate the literature about experiential learning and applied social research and see who benefits. They provide a framing for the rest of the book. Chapters 3 to 9, the 'How to' chapters, are the heart of the book. I will guide you through all the steps, starting with how to find and apply for an internship or placement (Chapter 3), including how to prepare for the interview and reflect on it (reflection is a key tool used throughout the book) (Chapter 4). I'll move on to how you can get through your first day (and week) (Chapter 5) and introduce how to use a framework for reflection (Chapter 6). Chapters 7 and 8 will focus, respectively, on analytical and research, and professional, skills, and show how to develop and reflect on these. The purpose of these two chapters is to help you think clearly about what you will get out of an internship, and to capture this employing the checklists and tools I provide, and use these to help inform what you do with your newly acquired knowledge and skills. Chapter 9 is dedicated to how you can use your placement learning to inform your future career and continuing study. This is an important chapter capturing multiple voices from early career social researchers and examples of the roles they do, and links back to how you can use your workplace learning to apply for these careers. Job adverts are provided too from three social research organisations – NatCen, Ipsos MORI and The Future Society – to help you see what employers look for. It assists you also to see where further study might be required, or be valuable to have. A very short Chapter 10 draws together what all the case study students did next, concludes with the main themes explored throughout the book, and presents suggestions for 'what next?'

I have not included here a chapter on how to set up an internship programme, even though many people have asked me how to do this. Nor have I included as much detail about what employers want as I could have, though I do reference other books that do this well. These omissions were deliberate; I think they would provide material for another book, and for a different audience. Focus is important. This book is for those who want to *do* an internship or work placement.

At the end of Chapters 1–9 I provide a Three Things You Can Do Next section, prompting you to action. Each of Chapters 3–9 will start with a set of learning objectives and many also include Top tips to help you identify which skills and attributes you can focus on. Checklists are also included throughout and Chapters 7 and 8 include personal development plans (PDPs) to assist you in self-assessing and monitoring your analytical and professional skills development whilst on a work placement. Collectively these learning tools will help you take the steps to gaining the most from your experiential learning and achieving a successful outcome.

I hope you find the book helpful. Most of all, I hope you will take encouragement from the many former interns that have paved the way for you. Enjoy, be brave and begin.

1

EXPERIENTIAL LEARNING AND APPLIED RESEARCH

Learning objectives

In this chapter you will:

- Learn what experiential learning is
- Be introduced to some theories of work-placed learning
- Learn what applied research and applied social research are and be shown two case study examples

'Tell me and I forget. Teach me and I remember, involve me and I learn.'

Xun Kuang (date unknown), translated by Dubs (1928: 113)

Overview

Chapter 1 sets the context for the book. Think of it as a 'What is?' chapter. Chapter 2 will then cover the 'Why?' question and Chapters 3 to 9 will be 'How to' guides.

When I started developing the internship programme that provided the impetus for this book there were very few examples, at least in the UK, of similar initiatives that were focused on developing applied research skills in the humanities and social sciences. Shortly after my work placement programme started in 2014 many other universities asked me to help them set up their own, and I presented widely on the successes we had experienced, reflected on some of the areas that required improvement, as well as thought hard about what didn't work (and dropped those parts). Within three years I had presented nationally and internationally at a large number of educational and research methods conferences, written an academic paper on the pedagogy of work placements, and started the proposal for this book. The contribution I discovered I was making to the field of research methods education was in speaking about 'learning by doing', and specifically in the application of research skills developed in the classroom and applied in the workplace. My programme was designed for undergraduate students to undertake data-driven, applied social research projects, but it has far wider applicability in research methods training more generally, and across all educational levels. My academic and scholarly contribution was recognised through a professorship in learning, teaching and scholarship in 2017, and then at national level in 2020 when I was awarded a prestigious National Teaching Fellowship. As a self-reflective practitioner and a teacher I am well placed to be capturing my experience and sharing it with you in this book.

As our programme developed and expanded it was clear to me, and others, that work-placed learning was becoming more prevalent in undergraduate and postgraduate programmes. I was so busy setting up and running the programme at my university, organising student paid summer internships and observing the subsequent success of those who undertook these in research organisations, that I slightly neglected the theory underpinning the approach I was taking. I too was learning by doing, and reflecting on my own as well as my students' learning. A smart student who was preparing for her work placement asked me about the theory behind experiential learning. She's right – it's important to know this. This chapter is my (belated) response to her, and she features in a cameo in a later chapter (thank you Grace).

This chapter, then, sets out what experiential learning and applied social research are. The purpose is to introduce you to sources if you are interested in reading about the theory behind learning in the workplace in more depth, to provide some introductory definitions, and to give you examples of applied social research. The referenced material will provide you with a starting point, and in so doing show how putting research into practice is a valuable pursuit. In the Three Things You Can Do Next section at the end of the chapter you will be invited to explore these readings further.

Chapter 2 will then focus on the benefits and beneficiaries of work-placed learning in the applied social sciences. The remaining chapters in the book will draw on these two chapters, and provide 'how to' practical information to get you started on your journey to learning by doing. The final chapter looks to the future.

What is experiential learning?

I would not be writing this book if I did not believe that experiential learning matters. I want to share my observations of how your learning can be transformed by situating it in a real-world, practical, working environment. Before doing so it is important to be clear what I mean by the phrase 'experiential learning', and to do that I introduce you to some of the literature that I think is relevant to setting this broader context.

An article by Jay Roberts, editor of the *Journal of Experiential Education*, describes experiential learning in the early twenty-first century as follows, explaining how the term has most often been used to describe learning that takes place outside of the classroom (and in many cases in the outdoors). I like Roberts' (2018: 6) summary:

> Experience, in Latin, comes from expereri, which means to experiment, test, or risk. It is time the field tested its limits and risked its identity to stretch to new possibilities. As experiential learning both metaphorically and literally comes 'in from the outside' in higher education, there will be exciting new opportunities for scholarship and research. From new curricular–co-curricular integrations, to internship programs, to active and collaborative learning in the classroom, to project and problem-based learning, there are a whole host of pedagogical approaches being developed on college and university campuses across the world. Each of these presents opportunities for study and research.

Roberts is right. There is an increasing number of Higher Education institutions that recognise the value of experiential learning, i.e. learning that takes place outside of the classroom. There is also no doubt, in my experience, that showing you have put your academic learning into practice will help you find and secure a future career. At the very least having work-placed experience enables you to speak about this at interview, but much more than that it can open doors to professional networks, provide inspiration for careers you have never even thought about, and give you the confidence to develop your analytical and professional skills and knowledge. This book is full of such examples with Chapters 3 to 9 featuring case studies from many students showing you how they accomplished a diverse range of experiences.

Careers services at universities place great store in helping learners find work placement opportunities. Look at any careers website (such as Prospects in the UK, which dedicates a whole section of its site to jobs and work experience, or GradAustralia, which has a section on internships), or sign up to LinkedIn (the social networking platform for professionals), and you will see that there is demand for graduates who can show they have prior applied experience. (A fuller list of such websites is given in Table 1.1.)

Table 1.1 Examples of websites with work experience opportunities

Name of website	Website address	Short description
GradAustralia	www.gradaustralia.com.au/internships	Describes itself as the best graduate jobs, internships and graduate programme in Australia
Graduateland	https://graduateland.com/jobs/internships	Graduateland is Europe's largest career portal for students and graduates. It has a section dedicated to internships
GradConnection	https://ca.gradconnection.com/internships	Website listing graduate jobs and internship programs in Canada
LinkedIn Student Careers	https://careers.linkedin.com/students/Internships	A sub-section of the LinkedIn website aimed at undergraduates, which is packed with information on doing an internship with LinkedIn
Milkround	www.milkround.com/jobs/internships	The part of the Milkround graduate jobs website that enables you to search for work placements or internships
Prospects (UK)	www.prospects.ac.uk/jobs-and-work-experience/work-experience-and-internships	Prospects work with UK Higher Education to support recruitment. This website lists work experience and internship opportunities
TARGETjobs	https://targetjobs.co.uk/internships	Lists opportunities, including internships, for the top 300 graduate employers and the leading employers across 19 different career sectors
Virtual internships	www.virtualinternships.com	Offers virtual internships with a range of global organisations

As Roberts says, internships are part of the experiential learning landscape. As this book focuses on work-placed learning, I want to delve a little deeper into why this is a smart thing for you, as a social-scientist-in-training, to consider doing.

Work-placed learning

You may have already done some work-placed learning. In the UK it is very common to have a week during the school year where you get to spend time working in an office or volunteering. Jones et al. (2016) analysed testimonies from 488 young British adults (aged 18–24) who had previously undertaken a work placement (some were still in school, others had left and were now in further study). The authors concluded that whilst some of these learners had benefited from a work-placed experience, the benefits to students differed depending on their socioeconomic background, particularly affecting those from less-advantaged backgrounds. The authors found that:

… benefits accumulate exponentially for some young people while leaving others increasingly detached from the capitals that are most important for labour market success.

Jones et al. (2016: 834)

The human, social and cultural capitals they refer to draw on the work of the sociologist Pierre Bourdieu (1986). More explicitly their work, based on a poll undertaken by YouGov in 2011, was able to investigate the extent to which nearly 200 (of 1100) respondents commented qualitatively on their former work-placed experiences whilst still at high school. They found that the majority of these 200 noted that the work experience helped boost their confidence and become more self-assured (cultural capital). In contrast only about one-third reported that making personal contacts (social capital) and developing evidence of application of skills (human capital) emerged from the opportunity. Nonetheless, all three capitals were present from those who commented, and hence it would seem sensible to pursue this outcome in Higher Education through work-placed learning. I will return to the benefits of developing these capitals in Chapter 2, but for now, notwithstanding the relatively small numbers of respondents polled, you can see that even at high school applied learning can be a worthwhile experience.

The Gatsby Career Benchmarks

It's never too early to start signalling potential careers. Schools are a good place to begin exploring how career guidance starts. A UK report published in 2017 incorporated eight benchmarks, known as the Gatsby Career Benchmarks, to support good careers guidance in schools. Published by the Department for Education in the UK, the report draws on international work and good practice. The career guidance strategy states under Benchmark 6, Experiences of workplace:

Every pupil should have first-hand experiences of the workplace through work visits, work shadowing and/or work experience to help their exploration of career opportunities, and expand their networks.

Gatsby (2017: 16)

Career guidance in schools is regarded as a vehicle for social justice, recognising that young people who lack social capital or careers support at home are disadvantaged compared to their peers who can access this support (Cullinane and Montecute, 2017: 23). In the light of research undertaken, especially where there are differential outcomes according to socioeconomic backgrounds, it is encouraging to see government take careers guidance and work-placed learning seriously.

There are many further published examples of work-placed learning internationally. *The SAGE Handbook of Workplace Learning* (Malloch et al., 2011) covers, in 34 academic papers, theory, research and practice, and issues and futures. Predominantly these papers focus on post-16 education. Dipping into this book alone shows the wealth of activities that work-placed learning addresses, and it is worth exploring a few of these now in setting the context for this book.

In Nicholas Allix's chapter on 'Knowledge and workplace learning', he concludes:

> … learning is a process that is continuous and lifelong, and is not confined to learning in the academy or the workplace, but is something that occurs in all contexts in which humans have to live or to survive … lifelong, and workplace learning, presents educators … with social roles of significance and consequence for both individual and social wellbeing.
>
> Allix (2011: 144)

This chimes well with the capitals introduced above. Allix goes on to say that in order to have an impact on learners and provide the best opportunities for them to learn from and apply their knowledge and skills in the workplace, educators need to develop opportunities for this type of learning to occur. He lists ways of doing this including internships, mentoring arrangements, establishing and developing communities of practice and creating work teams to problem-solve. In this book you will find all of these and whilst I focus on the first of these as a mechanism for enabling work-placed learning, the others listed by Allix occur as a direct result of undertaking an internship or work placement, as you will see.

Theories of work-placed learning

Different theories underpin learning, and likewise learning in the workplace. Section 1, Chapters 1 to 11 of *The SAGE Handbook of Workplace Learning* (2011) provides a comprehensive overview of different learning theories and how they pertain to workplace learning. This chapter cannot do justice to all of these, but one I think particularly resonates with the theme of this book is what Engestrom calls *expansive learning* (2011). This theory, which he develops building on previous scholars, argues that as the world develops technologically, organisations need better ways of working to use new knowledge. In Engestrom's words:

> The design of the new activity (externalization) and the acquisition of the knowledge and skills it requires (internalization) are increasingly intertwined. In expansive learning activity they merge.
>
> Engestrom (2011: 88)

I like this notion of expansive learning. It describes what I have witnessed over the course of my work in this area. It also connotes that learning needs to keep expanding and growing if we are to adapt to the challenges of the twenty-first century as the use of increasing volumes of data and evidence demand better understanding and application of research methods and skills.

Another experiential learning theory relevant to work placements and internships is that which describes workplace learning as *emergent*. In his chapter on 'Theories of workplace learning', Hager highlights this approach as the next area of research. He says:

> ... learning is emergent from its context in unanticipated and unpredictable ways. Thus context transforms learning in an ongoing creative process.

> Hager (2011: 27)

This captures the importance of the *context* of the learning, and as you will see throughout this book, context matters. All the work-placed learning I have witnessed, and the testimonies provided by interns and employers, exemplify this. In my experience, when learning research methods, social science students are rarely interested in, for example, data per se, or narratives divorced from their context, but they are enormously motivated by trying to better understand their subject. Whether criminology, politics, sociology, economics or business students, they are eager to learn how to systematically explore their research questions. And as they learn the theories that underpin their discipline, they want to explore how these theories can be tested in practice, and possibly to see how new theories can emerge. Experiential, expansive and emergent learning theories help explain how novice researchers contextualise their understanding by appealing to the substantive nature of their discipline. In other words, the research question drives the learning, and students are taught research methods, alongside theory, to equip them to attempt to investigate their question. Typically a student might be taught this in the classroom, sometimes through methods classes, but embedding the learning in the substantive subject provides a way of delivering a good learning experience (for example, see Buckley et al., 2015; Purdam, 2016). Assessing learning is another matter. A standard academic assessment might test an understanding of the learning through an essay, report, practical exercise or dissertation. Experiential learning is different, because the context is real-world, the learning has relevance outside the classroom and the outcome of the learning is no longer just academic. Although I do not focus on formal assessment of learning in this book, it is worth thinking about this as you progress through the chapters. What I do focus on though is self-reflection and this will help you develop self-awareness of your own learning whilst in the workplace, and bring this back to your studies.

Learning is a complicated process, with many, including some contrasting, theories that have been developed over many years and in many subjects. Work-placed learning, as a sub-discipline, also draws on different theoretical perspectives. Hager groups these into theories influenced by psychological literature, sociocultural theories influenced by sociology and social anthropology, and postmodern theories including emergent theories. There is also a huge literature on organisational learning, although I would argue that for work-placed learning the organisational context of the learning is accommodated in emergent learning theories.

The theories introduced above contribute to an understanding of workplace learning and offer a theoretical understanding for how work placements and internships help contextualise knowledge and skills development in a real-world setting. As this book shows you how to apply your learning, I will focus more on the practical application and understanding of learning through the main body of the book. Before doing so though, let's move on to home in on why this book matters, and the subject area that makes it different and hopefully useful, by defining what I mean by applied research, and then applied social research.

Applied research

What then, you might ask yourself, is applied research?

It seems that there is actually very little published information, at least in the social sciences, on *learning to do* applied research. Academic papers capture the outcomes of applied research. Policy documents provide examples of how research can be used to effect social change. Organisations such as NatCen (https://natcen.ac.uk), with the strapline 'Social Research that Works for Society', and the Australian Institute for Family Studies, which 'conduct research to increase the understanding of Australian families and the issues that affect them' (https://aifs.gov.au), have a plethora of research publications relevant to their audiences. Postgraduate research training provision in the UK is world-leading, and the research councils are huge investors in training postgraduates to conduct research. Academia is increasingly driven to evidence the societal and economic impact of our research. And governments worldwide are all looking for evidence-based policy research.

And whilst we know that the end goal of social and political research is to make a difference to society, we perhaps need to pay more attention to how to train our future social researchers – not all of whom will go into academic research – to undertake applied research. Whilst research funders are mindful of doing this through Higher Education doctoral training programmes, there is a lack of systematic evidence on how work-placed learning could contribute to the development of research skills. The UK Economic and Social Research Council (ESRC) is encouraging and supporting doctoral students to undertake internships with a range of public, private and voluntary sector organisations:

> Internships provide the opportunity for students to develop valuable skills and
> build networks outside of academia, which can provide important foundations
> for future collaborative research. We want our doctoral training to provide

a foundation for careers within and beyond academia, internships play an important role in developing employability skills and students' awareness of the value of their skills outside of academia and the range of employment opportunities open to them.

Deputy Director Skills and Methods at the ESRC

This is a welcome direction of travel. Chapter 9 provides multiple examples of what applied research looks like for humanities and social science graduates.

This book helps to fill the gap. My aim here is to contribute to the investment being made in research training at graduate level, by *developing the pipeline into research careers* for undergraduate social scientists. I am doing this by helping students, like you, to focus on learning by doing. Using student narratives to bring this learning to life, set in the context of applied research carried out in organisational settings, this book will provide tips and techniques to help you find, and then do, research in the workplace. It therefore provides a bridge between being taught how to do research and doing this in your future job, by showing you how you can become an applied researcher through a work experience.

I will say more about what applied research is and how you can learn how to do it soon, but first I want to introduce Anna. Anna is the first of my case studies who describes what can happen if you do a work placement, in her case as an undergraduate. Anna illustrates what applied research is, and how she started, and continued, doing it. This case study is longer than the others in the book – but bear with it. Anna is now five years out of her undergraduate degree. She was recruited to the organisation where she interned as an undergraduate, and whilst working there took a Master's degree in Politics and Communication. She has also mentored new interns. This virtuous circle, where former interns become mentors to new ones, is a satisfying and valuable outcome of work placements. Over to you Anna.

Case study 1.1

Anna: A personal view on applied research

I asked Anna to tell you what she thinks applied social and political research is, and how the internship she undertook helped her learn how to do it.

> When I was in the second year of my Politics & International Relations undergraduate degree I had very little idea about how I was going to apply all the theory I was learning in the classroom. Then I was lucky enough to get an

(Continued)

internship – having been initially unsuccessful at interview. The position was with a small consumer & social research company (called AudienceNet), who were at the time mainly doing research for the music industry but were in the process of expanding into political research.

Prior to starting my internship, I had no real knowledge of applied social research, other than some limited understanding through a few university course units I had taken. I had never considered a career in research, nor did I appreciate the extent to which data and evidence was used in politics and policy making. Five years on from writing my first report, as an intern, researching attitudes to the expansion of Heathrow Airport, I'd progressed to Senior Research Consultant. I've also now experienced the myriad of ways research is applied to help understand and solve real-world issues.

My work is extremely diverse. However, my favourite projects are those which help give a voice to groups who are usually marginalised or misunderstood within the mainstream. Research with such groups can help affect policy and behaviour change. In my career to date I have applied the skills I learned in the classroom and through my internship to a wide range of studies. For instance, I have interviewed 1,500 refugees to help challenge people's perceptions of them and worked with political parties to help them understand how they can help foster political engagement among young people. Having the opportunity to work on these, and many other, projects has taught me about the power of applied research. But for the internship, I doubt I would have pursued this career. I simply would not have had the confidence or skills.

Anna's case study is the first in the book. It's important for several reasons. First, it is included to inspire you. This student could have given up, believing she wasn't going to be successful (but was thankfully persuaded to keep going). She applied and did not get the first, or second work-placed opportunity she (thought she) wanted. As you can see this did not turn out to matter – she went on to find one that worked out. Second, Anna did not realise she had the potential to do applied research starting from what she perceived to be a low base (undergraduate training); this too proved to be an incorrect assumption. And third, not only was she capable of putting her learning into practice with this organisation, but she went on to be offered a position by them and become a Senior Research Consultant within a relatively short period of time upon graduating, and to mentor future Annas. Quite a nice case study to start with.

Ralph Hall (2008) draws a distinction between what he calls basic research and applied research. He characterises this as follows:

Basic research is designed to advance knowledge and understanding regardless of its application. [It is] curiosity driven, that is, the motivation for doing the research is to gain new knowledge without regard for any practical application of the results.

Applied research is designed to solve immediate problems where the results are to form part of the basis for decision making. The focus here is on problem solving rather than building a knowledge base as in strategic or basic research.

Hall (2008: 4–5)

Whilst we might question the use of the term 'basic research' and moreover whether separating it out from applied research is valid, this distinction turns out to be quite helpful. On the one hand, becoming a social scientist means you need to understand the norms and culture of your discipline – be it sociology, politics, criminology, economics, etc. You need to know how scholars have developed that knowledge and how you can critically evaluate it. In order to do this you have to read a lot, debate with your peers and teachers and form your own opinions to situate your learning in your disciplinary field. In short, you need to study and understand the epistemologies associated with your subject, the dominant paradigms, and how these together define your discipline and make it what it is. This contributes to the understanding of how knowledge is created in your subject area, and therefore supports further research, which develops new knowledge. In its conceived form this knowledge creation, or basic research, has no practical application.

This book, however, is about research in practice, and to practise your research skills you must have the opportunity to apply them. Thus, applied research is, put simply, the type of research that solves a problem that has direct application to the world. All of the examples in this book reflect real-world problems and applied research that has been undertaken to help organisations tackle these problems.

To do applied (or indeed any type of) research it is of course critically important to be able to design a good research question, develop a research plan, critique the data you use, select and apply an appropriate research method or set of methods, evaluate your analysis and communicate the results. There are many good books specialising in the full research cycle (e.g. Gray, 2018; Gronmo, 2020; Punch, 2014). This book will build on others by providing practical tips and advice in each chapter, based on real experiences, to help you understand what applied research is and how to do it. And all of these examples will be set this in the context of the workplace environment. My own introduction to applied research began during my PhD. I describe this below.

Case study 1.2

Author: My applied research

A personal story might help. I give you an example from my own applied research journey.

When I did my PhD many moons ago I was a mature student, having previously started my career as a schoolteacher. I was not your typical PhD student. I was, though, intellectually curious, analytically capable and extremely determined. My PhD was a 'CASE studentship', which means that an organisation has identified a 'real-world need' to solve a complex problem. I probably have the paperwork somewhere, buried in a box at home, which outlined the research question, but my memory is that I was asked to research an approach to predicting the radioactive fallout from a nuclear accident, so that the organisation would be able to make decisions on where to remove humans and livestock from to avoid harmful health consequences.

My PhD started in 1992. In 1986 there had been a catastrophic accident at a nuclear power plant, called Chernobyl, in the Ukraine. The accident occurred as a result of one of the main reactors exploding in an uncontrolled way. It took years for the full consequences of the accident to be discovered, and there is ongoing debate around the Russian authorities' handling of the extent of the damage (environmental and lives lost), resulting in a 2019 telling of the story in a TV historical-drama.

In 1992 investigations into the accident were still ongoing, and my host organisation had been involved with the nuclear fallout and public health advice in Britain. My research question was clear and carried very real benefit to the sponsor organisation, and potentially to society. My sponsor organisation (the National Radiological Protection Board, now part of Public Health England) and I worked hand in hand to find data we could use to inform the research, explore suitable research methods, and develop my skills to help them design and build an emergency response system. The result was my PhD thesis entitled 'An investigation into the applicability of geostatistical methods for environmental radiation monitoring data', and a prototype emergency response system that they implemented. I co-authored some academic publications. At least one paper by my industrial supervisor cited my PhD findings, and he continued to work in this area for a number of years.

Why am I using my own research as an example here? First, to show that I have conducted applied research. Second, to show that I have experience of doing applied research in a work-placed setting; my entire PhD was spent working alongside the organisation that sponsored it, and they had a vested interest in the results. This is still fairly typical in the natural sciences, and although this is less prevalent in the social sciences, as I indicated above, it is on the increase (see also Australian PhD students Ella and Sarah in Chapter 9).

And third, because at the time I had no idea that the results of my research might be of any use whatsoever. In some regards it could be described using Hall's term as 'basic research'; after all at its inception it was framed as being about finding new knowledge. In fact, using Hall's distinction, it turned out to be applied research as the problem was set in the context of a real-world challenge. As it happens the new knowledge I discovered was that a subset of techniques from geostatistics, based on a method called kriging, could be used to provide good estimates of interpolated data from point measurements. This set of methods *had not been applied before* to airborne monitoring data, although it had been used for mining data. What my research showed was that the limited numbers of radioactive readings taken on the ground after a plume dispersed across a landmass could be used to estimate where people and livestock ought to be evacuated from to uphold public safety standards. Hopefully you can see that no matter how uncertain at the outset the research you undertake is, there are unforeseen consequences for the findings. And seeking answers to real-world challenges motivates applied research.

There remains one further definition to introduce.

Applied social research

Whilst researching this book I Googled the terms I wanted to write about. I'm sure I am not alone in doing this, and it helps to know what common usage some terms have. I have written in this chapter about experiential learning, work-placed learning and applied research. I conclude by focusing on applied *social* research and to do so go back some years to a fascinating paper from 1979 (Barton, 1979). Barton writes about a deceased scholar, Paul Lazarsfeld (1901–76), an Austrian-born sociologist who was a professor of sociology at Columbia University in the US for three decades and founded four institutes of applied social research in his lifetime. The paper describes Lazarsfeld's work in this area. The following extract illustrates how different things must have been for researchers in the first half of the twentieth century.

> The characteristic of the work which [Lazarsfeld] did and which he inspired was attention to *social process and social context* along with individual attitudes and background, as determinants of *socially consequential behavior.*

> The use of surveys and other large-scale quantitative investigations of social phenomena by teams of researchers is taken for granted today, but when Lazarsfeld began to do this kind of work in the 1920s and 1930s there was literally no organizational base for it. … There was no organization for a social scientist who wanted to make surveys for scientific purposes. … And this drove Lazarfeld into the role of institutional inventor. What he invented was the university-related applied social research institute.

> Barton (1979: 7)

As someone who sits in an applied social research institute at my university, I was so happy to come across this article. It sets out how what we can easily now take for granted was a hard-won battle. Having access to robust nationally representative samples of attitudinal data, or polling data, or even anonymised records from the census, enables us to undertake empirical research that was once not possible. I did not know about Lazarsfeld before writing this book but I will be sure to look up his work now. Plus I like the description of him as an 'institutional inventor', and it turns out he was a mathematician by training who came to sociology and social science through an unconventional route. Not a million miles away from my own journey.

Applied social research then, for the purposes of this book, refers to research undertaken in an applied setting which explores human behaviour. The social sciences covered include sociology, anthropology, political sciences, economics and extend to application domains including education, policy and government, health research, marketing and market research, and research for social and economic development. In other words, applied social research covers a vast number of domains and places empirical analysis at the heart of its approach.

Applied social research institutes

Below I list some applied social research institutes that I am aware of through my own work. The following are based in universities and well worth checking out for their research outputs as well as the graduate programmes, summer schools and training courses that they run.

Applied social research institutes websites

- UK: The University of Manchester Cathie Marsh Institute for Social Research: www.cmi.manchester.ac.uk
- Australia: The University of Queensland Institute for Social Science Research: https://issr.uq.edu.au
- US: Harvard Institute for Quantitative Social Science: www.iq.harvard.edu
- Canada: University of Alberta International Institute for Qualitative Methodology: www.ualberta.ca/international-institute-for-qualitative-methodology

---

Whilst Lazarsfeld's work draws on quantitative research his comments are equally valid for qualitative and mixed methods research. The skills and understanding developed through experiential learning, applied research and applied social research are methods agnostic. Therefore, regardless of your subject, your methodological preferences, and your gravitation towards numbers or words, this book is intended to be useful for all.

Applied social research careers

I could have started this chapter with a list of the sorts of careers that social researchers do. That might have seemed more logical. Instead I decided to introduce a range of careers after explaining what this book is about, and who it is aimed at. Having defined my terms I move on now to the sorts of careers that are open to social science researchers. Chapter 9 provides examples of some of these careers, drawing on testimonies from early career researchers, to show how they apply their skills and knowledge in their roles.

There are some excellent resources on the internet that are valuable to help you see what you can do with a social science degree. For example, the UK Campaign for Social Science (CfSS) has researched the employment prospects of social science graduates and found that their prospects are very similar to those studying Science, Technology, Engineering and Maths (STEM) degrees (CfSS, 2018). This report builds on prior research, which found that social science graduates were highly sought after in the labour market (CfSS, 2013). Both these reports include case studies of social science graduates. The Social Research Association website (https://the-sra.org.uk) is another resource that provides a straightforward introduction to careers that recruit social scientists, although not exclusively to undertake applied social research.

Table 1.2 provides some illustrative examples of organisations that provide applied social research careers, and the roles that researchers do.

Table 1.2 Example applied social research roles

Organisation type	Sector	Applied social research role
UK national government department	Public	Government social researcher (GSR) Data scientist Government statistician Analyst
UK local government	Public	Social researcher Business intelligence analyst
University research centre	Public	Academic researcher Data scientist
University	Public/Private	Teacher and/or researcher
University administration	Public	Data analyst Market researcher Alumni researcher
Non-governmental organisation (NGO)	Not-for-profit	Advocacy role Researcher

(Continued)

Table 1.2 (Continued)

Organisation type	Sector	Applied social research role
Market research company	Private	Market researcher
Data consultancy	Private	Analyst
		Research executive
		Data scientist
Polling company	Private	Analyst
		Data scientist
		Polling analyst
Think-tank	Private	Data analyst
		Policy analyst
Media organisation	Private	Data journalist
		Investigative journalist
		Researcher
		Reporter
Banks and commercial	Private	Analyst
		Business engagement
Charity	Not-for-profit	Social researcher
		Campaigner
Social enterprise	Not-for-profit	Campaigner
		Researcher

Many of these roles and organisations are covered to a greater or lesser degree through the student experiences reported in this book. This world is open to you too, and in great need of trained social scientists who can understand complex social and behavioural issues. The next chapter will build on this one to cover the benefits of undertaking work-placed social research and show how this can open doors to the sorts of careers represented through the roles listed above.

Summary

The quote at the start of this chapter was carefully chosen. *Tell me and I forget. Teach me and I remember, involve me and I learn*. It derives from a Chinese Confucian philosopher, Xun Kuang. It has been used in more modern times by educators and I chose it to reflect the philosophy of this book.

This chapter has stepped you through what experiential learning and applied research is, honing in on the workplace dimension and on applied social research. The case for experiential learning in applied research was made through the introduction of Anna as the book's first student case study, and my own PhD experience. Some example careers are provided to help you see the sorts of openings that are available in different sectors, and how applied research skills are needed in the workplace to answer social and behavioural questions.

This chapter has set up the 'what is' part of this book. Chapter 2 will look at 'why' you might want to consider undertaking experiential learning in the workplace. Chapters 3 to 9 then proceed to guide you in how you can do it.

Three things you can do next

1 Take a look at one or more of the following applied social research websites and check out the types of research they undertake:

    a   https://natcen.ac.uk
    b   https://aifs.gov.au
    c   www.pewresearch.org
    d   www.iser.essex.ac.uk

2 Allix describes learning as 'continuous and lifelong, … not confined to learning in the academy or the workplace, but is something that occurs in all contexts in which humans have to live or to survive' (Allix, 2011: 144). Think about this and write down all of the opportunities that you have to learn that fall outside of formal education.

3 Think about a subject you are passionately interested in. Can you imagine a research project that you would like to undertake to explore this further? And can you think of an organisation you would like to do this in? You might feel ill-equipped to know how to start to do this. Two books that could help you get started are: (1) O'Leary, Z. (2014) *The Essential Guide to Doing Your Research Project* and (2) O'Leary, Z. and Hunt, J.S. (2016) *Workplace Research: Conducting Small-Scale Research in Organizations* (see References). Use these (or others, referenced in this chapter) to write a two-page brief on your research project.

THE BENEFITS OF EXPERIENTIAL LEARNING IN APPLIED SOCIAL RESEARCH

—Learning objectives—

In this chapter you will:

- Be introduced to the main benefits of experiential learning to students, host organisations and educators
- Be shown a typology of early career learning
- Be given examples of former students who have put their experiential learning into practice
- See how work placement programmes can provide opportunities to showcase your learning

'That all our knowledge begins with experience there can be no doubt.'

Immanuel Kant (1781)

Overview

In Chapter 2 I introduce you to the benefits of doing work-placed learning for developing applied social research skills and experience. The previous chapter provided some of the theoretical background to explain what experiential learning is, how it is underpinned by various learning theories, and a case study from a former intern to provide an example of how applied research can be done through an internship. I also introduced my own experience of applied research to show you how my own journey began.

You might have missed Chapter 1 and be diving straight in here curious to discover why work-placed learning is a good thing to do, or perhaps waiting to be convinced this is for you. Or you might have been so taken with the previous chapter that you are keen to learn more about the benefits before you decide to invest your time and energy in finding a work placement or internship. Whichever the case, this chapter is an important one to frame the rest of the book.

I set out to answer three questions: why do experiential learning? why does it matter? and who benefits? The chapter focuses on how work-placed learning benefits all those involved in the pipeline of developing skills for careers involving social research. To achieve this I draw on the three different perspectives that are represented in a triad of most internships or work placements. First, the student – what benefits will you accrue if you decide to undertake a work placement? Second, the employer or host organisation – what do they gain from providing people who might still be in formal education and not 'work-ready' with a work opportunity. And third, the educators that train and teach the students, why should they consider this as an option for their students? The overarching group, that connects all three of these, is employers. Ultimately the goal of an education is for you to contribute your knowledge and skills to the world, and most of us do this through paid employment. With that in mind, I have not included employers as a separate group here, although they are represented through the organisational perspective, but they are the ultimate beneficiaries, and necessary providers, of experiential learning. Employers can be from the public, private or not-for-profit sector with all three represented in this book.

The Three Things You Can Do Next feature at the end of the chapter is to provoke you to think about how, having been presented with different perspectives (students, employers and educators), you could act. You might not be so interested in your university's point of view initially, but if what you read persuades you to try to find ways to convince them to replicate the experiences illustrated through this book, then that's great. You will, however, be interested in and motivated by the benefits to you, and hopefully appreciate the value in thinking about the benefits to organisations that have taken student interns. Having their perspective, as well as your own, can bring insight to how you might want to frame an application, for a work placement or a future position for example. Case studies from students, and quotes from employers, will demonstrate why experiential learning and applied research does matter, and show how they can be used to your advantage. Unlike the previous chapter which focused on a single student case study (Anna) and my own experience of having done an applied research project for my PhD, this chapter will draw on testimonies from three of the book's case study students. Host organisations will share some of the benefits they see, and I provide an example based on my own work to show how educators stand to benefit.

What are the benefits and to who?

Steve Rook's book, *Work Experience, Placements and Internships*, entitles the first chapter 'Why experience matters' (2016). He describes experience as 'the oil that keeps your career on track', identifying five core areas that getting work experience will help you with (Rook, 2016: 5). These are to: research a role; develop your skills; build contacts; undertake the experience required; and open doors. You will see these areas appear time and time again throughout this book.

Nevertheless, I think the list misses out one enormously important area – and that's to help build confidence. I deliberately missed out the word 'you' in that last sentence. In my experience having the opportunity to undertake experiential learning is a confidence boost that has benefits to all involved. I used the term 'work-ready' above, and cringed when I wrote it. The notion of anyone who is ready for something before they have practised is somewhat a contradiction in terms. This book assumes you are not ready, as in fully-fledged, for anything, but that you are willing to put yourself out there and try. This chapter is written with that in mind. Indeed most of this book is written with that in mind too, although I expect you to use reflection as you proceed to evidence your new-found skills and confidence.

Experiential learning can benefit everyone, providing each party to it has an open mindset. You'll hear much more on mindset as this book unfolds, but it's important to frame this chapter with reference to that too. With a closed mindset, the benefits to all will not be fully realised.

Back to the benefits of experiential learning. Here is a list of what I propose are the main opportunities afforded to students, host organisations and educators through work-integrated learning, separated out by each group:

Main benefits of experiential learning

It enables students to:

1 **Practise** applied social research in a safe, supportive environment
2 **Observe** and **conduct research** in the workplace
3 **Acquire confidence** in applying knowledge to real research questions that matter
4 **Develop** and hone existing and acquire new **analytical and research skills**
5 **Collaborate** with professionals and **co-create new knowledge**
6 **Network**
7 **Learn** about new careers

(Continued)

It enables host organisations to:

1 **Create** and support talent pipelines – find bright minds
2 **Support** junior staff to develop their supervisory skills
3 **Understand** the research methods and software tools training that undergraduate and postgraduate students are learning
4 **Connect** with universities, especially around a corporate social responsibility (CSR) agenda
5 Fill **skills gaps**
6 Bring **dedicated resources** to business or academic research projects

It enables educators and universities to:

1 See how **research skills taught in the classroom are applied in the workplace**, and use this to enhance the curriculum
2 **Observe the types of outputs** produced by organisations, e.g. policy documents, briefings, executive recommendations, reports, etc.
3 Gain access to the latest workplace practices, improving their **understanding of how to achieve employability through the curriculum**: this can include recruitment and reward frameworks used in different sectors, software and methods used, better understanding of analytical roles, etc.
4 **Develop links with industry** and cultivate networks with external colleagues that could lead to business engagement or research opportunities in the future
5 Develop **employable graduates**

The list is a good place to start to draw out the advantages of putting your learning into practice in a workplace environment. You can see the different benefits for each group. It's not an exhaustive list, but as you work your way through this book you will observe how everyone benefits, and come to appreciate how important it is to start to regard this from multiple perspectives.

In his chapter in *The SAGE Handbook of Workplace Learning*, Michael Eraut 'starts with the proposition that both *knowledge* and *learning* should be viewed through two lenses: the individual and the social' (Eraut, 2011: 181). He analyses interviews collected from the workplace for mid-career business, healthcare and engineering professionals, concluding that 'learning at work derives its purpose and direction from the goals of the work, which are normally ... a combination of thinking, trying things out and talking to other people' (Eraut, 2011: 186). He goes on to say that consultation and collaboration constitute the most common form of learning from peers, and support from and observation in action of others, especially in the work team, are informal ways of learning. This is the experience of mid-career professionals, and begs the questions of how early career and more junior staff acquire these opportunities to learn.

The typology Eraut introduces to answer that question is useful here. Elements of this appear throughout the book and so I include Eraut's typology of early career learning here (Table 2.1). It provides a reference point for which types of knowledge, skills and learning can be acquired, and how, in the workplace. Experiential learning supports different types of learning, through developing your skills and knowledge in the workplace environment, rather than the classroom.

Table 2.1 A typology of early career learning

Work process with learning as a by-product	Learning actions located within work or learning processes	Learning processes at or near the workplace
Participation in group processes	Asking questions	Being supervised
Working alongside others	Getting information	Being coached
Tackling challenging tasks and roles	Locating resource people	Being mentored
Problem solving	Listening	Shadowing
Trying things out	Observing	Visiting other sites
Consolidating, extending and refining skills	Reflecting	Independent study
Working with clients	Learning from mistakes	Conferences
	Giving and receiving feedback	Short courses
	Use of mediating artefacts	Working for a qualification

Source: Table 13.2, A typology of early career learning in Eraut (2011: 187)

Later chapters provide examples and evidence of learning that falls into some of these groupings, almost all of which are covered in this book. The first two columns are most relevant for you as students starting your journey from education into the workplace. Let me now move on to describe the benefits of experiential learning to our three audiences.

Benefits to students

It is my intention here to persuade you that experiential learning is a worthwhile pursuit. As an educator I know full well that telling someone that something is good for them is not a good way to teach. I have to show you that experiential learning is going to be of value to you, and you should therefore invest some of your energy and time in acquiring it. This book is written as a result of my utter conviction and personal belief that you can do this. This conviction is based on my own experience of witnessing just how transformational experiential learning has been to the interns I have placed, the others I have interviewed, and my own experience which I was lucky enough to undertake part way through writing this book (more on that in Chapter 4).

Here is the subset of the list I provided above, this time just focusing on the main benefits to students:

1 **Enable the practice of** applied social research in a safe, supportive environment
2 **Observe** and **conduct research** in the workplace
3 **Acquire confidence** in applying knowledge to real research questions that matter
4 **Develop** and hone existing and acquire new **analytical and research skills**
5 **Collaborate** with professionals and **co-create new knowledge**
6 **Networking** opportunities
7 **Learn** about new careers

This list can essentially be distilled into two key interconnected factors, which act as fundamental drivers to students. Students want to acquire subject knowledge, skills and experiences that will help them find a post on completion of their formal education. That is to say, they want to acquire *employability skills* in order to gain *employment*. I consider each of these below.

Employability

One of the most obvious benefits to undertaking a work-placed research project or experience is to gain employability skills. Employability is a hot topic in Higher Education in the early twenty-first century (see Minocha et al. [2017] for a good overview of policy and practice in the UK). Universities globally are increasingly turning their attention to the employability attributes of their graduates as they are required to report on these through their career services and academic bodies. Nonetheless there is potentially a mismatch between what students want (and need) and what universities offer. How might you find out if a university course provides experiential learning, or for that matter how well a university scores on its teaching excellence? Different countries, with different educational systems, pay attention to employability in various ways. I include here an example of how this is factoring into a national framework in Great Britain (focused predominantly on England but including some universities in Wales and Scotland).

An example of measuring employability and employment outcomes

England introduced a Teaching Excellence Framework (TEF) in 2017, through the central Office for Students (OfS at www.officeforstudents.org.uk). The TEF assesses excellence in teaching at universities and colleges, and how well they ensure excellent outcomes for their students in terms of graduate-level employment or further study.

Universities that participate are marked on the basis of criteria they submit to OfS, and given a bronze, silver or gold award. Whether or not these types of frameworks accurately reflect a good teaching experience is hard to gauge, and it's too early to say whether students are looking at the TEF score when they select a university. Moreover, although employability metrics contribute to an institution's TEF award, no systematic evidence or comparison yet exists to show that universities that score highly on TEF offer extensive experiential learning opportunities. Until TEF is more mature it might be preferable for a prospective student to look at course-level data rather than a university-wide single metric to make an informed decision about the experiential learning component on that degree.

Notwithstanding that the TEF is not yet mature enough to conclude whether it is a useful way of measuring teaching excellence in England as it incorporates skills and employability, universities are now focusing much more carefully on how they are supporting this, not just through their careers services but within their course delivery too. This is an area that stands to receive more attention, and work-placed learning in Higher Education is firmly situated in this space.

The link between skills and employability attributes taught at university, and graduate outcomes, including employment and further study, is definitely of interest to policy makers and to universities for their reputation management. Global rankings for top universities as measured by graduate employment are published annually (see www.topuniversities.com/university-rankings/employability-rankings/2020). Not surprisingly the top universities in this list tend to correlate with excellent teaching and/or research profiles too. The methodology used also considers work placement-related partnerships reported by the institutions and validated by the research team. Work placements are therefore good for universities as they feed into these global rankings.

This book is not, however, exclusively about employability. Nor is it a generic book on work placements or internships (see Fanthome [2004], McCabe [2014] or Rook [2016] for more general work placement texts). Rather the idea here is to show how the students and employers included throughout have used work-placed learning to contribute to what are often referred to as 'employability skills and attributes' (Lowden et al., 2011) in careers and roles that involve applied social research. In Chapters 7 and 8 I return to graduate attributes to show how you can acquire these through a placement experience, and Chapter 8 gives examples of how they are used in applied social research careers.

You may be curious, however, to discover what these more general graduate attributes are. Normand and Anderson's (2017) book identifies ten graduate employability attributes, labelling them as follows: learning, adaptable, self-aware, resilient, agile, empathic, ethical, professional, digital and reflexive. Whilst all ten of these are relevant to experiential learning, I will focus predominantly on learning, resilience, professionalism and reflection and you will read more about these in later chapters.

The others could be said to be part of a professional's wider set of skills and behaviours that enable one to be a valuable member of the workplace. Chapter 8 focuses on these professional skills.

University careers services are excellent places to start if you are interested in understanding what they regard as the necessary basket of employability skills to acquire prior to graduating. My own university has a nice online tool, which helps guide students through a set of questions asking about their behaviours, to provide the best chance of getting into a good career. According to your responses, it profiles your areas for development, with friendly tips about how you can improve, and enables you to develop these over the course of your time at university, the aim being to ensure every graduate can find future employment. Although I cannot reproduce the questionnaire here (it sits on our intranet) I can share, with permission, a diagram (Figure 2.1) with the six categories of activity it encourages students to develop: explore, connect, communicate, take action, reflect and bounce back. I expect other university careers services have similar tools you can use – they are well worth a try, not least because they are developed from successful former students' experiences, and rather than being focused on technical or research skills alone, embrace a broader perspective.

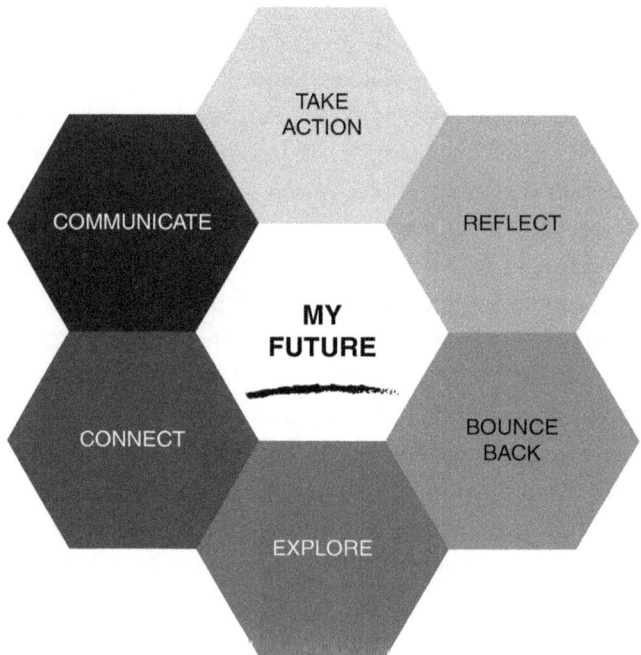

Figure 2.1 Graduate behaviours to develop for your future career

Source: University of Manchester, UK: MyFuture logo reproduced with permission

A senior careers service member of staff told me that she reduces these six categories to three by giving advice to students to be curious, connected and courageous. This sums up the advice I find myself giving to my students too. I encourage you to be curious, connected and courageous.

This section has introduced you to ten, then six, then reduced to just three attributes or behaviours to acquire for graduate employability. The next section considers the application of these to the labour market.

Employment

Employability is about acquiring the skills and experience to become employed, with employment being the end goal. Careers and business literature often refers to the 'right attitude' to work too. A 2018 Confederation of British Industry (CBI) report states 'clear drivers of success ... are attitudes and attributes such as resilience, enthusiasm, creativity and communication skills' (p. 23). You will read about examples of all of these throughout this book, using real examples, especially in Chapters 7 and 8. You should be starting to get a sense, hopefully, of what attributes you need to begin to develop to enter the workplace.

As this chapter is about the benefits of work-placed learning, and as the end goal of you doing (or considering doing) this is to gain meaningful and satisfying employment, I introduce here examples of experience gained by three of our students, which contributed to their later employment. All three were undergraduates when they did their work placements, with Chapters 8 and 9 providing examples from postgraduate students.

Marcus, Victoria and Zvi graduated with degrees in Politics, Philosophy and Economics, Criminology, and Sociology and Quantitative Methods respectively. You can read more about them in the Introduction. These three give a good spread across subjects, which might align with your own interests, and they interned in three different types of organisations: a think-tank, a government department and a data consultancy. Each undertook a paid, two-month long, data-driven, research-led summer internship. None of the internships contributed formally to their degree grade. All provided me with honest and powerful testimonies to say how the work placement impacted upon their learning. I pepper their stories as case studies throughout this chapter so that you can see how their experiences have relevance for each perspective covered: students, host organisations and educators. They feature elsewhere in the book too so you will be able to follow their stories in more depth as you proceed, and see how their experiential learning impacted their futures.

I hope they will not mind me saying that none of these students was particularly special in any way when they decided to apply to undertake an experiential learning opportunity, nor were they from privileged backgrounds. What they all had in common, however, was the courage to put their classroom learning into practice. And one of the common factors amongst all three of these students was the potential they saw in how a work placement could enhance their employability skills. What was much less clear when they each set off on their individual internship journey was how this would affect their employment prospects. As it turns out, all three progressed into careers that were opened up to them directly through their work placements. This is actually a very common outcome, and an enormous benefit.

Case study 2.1

Victoria: Benefits of doing an internship

Victoria undertook an internship in the public sector and now works in a national government department. I asked her to what extent the experiential learning she acquired impacted her further studies on returning, and then her employment choices and prospects. Here she gives me her response:

> The internship played a part in my journey [to my current role] as it gave me practical experience of working in a fast-paced policy environment. I didn't actually know that my current role existed so [the work placement] really opened my eyes up to that. I would thoroughly recommend an internship in the public sector as in my experience it provided an excellent insight into the central workings of government and how evidence and analysis is used to inform policy decision-making. During my undergraduate degree I realised that I was really interested in quantitative research but I had no idea what a career in research would involve or what it would be like. So doing the internship showed me how data can be used in real world social research.

I hope Victoria inspires you to believe that you too could benefit from a work placement or internship. Remember, the rest of the book will show you how. For now, take comfort that before she began her internship she had no idea of the opportunities it would open up to her. However, just from this short extract you can get a sense of how the internship brought benefits far beyond the duration of the placement itself.

Marcus, Victoria and Zvi are just three voices of students who have benefited through doing work-placed applied social research. Hundreds of others I have spoken to have told me similar stories. They talk about practical experience, discovering careers they never knew existed, acquiring confidence and skills, being paid for working (many students cannot afford to do internships if they are unpaid), having transformative learning experiences, putting this into practice when they return to university and understanding how research is done in the real world. All were curious, connected and courageous and have gone on to use their work placement experience in their lives after university. Adding to Victoria's words, you will hear from Marcus and Zvi below and meet all three of them again in later chapters.

Taking Eraut's typology of early career learning, I highlight, in Table 2.2, the learning that the three case study interns in this chapter demonstrated whilst on placement. If this is not enough to encourage you to undertake a work placement or internship, I'm not sure what is.

Table 2.2   Experiential learning undertaken for the three case study students (highlighted in bold)

Work process with learning as a by-product	Learning actions located within work or learning processes	Learning processes at or near the workplace
Participation in group processes	**Asking questions**	**Being supervised**
Working alongside others	**Getting information**	Being coached
Tackling challenging tasks and roles	**Locating resource people**	Being mentored
	Listening	Shadowing
Problem solving	**Observing**	**Visiting other sites**
Trying things out	**Reflecting**	**Independent study**
Consolidating, extending and refining skills	**Learning from mistakes**	Conferences
	Giving and **receiving feedback**	Short courses
Working with clients	Use of mediating artefacts	Working for a qualification

Finally, in this section, I refer back to Chapter 1 where the idea of social, cultural and human capital (Bourdieu, 1986) was introduced. All three of the case study students in this chapter reported that their confidence increased, and their testimonies confirm how they grew in self-assurance, supporting the claim that their cultural capital was improved by undertaking a work placement. Likewise they all increased their human capital through acquisition of new skills, and used these opportunities to access graduate careers, through the personal connections and networks they formed, showing their social capital also benefited. As you progress through the book you will be provided with further examples of this happening, through other student case studies. The benefits of undertaking a work placement go far beyond just acquiring skills.

While Eraut's typology focuses on processes, it is also really important as you undertake experiential learning to think about *outputs* you can develop to evidence your learning. I discuss in Chapters 7 and 8 the different outputs that you can develop to build your own profile as an emerging researcher and early career professional. If, whilst on or after a placement, you have the opportunity to present your work at a conference then do so. If you have opportunity to present your work with your lecturer or peers, do it. A nice example of this is a project that an English Language and Linguistics student worked on with a researcher, through his academic internship. The empirical work that the student undertook formed the basis of an academic paper that was then presented at an international academic conference. This work benefited both the academic and the student intern. The student progressed from this to do a PhD, supervised by the academic he co-authored the paper with. His undergraduate research internship was the start of his own academic career.

The last point highlights that a work placement is only a starting point. All the entries in Table 2.2 will be filled in over time. Marcus, Victoria and Zvi could now confidently fill in the entire table; I know – I have witnessed them doing 'all of the above'. The internships opened the door for them, the rest was down to them and we shall witness their development when we meet them later.

Benefits to host organisations

At this stage in the book I simply want to convince you that seeing the advantages of work placements through the eyes of the placement host is a good thing to do. In Chapters 3, 4 and 5 I spend a lot longer exploring why taking account of the host's perspective is worthwhile. Starting to step into the shoes of the organisation is a smart move, as you will see. The sooner you cultivate this habit the more you will realise that it's not just about what you bring to the internship, and you will develop an understanding of what they want from it, and from you, too.

How did I learn about the benefits of an internship to the host organisations? Well, when I started the internship programme that forms the basis for this book it was very much an article of faith. I speak elsewhere in this book about the need for evidence to inform policy making. Much of the research that interns and work placement students undertake is on collecting or analysing evidence, and later chapters show examples of this. When we introduced the internship scheme at my university we did not know if it was going to be successful, although I could not see why it would not be. However, I needed to think about how to evaluate it.

I started to collect evidence very soon after we set the scheme up. I employed a Research Associate to help carry out some interviews with the first cohort of students, and personnel from some of the organisations that they had been placed in. I introduced the term 'host organisation' rather than 'employer' as this was more accurate; indeed my university was paying the interns who were hosted by an organisation that was providing a data-driven, research-led project for them to undertake with support. We published a paper on our early findings (Carter et al., 2017) in order to learn from our first cohort. Extracts from one of the students who featured as case studies in that paper will be used elsewhere in the book to illustrate key points about what can be gained from a work placement.

What I was not prepared for was the benefits to these host organisations and their staff that they reported. I include here the main ones that I have encountered since we began, and illustrate some of these by example, drawing on interviews with and testimonials from some host organisations.

First, though, I want you to hear from Marcus, who speaks about what he gained from undertaking his work placement in a think-tank. He is several years post-internship now but the relationship he developed with his host organisation helped him eventually secure a research position with them.

Case study 2.2

Marcus: Developing professional know-how through an internship

I asked Marcus what he took away from his internship, and what he regarded as the main benefits, and you can see from his answer how it was far more than simply analytical skills.

> For me, the key benefits were actually seeing the things I had learned about and the skills I had gained in my studies being used in practice. I think it really helped build confidence for me to know that I could pull everything together and deliver something in a professional environment. I also think it helped me develop a deeper understanding of how the 'political' industry actually worked and to see space for me, with my degree, in that for the future. Finally, I think it's important to have got the kind of experience that helps you settle in when you get an office job – office manners, office politics – all that stuff that no one teaches you but it matters for enjoying your working life.

The benefits were not one-sided. His host mentor was so impressed with Marcus's work he included his name on the flagship report that Marcus contributed research findings to. The think-tank has taken an intern every year since then. Marcus was able to demonstrate the tremendous benefit of bringing an extra pair of hands, ears and eyes to an organisation that has a small staff, but an enormous quantity of research to undertake. His mentor had seen the value that Marcus was able to bring, in his role, providing a dedicated research resource to the think-tank just at the right time; they produce an annual report 'State of the North' and Marcus's work informed that (more on this in Chapters 5 and 8). Marcus and his host featured in a short film we made following his internship, and it's evident from that just how much value the organisation gained from having his input.

The main benefits to organisations of having a work placement student undertake applied social research are captured in the following list. They are based on the comments that arise consistently from speaking to our hosts. In the case of Marcus's host organisation they benefited from all six of these:

1   **Create** and support talent pipelines – find bright minds
2   **Support** junior staff to develop their supervisory skills

3 **Help to understand** the research methods and software tools training that undergraduate and postgraduate students are learning

4 **Help to connect** with universities, especially around a corporate social responsibility (CSR) agenda

5 Help to fill **skills gaps**

6 Help bring **dedicated resources** to business or academic research projects

Education is not and should not be beholden to the needs of industry. That said, a dialogue between what universities and colleges teach, and what industry reports are the in-demand skills, can be useful. A CBI report (2018) shows that whilst businesses are largely satisfied with the levels of education and digital skills new recruits present with, they are far less satisfied with the readiness for work of applicants and communicating and problem-solving skills. One in four employers are also dissatisfied with literacy and numeracy standards. And whilst they value workplace experience, only 38% of businesses questioned were satisfied with the level of experience of the workplace possessed by their applicants. There is clearly a demand then from the labour market for people with applied, work-placed learning experience, and developing these skills and attributes prior to entering the workplace can only be a good thing. Marcus talks about how he acquired these skills, and so once again the benefit is two-way: the student gains the skills, the future employer receives a graduate more ready for the workplace.

What do organisations say?

Three short testimonies (which intentionally do not align with the three students in this chapter) are introduced now in order that you can see what organisations say about having a student do an internship or work placement. Each was asked a series of questions to elicit their thoughts about the benefits of having an intern (and for some doing this year on year), and also whether there were any costs associated with this in terms of their staff time.

Employer perspective

Organisation's testimony: A large, national charity organisation

We still use the outputs of his work and of the other three interns. I estimate it took five days of staff time to set each intern up and induct him or her into the project and we generally got back four or more weeks of useful output. I think it helps with my own development having to explain to someone what we are doing and the processes involved. They frequently asked interesting questions which would not occur to me because I've been immersed in the project for so long. This can result in improvements to processes.

Organisation's testimony: A national government department

Employer
perspective

The interns are an extremely valuable resource as they help with projects that we wouldn't otherwise have the resource to do. They also offer a new perspective on methods and approaches to projects.

We have had previous interns return to work here permanently after graduating, which shows the value of these placements in helping develop future career choices and that the students enjoy their time with us enough to apply for a job! The placements help to break down the barriers between government and academia by offering an insight into government priorities and how analysis is used within government.

Paid internships provide experience for junior staff who wouldn't otherwise have the opportunity to manage someone, to take on the role of supervising a student. This helps them to build their own management and leadership skills and greatly helps with career development.

Organisation's testimony: Small start-up company

Employer
perspective

There was mutual learning on both sides and I think that she had to think quite creatively about the work … well this isn't a typical research environment. She helped us in that way and it was just hugely beneficial. She put in a lot of time helping us prepare for bids we were putting in and that was so helpful. Also the knowledge differs according to where we are doing the research so it was a very natural growth area for us [to take an intern] and exciting as there are always new research methods out there and we thought that partnering with an academic institution that's looking at these methods directly and contemporarily, we could benefit from it.

Overwhelmingly these organisations spoke positively about the benefits. Only one mentioned the costs – in terms of setting up and supervising the intern – although this does certainly need to be taken into account, and is discussed in the section on managing expectations in Chapter 5. Because these organisations did not fund the interns directly they did not comment upon this aspect. All of these organisations, representing three different sectors, praised the interns, said they contributed to the work that otherwise would not have been done without their input, and have all gone on to take a student again. Some even build incrementally each year on the previous intern's research. The small start-up company, which undertakes some challenging research in conflict countries, was especially pleased to have the opportunity to work with a bright, creative thinker who would help them better understand new ways of collecting and analysing data (which was indeed the outcome), and to be connected to a university known to have expertise in research methods.

It is evident from these three examples alone how different types of organisations gain benefit from offering work placements, and you saw from Marcus that this is a two-way process. The remainder of this book will provide further examples.

Benefits to educators

To complete the benefits, I show how your lecturers and universities can benefit from work placement schemes.

It will become fairly evident as you work through this book that the main beneficiary of a work placement is you – the intern or placement student. Although harder to capture, there is also enormous benefit to educators and educational institutions, colleges and universities. Many Higher Education institutions are beginning to use their student placement schemes as a way to reach out to their future intake, putting videos and testimonials online to showcase opportunities students have through these programmes. I know from my own experience how powerful it is to attend a university open day and hear from students who have benefited from doing work-based learning whilst on their degree. However, not all universities and colleges have a placement scheme. This section gives you information about why it would be beneficial for all Higher Education institutions to think about having a work experience programme, and how in particular this supports the teaching of applied social research. However, this is an ambitious goal and so this section also aims to help you consider how to engage with your own teachers to draw on their extended networks which could open doors for you.

My own university has a magazine that showcases the achievements of our staff and students across teaching, research and social responsibility, the three pillars that sit at the heart of our strategy. In spring 2016 this included an article entitled 'Giant steps for student interns' reporting on the work-placed learning programme that I had introduced for humanities and social science undergraduates. When our first student secured her graduate job with the organisation where she did a work placement, a piece was published with the title 'Student data-crunches her way to a new job'. This was Anna, who you met in Chapter 1. It is a positive step to see experiential learning opportunities highlighted in the humanities and social sciences, and very satisfying for universities to see the direct outcome of a programme that provides social science undergraduates with work-placed applied research experiences that build on their classroom learning.

Careers services have always shone a light on employability and employment success stories; after all this is their role. My own careers service has been instrumental in supporting the development of my programme. Now more and more universities and colleges are also communicating these success stories to attract good students to study at their institution. The important difference, from my observations, is that these benefit stories are starting to appear on course rather than careers webpages. The benefits to students applying to university are framed from the perspective of the academic achievements that can be accomplished, *as well as* future career prospects. Marrying research-led teaching with applied learning opportunities is a win-win scenario. Embedding employability into the curriculum is important and necessary.

In Chapter 7 I focus on how to develop research and analytical skills, and in Chapter 8 professional skills, and provide frameworks and examples to show how you can do this. Educators and universities can benefit enormously from better understanding how these skills are manifested in the workplace. The list of benefits for educators is perhaps naturally shorter than that for students and host organisations, although this is certain to grow as more educators recognise the value of this to their own students, and their own teaching. The benefits to teachers of applied social research skills acquired in the workplace are less evident in the experiential learning literature, but from my experience, and as noted earlier in this chapter, I would list the main benefits to educators, and to universities, as follows:

1   To see how **research skills taught in the classroom are applied in the workplace**, and use this to enhance the curriculum
2   **To observe the types of outputs** produced by organisations, e.g. policy documents, briefings, executive recommendations, reports
3   To gain access to the latest workplace practices improving their **understanding of how to achieve employability through the curriculum**: this can include recruitment and reward frameworks used in different sectors, software and methods used, better understanding of analytical roles, etc.
4   Universities can use work placements **to develop links with industry** and cultivate networks with external colleagues that could lead to business engagement or research opportunities in the future
5   Universities can use work placements to contribute to their **evidence of developing employable graduates**

One of the main benefits of experiential learning to lecturers is when a work placement inspires a student to undertake a piece of research they previously may not have felt able to do. Work placements have a way of alerting students to new ideas, giving them the skills and confidence to return to university to conduct a more ambitious research project. Here is just one example, from Zvi, of how this worked for him.

Case study 2.3

Zvi: Figuring out my dissertation topic through an internship

Zvi is the most recent graduate from the case study students. As with the others I asked him to what extent the learning he gained from his work placement in the private sector impacted his studies upon returning.

> Doing the internship really benefited me in so many ways. I did my internship in the private sector, and it was split into 2 weeks in London followed by 6 weeks in Washington DC. Before I did it I had started to get interested in sociological research and how we can use quantitative data to explore complex social questions. I was already starting to explore statistics and sociology in my courses and doing the internship gave me eight weeks to get practice in the workplace with this, and get paid for this too, which is really important. On finishing the placement I had decided what I wanted to do for my third year dissertation, and also I was far more confident in being able to do that when I returned to university. I ended up analysing technology use and sleep patterns of young people, using logistic regression, and there's no way I could have done that without having spent the summer doing data analysis. My dissertation was 100% influenced by my work placement. The experience also helped me land my first graduate job.

This case study initially reads as if all the benefits were for Zvi. Reframing it shows it is absolutely a benefit to his university and his lecturers as well. For one, as a result of his work experience his university has a powerful example of how his placement helped him decide on his third-year dissertation topic. Second, his lecturer can see how her teaching gave him the skills and confidence to apply for and do an internship, and moreover how he was then able to come back and use his learning in his dissertation (as an aside – his dissertation won a prize for his research). And third, his university established a strong connection with the host organisation, which led to a PhD student being given a work-placed opportunity two years after Zvi interned there. You can see how a single example starts to open up multiple opportunities.

I have not interviewed academics for this book, but here is an example of how I have benefited from my work placement programme. This provides an educator's perspective on how an applied social research work placement developed in the UK is helping develop a programme in Latin America to support the delivery of the United Nations Sustainable Development Goals (SDGs).

Case study 2.4

Author: The EmpoderaData Project

In 2019 I won a small grant to pull together an international team to explore the extent to which work placements could support a data fellows programme in Latin America. This led to an international symposium in São Paolo, Brazil, where a group of scholars and civic society professionals came together, to get involved in developing data literacy skills for the United Nations Sustainable Development Goals (UN SDGs). The EmpoderaData project team conducted an analysis on skills gaps and data literacy needs, delivered a workshop and a report, and secured funding for a follow-on project, EmpoderaData2. The final project report for EmpoderaData is available online (Higgins et al., 2019) and featured in DataPop Alliance's annual report (DataPop Alliance, 2019).

Figure 2.2   EmpoderaData project report

I then submitted a research proposal to take my work placement initiative to São Paolo and with a professor there we will be introducing work placements, calling

(Continued)

them 'immersion activities', for applied social research into the undergraduate curriculum for business students.

At the time of writing the EmpoderaData project lives on. I appointed a Research Associate on the project to help develop the work in Latin America, focusing on the single case study country of Colombia. We have just completed an academic paper on this work. The researcher was none other than one of my former interns, who in the meantime had undertaken a Master's and a PhD and has now secured himself a prestigious postdoctoral position.

This success story shows how experiential learning programmes can grow and develop and enhance the reputation of the academics involved and the universities that support this work. They can also support the pipeline of new researchers – as was the case with EmpoderaData, which appointed four early career research professionals through its two phases. The university has featured the project in a booklet highlighting colleagues' work on helping deliver the SDGs, and the project has helped me develop my own profile beyond the UK. The EmpoderaData project team proactively shared our findings, and we are excited about taking our learning to international audiences.

Why should you care about this section? Well, because educators benefit from students engaging in workplace learning in so many ways. In addition to the five items listed as benefits to educators, the personal benefits to watching our students become autonomous learners, developing their knowledge and skills in the workplace are enormously rewarding. Curiously the literature on workplace learning tends to mostly reflect the views of the employer or host organisations and the students who undertake the internships. There is much less written about how educators benefit. Maybe this is a gap that needs to be filled and will form the basis for a future book (get in touch with me if you would like to contribute to this!). Certainly work placements and the co-production of knowledge in the social sciences is an area that needs exploring further.

To finish this section I draw on the emerging work from Professor Melanie Nind and her colleagues in the UK. Their recent projects have focused on the pedagogy or teaching research methods to social science postgraduate students. In the conclusion to Lewthwaite and Nind's paper on speaking to experts, including educators who teach research methods, they say:

> We have crossed disciplines, national boundaries, and qualitative, quantitative and mixed methods to engage significant actors and informants within research methods in productive discussion of methods pedagogy. Through analysis of expert responses to the distinct pedagogic challenges of the methods classroom, the principles and illustrative examples generated can

form the knowledge and understanding required to enhance practice and
wider pedagogic culture.

Lewthwaite and Nind (2016: 428)

Whilst their work, which focuses on classroom and lab-based training for postgraduates, has not yet embraced experiential learning, there is clearly a gap in the literature that needs to be filled. This book starts to build the bridge between the classroom and the workplace, by exploring how we can develop the pipeline to future careers for applied social researchers. It would make for an interesting set of case studies to design a project to investigate how lecturers can learn from their students' workplace experiences, using a framework like Eraut's, which I introduced earlier, and incorporate this learning into the curriculum.

Creating a virtuous circle

This section brings the three previous ones together. I have shown how undertaking experiential learning benefits all those involved. I now want to show how you can work together with your lecturers and host organisations to create a virtuous circle so that everyone can see the rewards that accrue through undertaking a work placement experience. I provide a couple of examples below of how I achieved this, but you could think of others. For example, set up a student conference at your university, or work with your student society, or contact your professional society (ask your lecturers) to ask if they would support a student-led initiative. There are multiple ways you could be creative in sharing your own experience and put your collective experience on the map. Co-creation of knowledge is so important in this space, and I challenge you to get creative.

The EmpoderaData project example shows what can happen if lecturers share their experiences. It has always been important for me to share learning and after I set up the scheme at my university I was determined to ensure that as many people as possible – students, employers and other universities – could benefit from our experiences (good and bad). I have given many presentations based on my own learning through analysing my students' stories. However I wanted to do more – I wanted to co-deliver these with my students, and with my peers at other universities. This is why this section matters, because if I can do this so can your lecturers.

To help promote the experiences of applied social research interns I took four students, from England, Northern Ireland, Scotland and Wales, to present their work at the prestigious Royal Statistical Society annual conference in 2017. The international conference audience comprises statisticians and data analysts, academics, and professionals from various sectors. The title of the presentation was 'Getting down and dirty with data: Training students in the workplace'. In the presentation I introduced each of the four students, outlined the approaches the four universities had adopted to give their students work-placed learning skills and experiences, and led a panel discussion. Figure 2.3 is taken from a tweet.

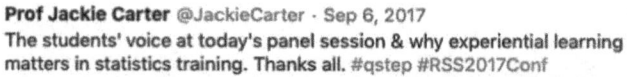

Figure 2.3 Photo tweeted by Jackie Carter, taken at the Royal Statistical Society annual conference 2017. Shared with permission of everyone pictured

The following year I presented again at the conference, this time with a panel of professionals and one intern (Grace) who has spent her internship working at an international organisation in Washington, DC. The Twitter picture here shows all four of us at the conference.

Figure 2.4 Photo tweeted by Jackie Carter, taken at the Royal Statistical Society annual conference 2018. Shared with permission of everyone pictured

Imagine if you could do this. What a great opportunity to present your work at a prestigious conference, prior to graduating. Your lecturers, like me, have professional networks that we can open up to you, in the right circumstances, and given appropriate resources (e.g. funding for conference attendance). Your voice is important. I think we can do more to help you connect to these networks, and this was my attempt to do that. In later chapters you will see many other ways that you can do this too, as doors open to you through your work-placed experiences.

I believe that as educators we should share what works – and what does not work – so that others can benefit. Since the RSS 2017 conference I have continued to present at as many educational conferences as I can. Sometimes I present my students' stories, in the way that I am doing throughout this book. Sometimes I try to get other educators to join me in order to share their own successes and failures. And sometimes, as above, I take one or more students to a conference to present alongside academics and professionals. It is my attempts to share these lessons with other educators that have helped develop my reputation in this space of applied learning for social research and earned me a National Teaching Fellowship.

In addition to external events I have established an annual Celebration Event where all interns present their work placement experiences in the form of a poster, a required output from their internship. Some also give a three-minute presentation, using a single slide, to tell a compelling story about their experience of applied social research. I have started asking academic colleagues to follow this format. As you can imagine it is challenging for them but it is also good to create an opportunity for students and their lecturer to hear from each other through a mini-academic conference. The academics thoroughly enjoy finding out about what all their students got up to during their placement; the university too welcomes this event as it supports the student experience, providing students with very tangible evidence they can go on to use in their future job applications. Perhaps you could propose something similar at your college or university. As well as presenting at academic conferences and internal events I use LinkedIn. (I introduced LinkedIn in Chapter 1 as a place to find internships or work placements.) I have authored a series of articles on LinkedIn to showcase what students can achieve when on work placement. LinkedIn is an excellent platform through which to connect with practitioners and professionals, and I use it increasingly to bring interesting careers and work-placed opportunities to the attention of my students.

Summary

In this chapter I set out to convince you why doing a work placement or internship is a worthwhile pursuit. I have focused on the benefits to three main groups: students, organisational hosts and educators. Student stories were included to persuade you that there are many benefits that open up to you through undertaking applied social research in the workplace. Organisations that host students, and educators and universities, also benefit in multiple ways. I propose that the symbiotic relationship between the classroom and the workplace requires further exploration. I hope you can start to appreciate ways in which you can play a role in persuading your institutions of the benefits of work-placed learning, drawing on these multiple perspectives.

A typology of early career learning was introduced to provide a framework for helping to understand the types of learning afforded by work placements and internships. The evidence for the capacity to develop social, cultural and human capital was presented through the inclusion of the selected case study students. Development of confidence through experiential learning is a commonly reported finding. And whilst I have said little about adopting a positive mindset in this chapter, I hope you can see that having an open mindset is a very good thing to start to cultivate.

The quote from Kant at the start of this chapter was carefully chosen. I hope you can see, through reading the examples I have included, that the value of acquiring knowledge in the classroom is to enable you to put it into practice. The benefits of putting your knowledge and skills into practice have been presented here. That, however, is only the beginning. The remainder of this book, as well as telling you how you can do this, is packed with stories of how applied learning is built on, and creates, a 'pay it forward' culture. It quite simply is a case of win-win.

Three things you can do next

1   Take a look back at Table 2.1, based on Eraut's typology of early career learning. Which of these do you already have that you can show has *been acquired in the workplace*? If none – the next chapters will definitely help you, so don't despair.

2   Develop your powers of persuasion. Read through the section on Benefits to Organisations or Benefits to Educators again. Write down all the things you can think of that would help you persuade an organisation to take you as an intern, or that would persuade your university or college to set up a work placement programme. Or if you have one already, think about how it could be improved or its profile raised.

3   Be bold. Start a conversation with your lecturer. Your lecturer is likely to be connected in ways you are unaware of. Ask them if they have ideas about organisations you might be able to work at in the future. Try to find out if your lecturer is doing research that you are interested in and explore whether there are ways you could contribute.

HOW TO APPLY FOR A WORK PLACEMENT OR INTERNSHIP

In this chapter you will learn how to:

- Find a work placement or internship
- Think about what relevant skills and experiences you have
- Articulate your skills and experiences on your Curriculum Vitae (CV)
- Think about the internship from the organisation's perspective
- Start to develop a support network
- Apply for a work placement or internship
- Do all of the above with a positive mindset

'I am always doing that which I cannot do, in order that I may learn how to do it.'

Van Gogh (1885)

Overview

Chapter 3, the first of the 'How to' chapters, will help you navigate the work-integrated learning landscape, whether or not you have a dedicated programme for this at your place of study. Examples are focused on applied social research, although anyone interested in work-placed learning can take something from this chapter. Taking your learning from the classroom to the workplace requires a brave leap, of both faith and action. You may feel you do not have relevant skills, but this chapter will help you think about the experiences you already have, within and outside the classroom, and show you how you can articulate these in a way that makes them relevant to a work placement or internship, especially one undertaking applied research. Your Curriculum Vitae (CV) is a good place to start and I offer practical tips on how to get your CV in shape, and how to get you started. As with the other chapters in this book, real students' and employers' stories are provided. Thinking about developing your support network is also included here, as you are going to need this before, during and after your placement. An often-missed trick is to think about why you should be the one chosen, and you can only do this if you start to consider the perspective of the organisation you are applying for. Seeing yourself through the eyes of the interviewer is a skill worth learning. Central to this chapter is the need for you to develop a 'can-do' attitude, a tenet that runs throughout this book. The overarching aim of this chapter therefore is to get you started, help you find that work placement, and give you the techniques to give you the confidence to apply.

How to get started

Applying for a work placement or internship is a bit like preparing to decorate a room. You might not have decorated a room before but anyone who has knows there is preparatory work involved. Paper over bumpy walls and the bumps will always show through. Forget to fill in the hairline cracks in the plasterwork and eventually they will reappear and you'll wish you had. Fail to put on an undercoat to the woodwork and you will get a less than satisfactory result. Why am I talking about decorating when you want to know about how to get started in applying for a work-based experience? Well, because the idiom 'preparation is essential' is true here too.

In order to get started you need to know where to look. You may have heard that your university runs a great scheme, or you have a friend who did an internship at their university, or someone suggested this would help you in your future career, or you read Chapters 1 and 2 in this book and thought 'I can do this.' Or it may be that you know nothing at all about work-placed learning but can't help thinking that having something else on your CV before you graduate would be a smart move. Let's start then by thinking about where you might go to find out more.

Where to look and who to talk to

Work placement and internship opportunities are springing up everywhere. You might have to do a little detective work at your place of study to find out if and where they are promoted, and how they might relate to your academic programme, but included in this section are some examples to steer you in the right direction. And because it's impossible to include the multitude of different offers across all universities here, I offer only a starting point. You will have to ask around and make further enquiries on your own and use the Three Things You Can Do Next at the end of this chapter. I will provide a few places you can go to get started. And to be clear from the outset, we are talking here about *applied opportunities to practise your research skills in the workplace*, not more general work placement schemes, as made clear in earlier chapters. This book is definitely not about generic work placements (see Three Things You Can Do Next at the end of this chapter for some pointers to books and online resources you can look at for more general material).

To get you started, and whet your appetite, here I introduce a number of links to international organisations that offer work-placed opportunities that align with those discussed in this book. These provide good examples of where you can look. You also need to know who you can talk to though, especially if you are undertaking this quest without clear support structures in place. The next section points you to some people and places where you can ask for help.

International research internships

Many large organisations offer summer internship and work placement opportunities. Table 3.1 lists some of the larger international organisations that advertise internships, providing opportunities for students to practise their analytical skills through undertaking real-world research. Others were provided in Chapter 1 (Table 1.1), so take a look back at those too. Whilst most internships offered are in-person, there are an increasing number being offered virtually.

Table 3.1 International research internship websites

Organisation	Description	Website
OECD	A summer and winter programme, for up to six months	www.oecd.org/careers/internshipprogramme.htm
World Bank	Lists many different programmes and internship opportunities for different nationals	www.worldbank.org/en/about/careers/programs-and-internships
United Nations	For final year undergraduates or Master's or PhD candidates	https://careers.un.org/lbw/home.aspx?viewtype=ip
UK government departments	Site enables searching across different departments and schemes	www.gov.uk/find-internship
Inter-University Consortium for Political and Social Research	Aimed at advanced studies and careers in data and social science	www.icpsr.umich.edu/icpsrweb/content/ICPSR/internship

(Continued)

Table 3.1   (Continued)

Organisation	Description	Website
Australian Internships	Offers internship programmes focused on 'hands-on' training and innovative real-world work experience in almost all academic disciplines, aimed at undergraduates and graduates	www.internships.com.au
Virtual Internships	Offers virtual internships with a range of global organisations	www.virtualinternships.com

The careers service

This is a sensible place to look for support as a first port of call. Your careers service may run a programme of work-based opportunities for undergraduates and postgraduates. If so they will provide a host of information for you as you navigate the pathway between study and work, and all careers services will be able to provide advice on all aspects of preparing yourself to enter the workplace. The trick is, though, to be focused in what you are looking for when you go to see them and figure out how they can provide you with targeted information.

To help you get started in your search for a work placement, you could approach your careers service with a direct opening question: 'I want to gain some work-integrated experience as a student. Can you help me?' Chances are they will have a leaflet, or a website, or an individual whose responsibility is to help you. This is good, but as this book is not intended for generic work placement opportunities, your question needs to be more focused. So hone your line of questioning. Ask your careers consultants if they have any opportunities for students who have a specific set of requirements, like you. 'Do you run work placements or internships that will enable me to develop my research skills?' is a good starter for ten. You might want to be even more focused – though don't start with too narrow a query, as it is usually easier to refine a larger question than expand on a smaller one. For example, show that you have thought about what you want to get out of this by saying something like, 'I have good research skills in using written materials, but really need some support in developing my analytical and numerical skills. Do you have any schemes that I could apply for?' I cannot overstate the importance of developing a targeted question like this. If you fail to do this then you risk drifting into a work placement that is not going to deliver the best experience for you.

Academics

You will, to a greater or lesser degree, interact with your academics during the course of your studies. You might only see them in lectures – and some of these might typically be hundreds of you in a room with your professor as the 'sage on the stage'. Or you might have regular slots in smaller groups (tutorials or seminars) where you get to know your teachers, and they you. Speaking to busy academics rushing between their teaching and research and administration tasks might feel intimidating, but remember they have your best interests at heart. They want you to become passionate – as they are – about the subjects they are teaching you. They also want you to become individuals who leave after your studies and become well-informed and critically enquiring citizens. In short, your lecturer or academic adviser or professor wants to assist you in becoming employable, educated and well-informed although employability might not be at the top of their priority list. The world for you is likely to be very different to the one that made it possible for them to become your lecturer, but they want to help you get your qualification *and* become ready for employment.

Your lecturer therefore has a vested interest in helping you gain the applied research skills that will help you become a successful graduate. Moreover they are likely to know about opportunities at your institution that will help you acquire these applied research opportunities. Ask them. If they volunteer this information in class, all the better. If they don't, approach them and enquire as to where you can find out more. They might point you to the careers service, but they're equally likely to suggest you speak to someone they know in your university who is aware of work placement opportunities; often these people are called something like 'employability leads'. This is how it works. You probably don't know who this person is, but by asking you are likely to find someone who does if this role exists, and if so where you can find that person. Again, be targeted in what you ask. Be brave in asking for what you want. Not just 'I want to do an internship' but 'I would really like to see how what you taught us in lectures can be applied in social research.' This approach will not only flatter them, 'what – you like my teaching!', but resonate with their sense of responsibility to help their students *apply* the knowledge they are being taught.

Employers

This is, of course, an obvious place to look. We look at employers and their needs throughout this book, but from the point of getting started let's consider an example in this section and expand on it later. If you are training to become a lawyer, or a social worker, or undertaking a Master's in Business Administration, or following a medical or veterinary degree, or nursing or health sciences, or other more vocational qualifications, you are likely to be relatively well provided for. Your programmes of study will have work placement opportunities embedded. The less vocationally oriented degrees are much less likely to include a work-placed learning element.

Below is an example of an applied research internship opportunity, and I show you how you can deconstruct this to understand what the position is, and what the employer is looking for. This advert was taken from a UK site called www.milkround.com, a go-to place for undergraduates looking for graduate opportunities.

Every year I promote an opportunity to my students to do a paid internship at YouGov, one of the most well-known polling and social research companies in the UK. To date I've had seven students go there for the summer to work with various teams on research projects including developing polling questions, coding these for their various panels, and writing blogs, reports and news items. These students are the lucky ones – they can benefit from my connections and the excellent working relationship I have with YouGov and its different divisions. Why am I telling you this, as you're not likely to be one of my students? Well, because this has exposed me – and by extension them – to the annual internship opportunity that YouGov advertises. Below is a screenshot of an advert for a year-long internship at YouGov.

A note of caution here before reading on. The advert below may feel a little overwhelming at this stage, and even out of reach. It demands a lot, and is aimed at ambitious, accomplished and capable applicants. It presents something of a conundrum. On the one hand, it requests some experience (e.g. of primary research) and you may be looking for an internship exactly with the purpose of acquiring that. Just relax. Subsequent chapters will take you through the steps of how to evidence what you have already acquired (even though you may not yet realise it). For now, be brave and trust me. Take a look at the example and use it to better understand what types of things a high-profile polling organisation like YouGov is looking for. And use this section to start to think about your own skills, and experience, and maybe gaps in those too.

I have broken the advert into four parts (Figures 3.1 to 3.4) and will walk you through each one.

Political and Social Research Internship

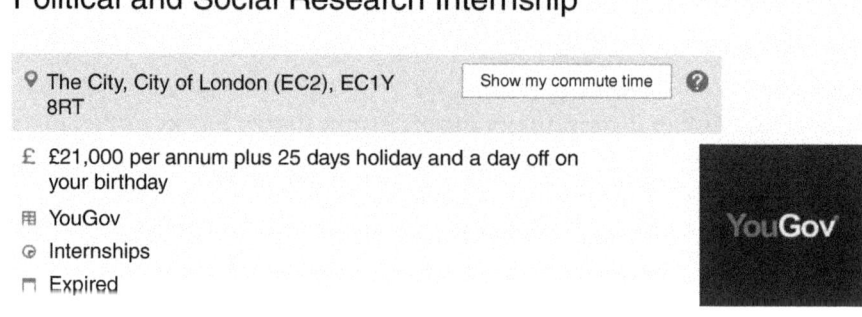

Figure 3.1 YouGov advert part 1

Part 1 appears at the top of the page. It gives a title, shows location, salary, a link to the organisation and makes it clear that this is an internship (rather than a position with the company).

We are searching for a very strong candidate to join our Political and Social Research Department for a one year student placement.

This role will involve working as a key member of the team, writing survey questions, scripting surveys, analysing data and producing results.

The successful candidate will assist on a range of political and social research projects, covering a wide range of subjects including everything from voting intention polling to Strictly Come Dancing predictions.

Clients will include major media organisations, academics, political parties, NGOs, charities, pressure groups, think tanks and 10 Downing Street.

Throughout the twelve-month placement you can expect to gain unrivalled experience of conducting primary quantitative research for one of the country's most successful, innovative and well-known research organisations.

The position would be best suited to a confident, well-organised, outgoing individual who has an understanding of primary research and a desire to pursue a career in either politics or political and social research.

The role is ideal for sandwich year students and 2nd year undergraduates looking for a placement.

Figure 3.2 YouGov advert part 2

Part 2 outlines which part of the organisation the successful candidate will join, a brief outline of what they will be undertaking in role, and what type of person they hope will apply. It lists some of the clients you will work with and describes the type of research that will be undertaken. It states clearly it is a 12-month long position. Finally it says at what stage of your education this is suitable for.

Main duties and responsibilities will include:

- Producing results for publication
- Writing reports for the YouGov website and clients
- Producing questions and proposing topics for research
- Creating surveys using our in-house software
- Working with social media to disseminate news and results

Candidates will need to demonstrate the following:

- Excellent written and spoken English accompanied by good numerical skills
- A strong interest in and knowledge of British politics
- An understanding of quantitative data and statistics
- A full working knowledge of Microsoft Excel and Word
- An ability to meet strict deadlines
- A keen eye for detail

Experience using the following is desirable but not essential:

- SPSS
- Microsoft PowerPoint
- PDF
- R
- Twitter

Figure 3.3 YouGov advert part 3

This section of the advert is what you need to pay careful attention to. I will use this part of the advert when I talk about how to write a letter of application later in this chapter. It outlines what the intern will do, and lists the criteria they are looking for. They will shortlist candidates on the basis of these. Note that not all the criteria are essential, but a strong candidate will provide evidence of **all** of the essential criteria and **some** (if not all) of the desirable ones too. You will be probed further at interview, if invited. We will come back to this in the next chapter.

To apply, please send your CV in PDF format and a covering letter.

Closing date: 31st December 2018.

Interviews will be held on 28th and 29th January 2019 at our London HQ.

Start date : Mid August 2019 (exact date TBC with the successful candidate).

Contact: Mark Hassan-Ali
Reference: Milkround/YouGov/PoliticalIntern
Job ID: 83989410

| ✉ Create alert | Apply | ☆ Save |

Figure 3.4 YouGov advert part 4

Finally in Part 4 details are provided to enable you to apply. There are some simple instructions here, but you would be surprised how many people do not follow these. I know from personal discussions. For instance, it says 'send your CV in PDF format'. If you fail to do this you risk having your CV not even looked at. This may seem harsh but it is the reality of the world of work, and gives the recruiter a very easy way to reject applications that do not follow this simple instruction.

The purpose of introducing this internship advert is to get you to start thinking about what an application would entail, and helping you decide whether or not you are eligible to apply. The YouGov example is a great one to start with, even if it does represent an ambitious internship, as it outlines everything required so clearly. This also serves as an opportunity for you to think about where else might run similar schemes. You don't have to rely solely on your university to get you an internship and indeed many universities will expect their students to find their own. With a little digging you can find one for yourself, and this chapter will help guide you to do so. And if it's a year-long one, like the one included here, you could approach your university and explore whether they have a year-in-industry scheme you could participate in, or whether you could take a year out of your degree to pursue a 12-month internship. The take-home message here is to be proactive and flexible. Go for it – employers want bright students who show initiative, and can fit in with the organisation. More on this later.

I also introduce here the important notion of starting to think about the work place-ment from the organisation's perspective. Later in this chapter, and elsewhere in the book, I expand upon this, but to give you some food for thought have a read of the following extract from an interview with the former head of political and social research at YouGov (the department that the example above is from). Note how he expresses the need for applicants to be able to understand the culture of the organisation, the 'way we do things here'. This further supports why companies like YouGov offer internship opportunities to students, in order that they can gain this precious experience.

> You need to learn the way we do things, the way that a commercial organisation does things and there's really no substitute for actually being on the job for doing that.
>
> And particularly, with interns of any kind actually, whether it's our year-long internship or our shorter work experience stuff, you need people who … intellectually from the interview, can think logically, can think through things, don't get flustered. All that sort of thing.

Employer
perspective

Former head of political and social research, YouGov

Friends and family

You may come from a well-connected background and have contacts and networks you can tap into to help you find opportunities external to your studies. If you are in that position you may feel you don't need this book, or at least not to find a work place-ment. The rest of the chapters should still be of value to you however. Do be careful though; if you do find a placement through friends or family exercise some caution. Ensure you create a professional working relationship and be aware that sometimes knowing people can introduce difficulties into a work relationship. Not only might your co-workers have opinions about nepotism, but you may feel less able to be objec-tive about the experience, and this could be self-limiting. My advice would be to try to find a work placement that you are not connected to through family or friends.

For most of us who are not well-connected at the stage in which we are acquiring our higher-level skills, a bit of help is welcome. We will come back to how friends and family can support you later, but the reason this section is included is because you may have networks you haven't identified as a potential source of opportunity yet. You also might not know what your family or friends actually do; you could start by asking them. People mostly like to talk about themselves, and if you precede this with a 'I'm thinking of trying to get some work experience so I can see how I can put my learning into practice in the real world of social research' you might be surprised what emerges from a conversation with someone you thought you knew, but didn't really ever know how they spent their working life. Be bold – ask and see what happens.

What to look for

Having stepped you through getting started, this section moves on to helping you think carefully about what it is you want from a situated-learning experience, and how you can think about this in a way that will help you find it. At the start of this chapter I used the decorating analogy to talk about being prepared. Imagine how frustrating it would be to sit in your newly decorated room but be constantly reminded of your lack of preparation because of bumpy walls or holes in the plastering, which could have been fixed with a little time and effort. Your time is much better spent if you are motivated *and prepared*, and putting the necessary time into planning always pays off.

Top tips

Start early

Whether you have a scheme at your place of study you can apply through or you are doing this alone, completely from scratch, ensure you build in time to plan for all the stages required to secure a work placement. Don't leave this to the last minute.

Get organised

Keep a record of what you are interested in – this helps you see patterns in the sorts of work placements that you are drawn to. Note down websites and adverts. It's easy to forget where you saw them.

It ought to be clear by now that there are various types of situated-learning. Your task is to find *one that is right for you*, or at least will help advance you in your quest to gain research skills that could benefit you during and after your studies. Table 3.2 shows the different types of work-integrated learning and tells you which of these this book will deal with.

Table 3.2   Types of work placements or internships

	Type	Assessed/non-assessed	Duration
A	Structured work placement or internship aligned to study	**Assessed** as part of your qualification Compulsory part of a structured course	Varies e.g. day a week across one semester, 6 weeks in a block, a year-in-industry
B	Structured work placement or internship aligned to study	**Not assessed** as part of your qualification Optional and competitive	Varies e.g. 2 months in the summer

	Type	Assessed/non-assessed	Duration
C	Work placement or internship not aligned to study	**Not assessed** For example, the YouGov one in this chapter	Often 3, 6 or 12 months full-time
D	More like a secondment, can form part of your continuing professional development	**May or may not be assessed** Could include different formats, e.g. shadowing another role, working in a different team for a period	Varies, 3 or 6 months common

Table 3.2 describes the four most common types of work placement or internships. You will find this book particularly helpful if you are interested in those described by types A, B or C, although if your placements falls into type D there is still much in these pages that will help you (especially the reflective framework). Indeed, it is hoped that anyone, at any stage of their study or career, will be able to dip into the chapters to take advice. The book is written very much from the point of view of those who do not know where to get started. It is intended to help those who may not have a formal work placement programme at their place of study and will help anyone who needs advice at various stages of the process. Multiple examples have been included to help you get started, although the book is not intended as a comprehensive source of *all* work placements; rather it focuses on applied social research opportunities. If you don't have an organised scheme at your university don't despair, use the resources supplied here to help you find one, then everything else in this book will help you put steps in place for how to get one once you've done this.

The questions shown in Table 3.3 provides some considerations you need to think about when seeking a work placement. Consider these questions before you start your search – and we will come back to these throughout this chapter.

Table 3.3 Considerations when seeking a work placement

Consideration	Question
Practical matters	• Do I want (need) a paid or unpaid placement?
	• Time: What duration can I commit to?
	• Location: Where can I feasibly work?
Type of internship	• What type of internship do I want?
	• What working culture am I seeking? (consider expected hours of work, and sector – commercial, educational, public, voluntary)
	• If assessed, how will this fit into my studies?
	• If not assessed, how would this contribute to my degree?
Skills required	• What are the essential and desirable skills for the role?
Eligibility criteria	• Are there any special requirements? (e.g. security clearance, need to be a citizen of the host country, studying a certain degree subject)
Fit with my plans	• Does it fit with what I want to do in the future?
	• What, if any, on-the-job training might I be offered and so what could I learn?

This list of questions is non-exhaustive, but will help you narrow down what you are searching for, and then when you find something it will help you decide whether to proceed to the next step, in other words whether to apply. In life, including student life, things rarely match our carefully thought-through plans. One of the recurring themes of this book is to be focused, and at the same time flexible and open-minded. If you apply for an internship that doesn't quite measure up to your perfect idea of what it should be, you may find you end up being pleasantly surprised. Anna's case study in Chapter 1 is a prime example of this. On the other hand, if you proceed to apply for something that you have no interest in, and no skills for, this is likely to be a waste of your time and can lead to self-defeating behaviour. You need to draw breath before diving in.

What's your motive?

There is a useful book I recommend to many of my students and postgraduates, called *Thinking, Fast and Slow* by the Nobel Memorial Prize winner Daniel Kahneman (2011). He distinguishes between fast, intuitive thinking and slow, rational thinking, and provides copious research to demonstrate how humans are prone to make quick, instinctive decisions, which can be improved if we pause and think, instead of rushing to act. One of the key ideas he proposes is 'Prospect Theory', which shows how humans hate losing more than they like winning (Kahneman, 2011: 278–88). I offer the same advice here. Before rushing into an internship or work placement it's important to stop and think about why you are doing this, what you want to achieve, and why. And as you will be investing your precious time into this it is important to be realistic about the outcome, based on your own assessment of your skills and experience. The 'how do I do this?' then becomes a series of logical steps, and the self-assessment of your potential informs your preparations.

Table 3.2 introduced *types* of work-integrated learning you might be able to apply for. The most important question for you to answer though, is 'what's my motive?' You need to be clear why you want to expend your energies in this way. Figure 3.5 offers a series of questions you need to ask yourself before you start searching the university website or internet for your perfect work placement, and definitely before you put pen to paper. All of these are good reasons to consider undertaking a placement. If on the other hand you really are not sure why you are doing this (because everyone else is/your parents told you to/you think you should but you're not really sure why), you might like to give this some more thought and make sure it's the right step for you.

Case study 3.1 makes this more real. I introduced Anna in Chapter 1, so you already know that she was successful in securing an internship.

Figure 3.5 What's my motive?

Case study 3.1

Anna: My motivation for applying for an internship

One of Anna's friends, from the same degree course, was applying for an internship and Anna thought she would take a look into this too. Anna was an international student studying in the UK. She was not actually planning to do an internship, having expected to spend the summer earning money through a holiday job, as she had done previously, probably returning home to do so. But her head was turned when she realised she could have the possibility of working for an organisation that would help fill some gaps in her CV, *and* earn money doing so.

When asked about what motivated her to apply for a summer internship, Anna said:

(Continued)

> I think it was the prospect of being able to do your own research that would be relevant to your degree that persuaded me to apply. It's quite difficult to find anything that is relevant to politics research as a second year student as most of the big organisations don't want an undergraduate. … NGOs and think tanks seem to prefer Master's students. I think they want people with a bit more experience than I had. Anyway, I applied for a placement at the Social Action Research Foundation but didn't get it.

Hopefully you can see how Anna's motivations spurred her on. And even though she was not successful with her first attempt, this did not stop her gaining a placement subsequently. You will see how Anna's journey unfolded throughout this book. Having contemplated your reasons for doing this, like Anna did, and assuming you have decided this is a good move or at least you want to continue to explore this some more, the next stage is to consider what *you* have to offer.

Evidencing your skills and experiences

As an educator I am always astounded by the skills that our undergraduates already have. What puzzles me though is that they don't know this, or more accurately they don't know how to express these skills and attributes in ways that employers look for. Perhaps academics are less well-versed in knowing how to express academic skills as employable skillsets because many of them have not worked outside of education. And education is not simply about creating employable graduates (as discussed in Chapter 2). Most academics will have excelled at school, college, and now university, and some will not have worked elsewhere, so it is not surprising that they often do not have a full and current appreciation of the labour market outside their sphere of expertise. Fortunately for you I have vast experience of knowing what employers are looking for, have thought long and hard about how students can articulate their learning in ways that chime with what organisations are seeking, and have first-hand testimonies from employers about their needs. I cover this in more detail too in Chapters 7 and 8. Careers consultants are also experts in this area and are a natural place to turn in the first instance, but may be less focused on the types of work experience covered in this book.

Surfacing your work-relevant skills

Let's take a typical day in an undergraduate social science student's second year and see what sorts of skills that student might have (see Table 3.4). I expand on this further in Table 3.5, but for starters consider the following activities on a regular teaching day.

Table 3.4 Skills gained through studying

Task	Skill
Get to lectures	Time management
Listen to lecture, take notes, attend tutorial, give informed response to pre-set course reading	Writing, assimilating knowledge, reflection, critical argument, verbal presentation
Start essay assignment	Planning research to develop main arguments, understand marking criteria, written skills

These cover some of the main educational activities at undergraduate level. Fold into this that many students will also have a job, and enjoy an active social life, and you can start to develop this into a longer list. Table 3.5 shows in the left hand column some activities that students typically undertake. The right hand column then translates these into language describing employable, or work-relevant, skills. Take a look and see how you too can evidence far more than you think you probably can simply by reframing your educational and life experiences into work-relevant skills and attributes. We will do more of this in later chapters, as you further develop these skills in the workplace.

Table 3.5 Work-relevant skills acquired

Things I do/have done	Work-relevant skills I have acquired
Studying	Developed a strategic learning approach
	Developed critical thinking and reasoning skills
	Practised argumentation and persuasion
	Understood the need to submit work on time
	Learned how to credit and attribute other people's work
Being a student, assessment submission and dealing with feedback	Developed resilience
	Learned to prioritise tasks and manage competing demands
	Learned how to accept, incorporate and learn from feedback
Work in a pub/shop/café	Delivered good customer service
	Developed good oral communication skills
	Practised diplomacy
Balance a busy study/home/family life	Developed excellent time management and problem-solving skills
House-share	Managed people and resources
	Showed leadership (e.g. organising a cleaning rota, being responsible for ensuring bills are paid on time)
	Developed emotional intelligence
Make money go a long way	Budget management (even better if you keep a spreadsheet to do this)

(Continued)

Table 3.5   (Continued)

Things I do/have done	Work-relevant skills I have acquired
Deal with the unexpected	Dealt with adversity and unanticipated events (illness, personal difficulties when essays due, requested an extension)
Move house, change courses, etc.	Change management
	Developed adaptability

Once you start to think about everything you do, and put yourselves in the mind of an employer who doesn't know you, you can start to appreciate that actually much of what you do is useful and applicable to a work context. After all, studying is hard work, you're just (usually) not paid to do it. Later in this book I will encourage you to think about the skills you particularly want to focus on when you take up a work placement opportunity. I hope you are already beginning to think about this. For example, you may particularly wish to focus on a type of analysis, a research topic, or learning a particular piece of software and be seeking a work placement to enable you to do this. Or you may be more interested in acquiring experience in a particular sector, perhaps to help you better appreciate whether this is an area you would wish to pursue on graduating. To enable you to start to think though these motivations you need to be able to express your skills and attributes on your Curriculum Vitae (CV). This is your starting point for being able to see what you have to offer an employer or host organisation.

Getting skills down on your CV

The intention here is not to teach you how to write a CV. There are many fantastic resources on the internet for that, some of which are included in Three Things You Can Do Next at the end of this chapter, and careers services are masters at helping with this. Rather this section is to help you understand how you can *evidence* your skills and attributes in a way that will convince an employer that you could apply what you know in a way that would be useful to their organisation.

This example, from an employer's perspective, demonstrates why evidencing your skills in a way that helps an employer understand how you can *apply* those skills matters. Sam is a data analyst in a large university undergraduate planning department. He had the opportunity to interview three interns for just one post. Here is what he said after making his selection, when asked why this student was suitable.

Employer
perspective

The quality of students was quite impressive especially when I think about myself as an undergraduate. I don't think my CV, and the way I presented myself, was up to their standards. We could have probably taken any one of the three to do the placement but H stood out in terms of the data skills he had and he also came across a little more confident. He had a lot of work experience outside of the university too, so we thought he would integrate into a team quicker than the others. And also with an internship you accept that there is a certain amount of supervision that you will have to give the students but he convinced us he would be able to pick up things quickly.

There's a lot packed into this. First, the student's CV had got him shortlisted – and looking back at it he evidenced that he talked about what he learned on his courses and also that he had a job (in a fast-food outlet, not a professional or office setting). He had also sought support, from me and the careers service, and we had made suggestions to him, which he had acted upon. The academic and non-academic aspects in his CV were both picked up at interview. Importantly not only did he say what he had studied, but *what he had learned and how he could apply it* (e.g. tables in Excel using social survey data to analyse crime patterns in London). And he came across confidently – more on this in the next chapter when we introduce interviews, but it is absolutely possible to put yourself across confidently in your CV too. His ability to 'pick things up quickly' was evidenced by his non-academic skills, he had worked in his job for two years and been made a supervisor, and shown leadership. The point is that all of these things matter. Employers are looking for people who can get on with the job, albeit with some supervision, and in an internship this is a primary concern. Hence, indicating you are a fast learner, and demonstrating on your CV how you can show this, is important.

An example CV

The fictional CV shown in Figure 3.6 is based on a combination of good CVs I have seen. Treat this as a CV to aspire to. This one provides a name and address, but increasingly this is becoming non-standard practice, as organisations are moving towards blind recruitment processes. I have included name and address here, although not date of birth. You must decide what personal data you choose to supply, and be led by the requirements of the organisation you are applying to.

Carlotta Russell

Address: 23 Bridge Street, Manchester, M20 9PP, UK

Contact details: carlotta.b.russell101@gmail.com | 077 2345 6798

PROFILE

I am a second year undergraduate keen to work in a future role in Social Policy or Social Research. I have a broad range of skills and interests and most enjoy being stretched through challenges that enable me to work in a team, whilst taking personal responsibility for a task. I am keen to apply my academic learning to real world complex issues such as climate change or global inequalities.

(Continued)

Figure 3.6 (Continued)

EDUCATION AND QUALIFICATIONS

University of Manchesterford, UK

Bachelor of Social Science (BASS) Politics and Philosophy

First Year Result: 68%, Second Year results: 74%

Expected Result: First Class Degree, Graduation 2020

Relevant courses: Introduction to Data Analysis; The Social Survey; Research Methods; Making Sense of Politics; Introduction to Philosophy; Globalization in the 21st Century

South Chesterford High School, UK

A Levels: 2017: Geography A, Politics A, Biology B

GCSEs: 2015: English A, Maths B, Biology A, Chemistry C, Physics B, French B, Geography A, Art & Design B, Religious Studies B

EXPERIENCE

Student Representative, University of Manchesterford, UK *2018–*

Elected role, act as active link between students and the university to represent the student body. Gather student opinion by conducting surveys and developing statistics via reports, which I then present to University Board of Governors.

Volunteer, Citizens Advice Bureau, UK *2017–2018*

Worked in local branch of Citizens Advice Bureau. Supported members of staff to handle queries from citizens seeking advice. Observed multiple examples of social justice in action. Supported the team with data collection and processing.

London International Model United Nations (LIMUN) High School (HS), UK *2016*

One of 500 delegates in the 2016 inaugural event. Discussed global issues, diplomacy and mediation on pressing world problems including climate change and global inequalities.

Part-time barista, Nantwich, UK *2015–2017*

Worked in the local gym café in a team of 8 people during weekends, evenings and holidays.

SKILLS AND INTERESTS

- Data Analysis (SPSS-Statistical Package for the Social Science, STATA, R, NVivo)
- IT (Microsoft Word, Excel, PowerPoint)
- Teamwork, Leadership, Public Relations
- International Politics, Gender Politics, Development Studies, Global Justice, Global Inequalities
- Excellent written and verbal communication skills, highly organised, creative and resilient
- Languages: English, conversational French
- Member of the University hockey team

REFERENCES

Can be supplied on request

Figure 3.6 An example CV

The CV is well structured and has all the essential information required. *Name and contact details* are clear. The *Profile* provides a brief summary of the person and sets out what she hopes to achieve, as well as her key interests, in just a few sentences – this gives a sense of the person behind the CV. A reader can quickly ascertain what level of *Education* this student is at and what formal *Qualifications* she possesses, as well as her degree subject and how she is performing in her assessments. She also includes some information about the university courses she has taken that are relevant to an application for a research placement. Her school-level qualifications are also clearly presented. There is some detail about relevant *Experience*, in chronological order (most recent first) and how, even with limited experience, she is developing and availing herself of opportunities. The *Skills and Interests* section separates out technical and IT skills (note she lists the software packages she has used) from her substantive interests, and also includes a bullet (not obligatory) about language competencies. Finally a section is included for *References*, which in this case invites further details but could easily include names and contact details of referees (although note you should only include these with permission).

Competency-based frameworks

Some companies and organisations use *competency-based frameworks* during their recruitment processes. These companies not only want to understand what you know, but how you can apply it. You will likely be asked to give lots of examples at interview in a 'give us an example of when you had a difficult situation to deal with' and the answer needs to include sufficient information for the interviewer to determine your potential for responding in a given situation. In Chapters 4 and 9 I talk more about competency, and other frameworks, used by recruiters.

This section is about CVs, not interviews, but it is well worth thinking through the four pillars of response for a competency when writing your CV. The four pillars are captured in the acronym STAR representing: the *situation*, the *task* required as a result, the *action* you took and the *result* of that action. I am not suggesting you have to write each of these on your CV; rather that if you describe a skill on your CV (e.g. analytical thinking) you could construct an example of a situation, task, action and result that would demonstrate that particular skill. For example, I needed to think analytically about how to approach this book (task), whilst working full-time (situation) so I found a peaceful place to write during weekends (action) and developed the outline for the book which was written incrementally over a number of months (result). See where I'm going with this? The writing of the book/essay/dissertation/thesis is the end product – you need to think about all the stages in between and capture on your CV the skills that you used to get there. In Chapter 4 I will look at STAR applied to interviewing.

Do you meet the criteria?

Once you identify a placement or internship suitable for you, the next step is to consider the information provided carefully. If this is written down, read the description in detail; if it's not available in a written form then either request this or make notes and ask the organisation to confirm if your understanding of the placement aligns with theirs. For the purposes of this section let's assume that there is a written expression of what is required.

Eligibility criteria

If your organisation has a work placement programme, they are likely to have criteria for applying for an internship through this. You may be required to be in a particular year of study, or on a specific degree programme, or have achieved a certain grade or mark in your studies at the time you apply. Check that you meet these requirements before doing anything else. If you do not, then by all means ask the internship coordinator if you can apply, but be mindful that these eligibility criteria are governed by valid reasons (e.g. due to the funding source, or the need to fill the gap for certain skills, or the strategy implemented by the institution) and hence you may receive a response to explain why you are not eligible. At this stage don't give up – as universities increasingly recognise the enormous value of providing work-placed experiences, more and more opportunities are being made available. Enquire about other possibilities (e.g. through your careers service) and check these out, and use the resources provided earlier in this chapter.

If you have to find an internship for yourself (as discussed earlier in this chapter), you will need to check whether the position you have found has specific criteria attached to it, so this section is still relevant to you.

Here's an example. The University of Manchester has an internship programme designed for social science students to fill the need for more quantitatively trained graduates. This programme, called Q-Step, has two levels of eligibility. The *first* is the degree studied; the *second* is the course units being studied as part of the degree. To be eligible to apply for an internship you would need to be studying a selected degree (at the university) and also, on that programme of study, some specific course units (sometimes called modules). You are expected to be achieving at 60% or higher in your coursework and exams at the time of application. This is all made clear during the application process, but each year enquiries arrive from students who do not meet one or more of these criteria. These students are directed to other opportunities that they can explore, and/or to the careers service.

Do you have the required skills and experience?

I introduced evidencing your skills and experiences above, in the section on developing your CV. Having done this you need to check the required skills and experiences for the placement.

Having a flexible approach to reflecting on and updating your CV introduces good practice for future job applications. Most internship documentation will state clearly the essential and desirable skills sought for the position (as the previous YouGov example did). Read these carefully. If you do not meet the *essential* skills then you should not really apply for the role. Some people will do, regardless of not meeting the essential criteria, but I would not advise it *for an internship*. The shortlisting panel will sift the applications and discount those that do not meet *all* the essential criteria, so you are not using your time wisely by applying. If, on the other hand, you do have all the essentials but do not have the *desirable* skills then don't let this stop you. By definition these are looked for but not necessary. You may have all, or some, or none of these. Whatever you have, providing you meet all the essentials, then you can apply for the role.

Here is an example to illustrate this.

Essential: Numerate, punctual, reliable, committed, proactive, good communication skills, ability to work in a team

Desirable: SPSS knowledge, analytical skills, ability to multi-task, attention to detail

The essentials can all be covered by your CV (so in the example above you would include this in the Skills section) and/or covering letter (more on this in how to apply). And of course be prepared to defend what you say on paper if invited for interview. In the list of desirables you may feel you can make a good case to say you have all of these except perhaps one, for example the 'SPSS knowledge' (SPSS is a statistical software package created by IBM and often used in the social sciences). You can, if you choose, be upfront in your covering letter about this whilst drawing attention to the skills you do have that would enable you to learn this on the job. And be sure to indicate your willingness to learn new skills and software. More on this in the letter of application extract below.

Ensure you can commit

Finally, this is an obvious consideration, but apply for an internship only if you fully intend to commit to it. Commitment takes a variety of forms, but the two most important ones are time and attitude. If you cannot give the number of weeks required of the internship then it might be wiser not to put yourself forward for it. I have experienced students who gain work placement opportunities at prestigious organisations and then drop out. This reflects badly on them, is not good for the relationship with the university and the academic who established the opportunity, and can be irritating and inconvenient for the organisation that needs to find someone else. If you cannot commit the time then don't apply. If on the other hand you can, but you have a reason to need time away during the period of the internship, that is usually fine providing you are upfront about this from the start.

Second, you require a commitment of attitude. Time and time again the employers I work with refer to this, making it clear that they look for enthusiastic, smart, committed students, and they want people to stand out on application and at interview. When asked why YouGov put so much emphasis on work placements, here was the response:

Employer perspective

… as a commercial organisation, we are really up for having interns but we need to minimise the amount of time this takes up. People really, really want to work here and so if you don't put the effort in, or seem like you're not bothered, then we can't be bothered with you. I speak as an employer who has to frequently go through 500 CVs … so many of them look the same and often not in a good way. What we are looking for is differentiation. Someone who stands out. Someone who can point to something in their CV that convinces you they can work in your environment.

Former head of social and political research, YouGov

How to apply

Now, you've reflected on your skills and experience and developed your CV, you've found a work placement opportunity that aligns with what you want to do, or at least a site where you can search for one, and you're committed and have allocated time in your diary to do this. The next step is to prepare to make the application. This might be a structured process, typically requiring a CV and letter of application, or, depending on the internship, it may be more loosely defined. Either way it will require you to do two things: one get yourself mentally prepared, and two get everything together and submit your application.

This section will step you through the process of applying. Before doing so though you might want to think about your strategy, and start to develop a positive frame of mind, or mindset, to help you. As you know, from the first case study in this chapter, Anna's first attempt was unsuccessful, but she did go on to find a placement that worked out well for her. By her own admission, initially she had only applied for one internship and when she did not get it she was almost ready to walk away. She and

I spoke about her wish to continue, and what she had to offer, and she went on to apply for more, casting her net more widely. We both learned a valuable lesson – to keep options open and not despair if the first opportunity does not bear fruit. Pick yourself up and keep going.

Case study 3.2

Ryan: Applying for several internships

Ryan's strategy was to apply for three internships with three very different organisations: an economic think-tank, a national charity and a standards-setting agency for medical education and practice. Partly this was, as he says, because his degree and his interests were very broad.

> As an interdisciplinary student I was interested in the interconnectedness of the fields I was studying (politics, philosophy and economics). I also had a great interest in computation and knowledge representation and all of the positions I applied for were interesting in different ways. I saw an internship as a great way to evidence how I could put into practice my learning, and to use this to build my CV as well as my experience. I adapted each of my applications to reflect the internship I was applying for.

Ryan took an internship at the General Medical Council (GMC). This was after he was interviewed for all three and offered two. He chose the GMC one as it allowed him to be in London for the summer and learn a range of new software tools and skills, which aligned with his motivations for undertaking the experience.

Both Anna and Ryan were successful in the end. They are both included here to show that whilst each approach is valid, Anna needed to revisit hers to achieve success. By changing tactics, broadening her options, whilst not compromising her interests, and keeping going, Anna achieved an excellent outcome. Importantly, they both had a positive mindset before applying for their internship. They had thought about their degrees, the reasons for undertaking an internship, and the value to them in terms of their graduate prospects. Interestingly too they had both thought about the gap in their CVs (skills and experience) and were using the chance of an internship to close these gaps. Moreover, they knew what was required of them to enable them to make a strong application, in part informed by their having drawn on their lectures, but also speaking to people (me, their lecturers and their friends). They also both had to handle not being given an internship they were interviewed for. This is such an important part of the whole process I devote a section to discussing this in the next chapter. Dealing with failure is important. Dealing well with failure is essential.

We will return to 'where to get help' later in this chapter. Let's move on to putting everything together to make an application.

Starting your application: pulling everything together

The actual process for application will differ depending on your institution and on the information requested. It is likely though that you will need to think about the following in terms of bringing everything together, to enable you to apply:

- An outline of the internship/work placement
- Your CV
- A tailored letter of application or covering letter
- Information about the interview

That's all quite straightforward. And actually you could replace the first bullet point by 'job description' and see that this just mimics the steps involved in applying for a job. I cover this in more detail in Chapters 7–9. In fact, if you see this as an opportunity to try out a job, that helps frame the experience in a way that can help guide you in your future choices. See, always thinking positively about the value of your time helps you deal with why you are doing this. Nothing is ever wasted.

Letter of application

Creating a tailored letter of application is essential. In this section I focus on how you can write this to target the position you are applying for, drawing on the YouGov 12-month long internship example introduced earlier in the chapter.

Our fictional character, Carlotta (whose CV was introduced above), wishes to apply for the YouGov internship introduced earlier. For the sake of this section we can assume that she is eligible to apply, and can take a full year to do this. Below is an *extract* from her letter of application (also called a covering letter). It focuses on her motivation for applying, shows what differentiates her, and covers her skills and experience to match the essentials and desirables specified for the post.

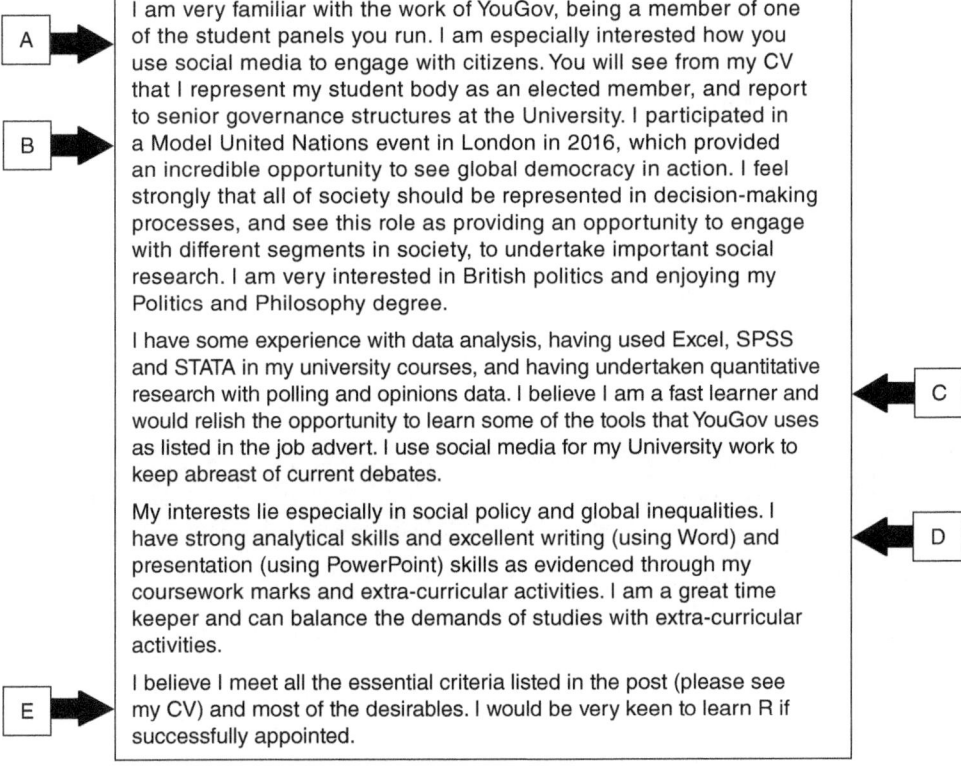

A I am very familiar with the work of YouGov, being a member of one of the student panels you run. I am especially interested how you use social media to engage with citizens. You will see from my CV that I represent my student body as an elected member, and report to senior governance structures at the University.

B I participated in a Model United Nations event in London in 2016, which provided an incredible opportunity to see global democracy in action. I feel strongly that all of society should be represented in decision-making processes, and see this role as providing an opportunity to engage with different segments in society, to undertake important social research. I am very interested in British politics and enjoying my Politics and Philosophy degree.

I have some experience with data analysis, having used Excel, SPSS and STATA in my university courses, and having undertaken quantitative research with polling and opinions data. I believe I am a fast learner and would relish the opportunity to learn some of the tools that YouGov uses as listed in the job advert. I use social media for my University work to keep abreast of current debates. C

My interests lie especially in social policy and global inequalities. I have strong analytical skills and excellent writing (using Word) and presentation (using PowerPoint) skills as evidenced through my coursework marks and extra-curricular activities. I am a great time keeper and can balance the demands of studies with extra-curricular activities. D

E I believe I meet all the essential criteria listed in the post (please see my CV) and most of the desirables. I would be very keen to learn R if successfully appointed.

Key:

A. First three sentences show her interest and active participation in the organisation. Writing is good and succinct.
B. Indicates knowledge and interest in politics, and in British politics which is specifically requested.
C. Evidences interest and experience in quantitative data and statistics, a requirement of the post.
D. Speaks to the requirement for an ability to meet strict deadlines and have a keen eye for detail (analytical skills), as well as references two of the software packages sought.
E. Points out that although she does not have R (one of the desirables) she is keen to learn it if successful.

Figure 3.7 Letter of application – an extract

This extract shows how her letter of application has brought together relevant information to help the task of shortlisting easier for the organisation. She has looked at the requirements in the job advert, the skills and experience on her CV, and addressed these together with her motivation to apply and her suitability for the position.

Hopefully her application will result in an interview. But remember that if she forgets to send a PDF document (as requested) she is likely to be rejected at the first pass. Perhaps YouGov use this precisely as a filtering mechanism, and if they do you don't want to fall foul of simple instructions.

Nearly there – check your checklist

Back to getting everything together. You will have your own preferred style of planning and getting organised, but for those who like checklists, Table 3.6 offers a blank one for you to work with.

Table 3.6   Checklist – preparing to submit an application for a work placement or internship

Title of internship:		
Task	Action: What I need to do and when	Date completed
Schedule time to find an internship – allow more time if no formal programme is available		
Schedule time to make a good job of my application		
Save everything related to the internship/work placement in a folder (virtual or physical)		
Read the information carefully, then read again		
Make a list of what I need to do		
Make a start on the application, don't worry where, just make a start		
Tailor my CV so that it highlights the criteria I will succeed or fail on		
Write my draft letter of application with the organisation I am applying for in mind		
Find a trusted friend (I need another pair of eyes and a sounding board) and ask them to read my application		
Do a check – have I collated everything I need?		

That's it. You're nearly ready. You've allocated time, got organised, done the preparatory thinking, mentally prepared yourself for developing your application, and you have everything in one place, and have started your application. A few more steps and you'll be close to completing your application, and almost ready to submit it. Two things remain. The first, to ensure you have a support network, and the second – and this is really important before you submit – to put yourself in the shoes of your prospective host organisation.

Who to go to for support

Every successful person relies on a range of people to support them in what they do

icould.com (2016)

Support networks are important for helping you think about applying for an internship. You might want to refer back to that section now. I revisit this here, as it is such an important part of assisting you to become, and be, successful.

We all need support networks and undertaking an internship is no different. But you're not there yet, so let's stop and think about who can help you get there. You will no doubt be surrounded by other people like you, but you will have access to others too who can undertake an important role in your endeavour to get that prized work-based opportunity.

Developing your support network

You need to work out who you can turn to as you develop your application. Friends may be willing listeners but are they the best people to provide advice that will help you hone your offer to your prospective host organisation? Maybe they are, especially if they have good attention to detail, can write well and offer constructive feedback. Be prepared to think about other people in your life too. Lecturers, as we discovered above, have your interests at heart and are often willing to give constructive advice on aspects related to your prospects of being employable after you graduate. You will most likely have an assigned individual (academic adviser or mentor) who can be a sounding board. They are busy people though, academics, and so do not be disheartened if they do not or cannot respond to your requests to help. Your careers service are trained in this and will do everything they can to support you find gainful employment (and anything that leads to this). Outside of your studies think about who you know who is already successful (not necessarily just in terms of a career). Who do you know who can multi-task, has handled difficult times in their lives, always seems organised, or who you know to be a supportive critic? Approach them, ask for help. Whatever you do, do not submit an application that has not been seen by another human being. We all miss things, and the last thing you want to do at this stage is to submit a letter or CV with silly spelling mistakes or grammatical errors or in the wrong format (check this carefully). Remember – this is not a university essay you are submitting but an application for a professional position. You want to get past this first hurdle and secure an interview. You need to pay attention to this so take advice and put it into practice.

Put yourself in the employers' shoes

> You never really understand a person until you consider things from his point of view – until you climb into his skin and walk around in it.
>
> Harper Lee (1960)

One of my favourite books is *To Kill a Mockingbird* by Harper Lee. I first read it as a teenager and to be frank didn't really understand it other than on the level of a story about two children growing up in America's Deep South, with an awesome single-parent dad. Anyway I then re-read it as an adult at a time when I was working increasingly with organisations that were willing to offer students work-placed research opportunities and the central theme of considering matters from different perspectives resonated enormously. I see this played out constantly in my interactions with employers. They want to know what you can bring to their organisation, and how you will both fit in and do the role, often at minimum cost (time-wise) to them. The employer quotes in this chapter show this.

Right – that's not really a revelation is it – but how can you convince them you will add value, get the task done and help them deliver a valuable piece of applied research?

Why should they take you?

We've explored in this chapter the steps needed to get started. There is one very important element we need to cover before concluding. Indeed this provides a starting point for something that should form a cornerstone of your mindset about employment more generally; what's in it for them and why should they consider you the right person for the role?

Start by imagining yourself in the role of the person who, if you're successful, might end up interviewing and appointing you.

Imagine you are the internship recruiter

You're a busy professional, sitting at your desk with just 30 minutes to look through some CVs and letters of application for the internship role you are hoping to fill.

You've had a very busy morning, but you're determined to go through this pile and find someone who will help you deliver this important piece of applied research that you have wanted to do for months, but simply not had the resources to devote to it. You have a pile of applications in front of you and just hope there is one in there that will be suitable. You are excited about this prospect – it would really make a difference to the team and help the organisation you work for progress. There might even be an opportunity for your newest member of staff to supervise this intern, and for the team to get a publication out of it. You are motivated to find the best of the bunch, inter-view them and see where it goes.

You start looking through the applications with these questions in mind:

- Does this person's CV and letter of application instil confidence?
- Do they write well?
- Do I think they could take on the research we have in mind?
- What differentiates them – do they stand out and how?
- Does their academic record of achievement (grades) align with the skills I need them to have to do the research?
- Do they evidence the essential skills for the post?
- How many of the desirable skills do they have?
- Do they demonstrate anything (skills and experience) over and above other candidates?
- Do they talk about how they have applied their learning, not just what they have learned?
- Do they show sufficient enthusiasm (in their covering letter) for the role?
- Do they inspire confidence that they would be a self-starter?

The list could go on but these are the most important points to consider. In other words, if your CV and covering letter is just one of several tens or hundreds, how can you evidence what the recruiter is looking for? If you show your application to a trusted friend asking them to role-play the prospective shortlister, will you be placed on the 'proceed to interview' or 'reject' pile? And if the latter what can you do to make it onto the former?

A few final tips. Remember this book is about helping you to get a research-focused work placement. Think carefully about what you have done that will highlight this for the shortlisting recruitment panel. We will look in the next chapter at how you can talk about this if called for interview, but if your application does not cover this adequately then you need to revisit it and make this apparent. Never, ever assume that the people reading your application know anything about you. They do not. Start from this premise. Also bear in mind that increasingly for job interviews a machine could be reading your CV. Follow the advice in this chapter, and you will be one step closer to success.

Bringing it all together

In wrapping up this chapter I hope the steps outlined have led to a systematic way of thinking about undertaking a research work placement or internship. If you follow this advice there is no reason why you cannot find yourself on the way to spotting a suitable opportunity, submitting a strong application and receiving confirmation inviting you to interview. And if it doesn't happen on your first attempt, just keep trying. It's incredibly common to not be successful on your first attempt. Some students find it hard to deal with rejection, especially when they have always got straight As in their work, passed their driving test first time, got into the university of their first choice and so on. But rejection is part and parcel of life and not getting the first external opportunity you apply for is fine, just fine. Reflecting on feedback is a learned skill – few of us like to be told we were unsuccessful, or that we could have done better. Nonetheless, improving at anything requires us to be honest with ourselves and face up to what others think about us – even if we don't agree. Sometimes applications or interviews do not go well, and we're not shortlisted or selected, but the sooner we choose to learn from these experiences the more likely we are to improve next time. As a general rule, let us note here that we can all improve on everything we undertake, and accepting that early on may open up opportunities in the future.

The checklist in Table 3.7 follows on from Table 3.6 earlier in this chapter but takes you up to the point of completing the application and submitting it. Obviously if you apply for more than one role then you need to do this multiple times. Use this checklist as a final means of ensuring you have followed the advice presented here.

Table 3.7 Checklist – applying for a work placement or internship

Question	Answer: Yes/No/ Unclear	Action: What you need to do and when
Does the internship match my own requirements and motivations?		
Have I adequately addressed the essential and desirables elements of the post in my CV and/or letter of application?		
Have my documents been proofread by a trusted person?		
Have I considered my application from the perspective of the organisation I am applying to?		
Have I developed a support network?		
Have I developed a positive mindset to help me deal with this and the next steps?		
Have I done all of the above with good grace, and kept a steady head?		

Well done. If you have followed the advice here and done all of the above you are ready to submit your application and await a hopefully positive outcome. Or if not successful the first time you are ready to try again. And possibly keep trying. Good luck.

Summary

This chapter has provided information to get you to the point of finding an internship, evidencing your skills, writing a CV and a letter of application (or covering letter), thinking about all of this from the perspective of the host organisation, developing a support network and finally getting ready to apply. All of this needs to be done whilst cultivating and maintaining a positive mindset. The various tools provided throughout will help you get started and both prepare for and apply for an internship position. Use these to ensure you have everything covered, before you press 'send' on that application you have so carefully crafted.

Three things you can do next

1 Find a copy of Steve Rook's *Work Experience, Placements and Internships* (2016) and take a look at Chapter 3: 'Managing your networks and social media' and Chapter 9: 'Applications and interviews'.

2 Take a look at one of the following websites, or find your own university or college equivalent, for more information on developing a model CV. If you don't already have one, draft your first CV. If you do have one use these resources and the sample CV in this chapter to help you improve yours.

   a CV advice from Monster: www.monster.co.uk/career-advice/cv-writing-tips/cv-advice

   b Writing a CV first steps, University of Manchester: www.careers.manchester.ac.uk/applicationsinterviews/cv

3 To learn how Artificial Intelligence is being used in recruitment practices take a look at the article 'AI in recruitment isn't a prediction – it's already here' by Riaa O'Donnell at www.hrdive.com/news/ai-in-recruitment-isnt-a-prediction-its-already-here/514876/. Then return to the section on completing your CV and letter of application and ensure it has captured the keywords required for the post.

4

HOW TO PREPARE FOR, DO AND REFLECT ON AN INTERVIEW

—Learning objectives—

In this chapter you will learn how to:

- Evidence your research skills
- Describe your research skills for an interview
- Prepare for an interview
- Get through an interview
- Reflect on your interview
- Do all of the above with a positive mindset

'First we make the beast beautiful.'

Wilson (2018)

Overview

Chapter 4 focuses on the interview. Initially I called this chapter 'how to get an interview', but I think that's too bold a statement – and much better left to careers services and other professionals in this area. What I can do though is help you put all the necessary steps in place that will help you be supremely well placed to prepare for, get through and reflect on an interview for an applied social research work placement.

An interview can be an anxiety-inducing experience for students, and indeed many accomplished people also find this to be the case. The quote at the start of this chapter is taken from the title of a book on how to deal with anxiety. Psychologists and neuro-scientists have written extensively about the anxiety disorder spectrum, and described how anxiety can be a defence mechanism (e.g. Lang and McTeague, 2009: 6; McNaughton and Corr, 2004: 286). There is also empirical evidence to show that anxious interviewees fare less well in terms of the impression they make on, and the feedback they are given by, interviewers (Feiler and Powell, 2016: 156), although these studies do not show that anxious candidates would be less capable of performing in role.

In my experience the interview is probably the aspect of finding and doing a work placement that students worry about the most. After all, a lot depends on it so the stakes are high. Please try to relax, this book is here to help you.

This chapter will guide you through all stages of preparing for and undertaking an interview. Before you can even prepare for an interview you will need to reflect on your skills and experience to date, and understand how you can evidence these in a manner that will help you get an interview, and talk about what you can offer. I will pay particular attention here to helping you reflect on your research skills and show how you can give examples of these if asked. Chapter 3 helped you think about your more general skills and you may want to refer back to that. Once again, examples from students and organisations are included here. Humanities and social science students are taught applied research skills through a variety of different pedagogic approaches. They may be taught in methods classes or embedded into their substantive courses. This chapter will reflect different approaches and illustrate how students can talk about these skills during interviews. The examples provided will enable you to think about how you can demonstrate in an interview that the research skills you have learned in the classroom translate into subject knowledge and analytical skills that can be applied in, and are relevant to, the workplace.

This chapter does not cover, in any great depth, the questions you might be asked to elicit your professional skills. There are many excellent books and websites that can help you with that and some will be introduced at the end of this chapter, and Chapter 8 will focus on these professional skills. The strength of this chapter, which will help you differentiate yourself from your peers, is its focus on research skills and methods, and their potential for application in the workplace. Very few careers guid-ance or work placement books provide this important advice. Showing you how to recognise your research potential is critically important. In common with other chapters reflection takes centre stage, this time on the interview, and I will start to introduce the reflection framework that I expand upon in Chapter 6. Having a positive approach and mindset to the interview is interwoven through all the examples. My aim is to help you enjoy the experience, encourage you to bottle that feeling, and whatever the outcome teach you to see this as a necessary part of personal and professional growth.

How to evidence your research skills

Let me share with you a personal anecdote. Part-way through writing this book I decided I would like the opportunity to undertake a work placement myself. Having seen the transformational change some of my, and other universities', students had gone through during their internships, I thought it would be a good move, for my personal and professional development, to spend time in an organisation whose work I admired, and felt I could both learn from and contribute to. I approached the UK Office for National Statistics Data Science Campus team, and we discussed a chance for me to spend four days a week with them for six months on secondment.

As part of setting this opportunity up, I needed to develop a business case to demonstrate the value that I could bring to their organisation. This needed to be broader than simply submitting my CV. Here is an extract of what I wrote in my proposal to undertake a secondment:

> Jackie Carter has a background in maths, applied computing, social science, data analytics and education and an international profile in developing statistical skills training for university-level social science students. Starting her career as a secondary school maths teacher, she then gained a Master's and PhD in Applied Computing. Her career includes roles as: Data Visualisation Support Officer, Director of Teaching and Learning and Socioeconomic National Data Services; Senior Lecturer in Social Research Methods; and currently Professor in Statistical Literacy. She has developed a prestigious, high-profile paid internship programme for undergraduates to practise their data analysis skills through data-driven, research-led projects in the workplace. She has won numerous grants, published and presented internationally, is an active member of the statistical education community and a leader in experiential learning.

This overview enabled me to demonstrate how the skills I have developed over the course of my career were relevant to the position I was seeking. The detail of the teaching and research I have undertaken was covered separately in my academic CV. What this extract enabled me to do was highlight the main skills for the organisation in order to help them make a decision about whether or not to take me on. Think of it as a précis of my CV.

I include this extract here to help you see that even as our careers develop we need to keep in mind that our research and professional skills need to align with the positions we seek. Importantly, we need to be able to evidence these for a prospective employer. By writing this document I was able to think carefully about my own skills and experience that would be of value to the secondment organisation, and importantly omitted the ones that were not as relevant. Being succinct and on point is an important skill to acquire.

You, being at an early stage in your career, are likely to have a much smaller set of research experiences than mine. My task now is to help you appreciate what research skills you do have, and how you can evidence and draw on these in a way that you can then talk about if invited for interview, which is after all the end goal of this chapter.

Chapter 3 covered content on your skills and experiences generally, and provided a list of how you could think about these as work-relevant skills. I extend this now to focus on research skills. I write this section under the assumption that you have not done a work placement before, but if you have please do use your experience to contribute to what this chapter covers, and ensure you reference that experience.

Identifying your research skills

Since beginning your studies you will have been trained academically to ensure you can understand and critique theory, undertake a literature review, develop a research question, gather data (qualitative and/or quantitative), analyse the data and literature critically, write up your findings and draw a conclusion. In other words you have been taught how to do research. Social science is a field full of multiple perspectives, competing literatures and is often complex. Unlike in the natural sciences, there is rarely a 'right answer' and even if you do provide an answer it is usually caveated, or expressed in terms that show the uncertainty associated with the findings. Recognising this is a good place to start though, as the types of organisations that undertake social research are used to working with complex problems. To quote Laurence J. Peter: 'Some problems are so complex you have to be highly intelligent and well informed just to be undecided about them' (Peter quoted in Ratcliffe 2017).

In Chapter 1 I introduced you to the definition of applied social research that I use in this book. I differentiated this type of research from 'basic research'. Most universities teach research skills through methods classes, or embed the teaching of these skills through substantive classes. In the social sciences, the study of how to teach research skills is an emerging area of research, and there remains far more to be written on this. Of particular note is the work of Kilburn et al. (2014) who, drawing on other literature, list five categories that need to be considered when discussing the pedagogy of teaching research methods. These are as follows.

Five categories to consider when teaching research methods

1   The substantive nature of the subject taught
2   The knowledge and skills of the students and teachers
3   The organisation of the course
4   Fears and beliefs
5   The wider environment, including non-classroom teaching

Interestingly, although applied research through experiential learning is referred to in point number 5, there are few examples of where this learning has been systematically captured and researched. This book is one of the first examples of highlighting through narratives how this is being achieved through the workplace. For now, though, and before you apply your learning in the workplace, it is helpful to capture how classroom-based methods classes have approached the teaching of research methods.

The graphic representation in Figure 4.1 depicts how you may have acquired these skills through your education, in the classroom, the library and computer lab.

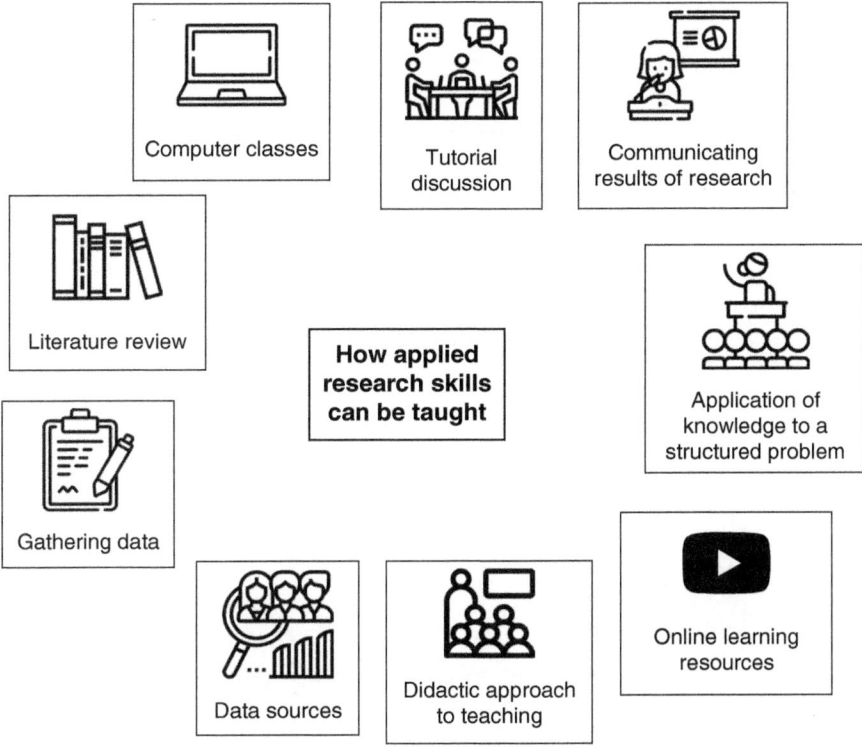

Figure 4.1 Examples of how applied research skills can be taught

Listing your research skills

Identifying your research skills will help enormously when you come to preparing for an interview. Table 4.1 extends what I started in Chapter 3, when I spoke about surfacing your work-relevant skills. . You may not have done all of the things listed in the table, but there is a good chance you have done some of them. The others might form a checklist you want to start for yourself so that you can add to your skillset before you complete your formal studies. Chapter 7 focuses exclusively on analytical and research skills and provides a framework and tools to help you elicit and capture yours, and think about how you want to develop them further.

Table 4.1 Checklist of research skills

Things I do/have done	Research skills I have acquired
Writing essays	Literature review
	Ability to attribute work to original authors, and knowledge of referencing systems (e.g. Harvard)
	Structuring an argument
	Writing, respecting the word limit
Taking exams	Planning a structured response
	Communicating salient points
	Answering a question with reference to learned knowledge, acknowledging the sources
	Time management
	Dealing with pressure
Preparing reports	Understanding how to structure information
	Working with others to acquire relevant research
	Understanding your audience
Collecting data	Understanding research design
	Understanding sampling frameworks, questionnaire design, bias, segmentation
	Ethics approval (if collecting data for research)
	Qualitative data collection methods
	Undertaking primary research
Analysing data	Quantitative or qualitative software
	Missing data
	Theoretical framework to design and make sense of the analysis
	Hypothesis testing
	Undertaking secondary data analysis
	Gaining insight from data analysis
	Interpreting results of statistical or other analysis
Writing a dissertation	Planning the thesis
	Structuring the dissertation
	Ensuring the reader can follow the story and the findings
	Identifying follow-on research
Presenting research findings	Preparing slides or a presentation
	Using visuals effectively and persuasively
	Adding to knowledge

There are many books on research skills development. I think there are three main things you need to bear in mind to be able to demonstrate that you understand what research is, in particular in the context of applied social research projects:

1   It builds new knowledge on top of existing knowledge. This is why attribution is so important, and why we spend so long as academics teaching students how to reference correctly.
2   Research is a process. It starts with a question, uses theory to frame this, and usually requires data (at least for applied research), methods for analysis and leads to findings and conclusions. Good research design is essential.
3   The communication of the research findings is just as important as the actual research. You will know from your own experience that there is a world of difference between a brilliant researcher and a brilliant researcher who can enthuse you with their findings because they communicate so well (think of all the lecturers you have encountered). Communication takes place in many forms and the more of these you can acquire in your studies the better.

I will come back to these three core elements of doing research throughout the book. For now though, back to the matter of concentrating on how to evidence that you have these research skills – or some of them – in an interview.

Here is Anna again, who you met in Chapters 1 and 3. Hopefully she is quite familiar to you by now.

Case study 4.1

Anna: Eliciting your research interest and skills

Following Anna's first internship interview, which did not result in an offer, she and I met to discuss how she could evidence her research experience, to position her to apply for other work placements. Anna had finished her second year of a Politics and International Relations degree, taken the compulsory research methods classes in her first two years and understood the concept of doing research but felt she had limited experience of putting it into practice. She had done a data analysis unit, and had read widely around international migration in which she was very interested; knowing this is what she was passionate about, we had the following conversation. I told her that in answering my question she was to think about her research skills and experience.

Me: Hello Anna, tell me what it is about your degree you are enjoying?
Anna: OK, I really like the international relations part of my course. I am fascinated by international migration, and how people move from country

(Continued)

to country in search of stable employment. I'm from overseas myself and have come here to study so I guess I'm motivated by why people settle in a country, and what the challenges are.

Me: That's interesting. Can you tell me something about how you have studied this from a research perspective, and what you have learned?

Anna: Hmm, let me think. Right, well in my first year we did a course unit on research methods. It was quite general – but also interesting as we had a different lecturer each week talking to us about how they do research in their subject area. So for example the social anthropology lecturer was talking about using films as an ethnographic technique, and the politics lecturer spoke about using international surveys. It was good to see the diversity of approaches. I'm mostly drawn to the qualitative methods. Actually the numbers [the data] scared me a bit but it was also fascinating to think what they represented, and how people had been counted. And so in the second year I took a course called 'politics project' and decided to look at some international data on migration.

Me: Fascinating. Tell me more.

Anna: We had been learning SPSS [statistical software] in the computer lab, and so I decided to download some data from the European Social Survey to look at attitudes across Europe to migrants. I can't remember what I found exactly but it was a really good way to use quantitative data to explore a complex social and hugely political issue. And what it made me realise was that this is an area I would like to explore further. I got a high mark for that coursework too so I was really pleased – it was my first piece of data analysis and I enjoyed doing it.

That conversation enabled me to help Anna see that she was passionately interested in an area of research, had already done some reading around it, and had acquired some research skills to enable her to talk about this at interview. The fact that she went on to get an internship in a social and research organisation – and did not do a piece of research on international migration until after she graduated – is neither here nor there. She had successfully articulated her research skills in a way that next time she was interviewed she was able to use the thinking she had done with me to put into words sufficiently well how she *did* have research experience, and she was ready to apply this. More on this later. Just to note too that I encouraged Anna to go back to her politics project and look at what she had found so that she could talk about this at a subsequent interview, which indeed she did and with a successful outcome, as we have already seen.

Top tips

Do what Anna did. Find someone to practise with. Ask them to ask you questions about your research interests, experiences and skills. Tell them you need them to be brutally honest. If they don't seem to understand you, keep practising until they do. Imagine the person knows nothing about your subject – how can you convince them to care about your findings, no matter how inconsequential they may seem?

How to describe your research skills for an interview

Hopefully you can now start to think about how you could describe your research skills if asked at interview. Evidencing them is one part of this; you will be more confident about answering questions in this part of the interview if you have given some thought to what it is you have actually done. The inclusion of Anna's story above was intended to help you think about how I was able to help her *elicit the skills she had acquired in her studies* that related directly to research that she was substantively interested in. The final part of this section therefore is to give you an example of an actual interview, and this time to present this through the eyes of the prospective host organisation. As I have said before, the organisations don't feature as characters in this book, although the example in the box below is from an actual interview. Rather than introduce an example Q&A response here though, I am going to list the questions that were asked at interview in order that you can practise the techniques given above. Underneath each question I make a suggestion about how you could answer. This will also lead into the next part of this chapter, which is about preparing for an interview.

The series of questions listed in the box below are typically asked by organisations that host students to undertake an internship. It's a set of generic questions, and can be used by any organisation in any sector. Use this list to help you think about how you might answer.

Interviewer: I'd like to start by asking you some questions about any research you have undertaken. Please answer each with reference to your own experience, no matter how limited you think that might be.

Interviewer: Can you describe a research question you had to tackle? What was it about this research question that particularly interested you?

(Continued)

Think back to your methods classes. How can you draw on these to describe an interest-ing piece of research you were presented with (by your lecturer) or preferably were required to undertake yourself? Be sure to talk not just about the research methods but the substantive topic (e.g. investigating the possibility of elections being rigged, explor-ing attitudes to crime in different groups of the population, understanding how young people feel about their university education, discovering whether attitudes to climate change vary by levels of educational attainment). In other words, describe the context in which the research was being undertaken, and say what interested you about this. Get the interviewer's attention – look at the Top tips above to see how you can practise this. Most of all, explain why you were drawn to this research. Even if it was a compulsory part of your course use this starter-for-ten question to make the research sound interesting and draw in the questioner.

Interviewer: Where did you start with the research? How did you set about finding out what had already been done in this area of research?

This is your opportunity to talk about undertaking a literature review. Remember, research builds on previous knowledge, so make sure you show that you know that, and that your work is adding to what has come before.

Interviewer: Can you describe to me how you planned to do the research?

Now it starts to move into how you planned the research. Think carefully, what did you do? You might have written a statistical hypothesis, or expressed this in words. You may have planned to look at a range of sources and compare them. Or gather primary data. Or use secondary data. Whatever it was, you need to be able to articulate this in a few sentences. And focus on the 'how you planned to do' part of the question – how you did it comes later.

Interviewer: Did you use any data? Or did you collect data for the purposes of the project? Tell me about this, and how you analysed the data.

This is a perfect opportunity to say what you did, and how – if at all – data featured in your analysis. You may feel you have already answered this (with the above question) but if so try to go into more detail now. Look back at Anna's example above, and others in the rest of the book, to see how people have used all kinds of data to explore their research question. If you did not use data in your research be prepared to say this, but also to make it clear how you carried out the research (e.g. by comparing two primary sources).

Interviewer: Leading on from the last question, what software did you use?

This is a good chance to rehearse what software tools you used. Interviewers will be looking out for this. Here are a few listed to prompt you, and be specific, so don't say 'Microsoft packages' but say 'Excel' or 'Access', SPSS, Stata, NVivo, MatLab, R,

Python, QGis, ArcGIS, SQL, Tableau and so on. Again, if you did not use software, say so, although most placement opportunities will expect you to have used some digital tools for your analysis.

Interviewer: Now tell me what you discovered. Were there any limitations to your findings?

This is a question to help you prepare how you can summarise your findings in a few sentences. There is a real skill to doing this and practising it will pay off. It's a two-part question. In the first part you need to be able to sum up your main (headline) findings. In the second you need to be able to say whether the findings are limited, and if so why. In addition this gives you the opportunity to think through what else could be done to extend the research (so that if you, or someone else, were to build on it you would be able to instruct them about what else could be explored).

Interviewer: Did you have an opportunity to present your research findings? If so how, and what tools did you use to present the results?

Chances are you wrote an essay or assessment. At the very least this gives you a chance to say what mark you got (hopefully a good one). They will be really interested though if you managed to write a report or a blog post or something that had relevance beyond your studies. If you did this that's great – talk about it. If you did not do this then use this prompt to maybe think that this could be a good thing to consider doing. The translation of your academic findings to a real-world context will really set you apart – and even if you haven't achieved this (yet) it is well worth thinking about how you could. In Chapter 9 I include an example of a PhD student whose placement helped her do exactly this. Setting yourself apart, getting noticed, is something you can work at. Having skills and experience that an organisation values is a tremendous asset to develop.

Interviewer: Finally, what did this experience of research teach you?

I will leave this question dangling. This is a really important one though – and once again requires you to actively reflect on your learning. You will see many examples of this throughout the book.

Prepare for an interview

The content in this chapter so far has been written to help you think about what you have done by way of acquiring research skills, and how you can talk about these if invited for an interview. This section will help you prepare for an interview, in the expectation that you will get one.

Make the beast beautiful

I said at the start of this chapter that many students I have encountered find the prospect of an interview a stressful one. In keeping with the quote at the start of this chapter – which comes from the title of a book about dealing with anxiety – I want you to indulge me (again) in a personal anecdote.

Several years ago I met a really successful businesswoman. I'll call her Jess. She was young, about 25. We got talking and I told her how confident she appeared. We started talking about things that had made us anxious in the past and I confessed that I used to hate going to the dentist (in fairness I had a lot of dental work done when I was young), and to this day I still don't like it. Not an uncommon experience I imagine. She laughed and told me that when she was little her mum used to dress her and her sisters up on the days they went to the dentist in their 'Sunday-best' (this phrase will really age me, but this just means your best clothes). After they had had their appointments her mum would take them to the park, or the cinema or shopping for a treat. As a result, she still associates the experience of going to the dentist with a positive outcome.

Isn't this a great story? I've never heard anyone talk about visiting the dentist in this way before or since but it stuck with me. I try to use this approach when I talk to my students about interviews for work placements. In a way the outcome (whether they get the placement or not) is not the end goal, but the experience of having the interview should be a pleasant one. If they can learn to go into it with an open mind, and be prepared to think of it as necessary experience, it will alleviate much of the tension that would otherwise build up. I offer you this advice too. In fact I would even go so far as to ask you to try to enjoy it. Is that going a little too far, maybe? Well even if it is, I would like to frame this part of the chapter about preparing for an interview at least by suggesting that suspending your worry about it will take you a long way, and open you up to possibly having a very positive experience. I'm not asking you not to get nervous, or dismissing your concerns that interviews can be nerve-racking, but I implore you to at least take a breath and read on in the hope that this will help you cope a little better.

As I said at the start of this chapter, comprehensive information about preparing for interviews can be obtained from careers guidance services, and this book does not aim to repeat that advice. What I do here is to offer some thoughts and experiences based on seven years of helping students prepare for interviews with organisations that have shortlisted them on the basis of their CVs and letters of application, for applied social research positions.

Learn from failure

You will not always be successful. In Chapter 3 I wrote about the need to learn how to bounce back if you are not successful initially. Ryan and Anna's stories were used to show how they dealt with this. I introduce a vignette here of a student (not one of our main characters) who was forced to develop quite a thick skin early on. Her story is not untypical and it is really important for you to realise this. Here is what she says.

---Student vignette---

I applied for one, then two then three internships. Each time I failed to get an interview. I knew it was going to be tough but I didn't think it would be quite so, um, dispiriting. But I was determined to succeed. I knew I had good grades, had a lot to offer, really, really wanted to do this, and just needed a break. I asked the internship coordinator for feedback on my application form and letters, and she gave me some great advice. I also made myself do some practice interviews with her and with the careers service. That was really tough, but I'm pleased I did it. I listened to all the feedback, took a long hard look in the mirror with new eyes, and made some changes. On my fourth attempt I got shortlisted. Looking back, what I was not doing well was selling myself … I was failing to show I had the skills they needed and that I could apply them. On my fifth attempt I got an internship.

See how she recognised, through seeking help, how she could improve, especially on making her research skills evident? It was hard for her to do that, as she had to make herself open to listening to how she came across. She was brave though, and it takes bravery to listen to what others say about us. She did it, persevered and it paid off. I hope this chapter will help you learn from her and others' experiences.

Get organised

Be prepared is the most important advice you can take away from this chapter. You are likely to have many interviews during the course of your professional life, so getting into the habit of organising yourself before a work placement interview will stand you in very good stead. All of the chapter content so far has been about getting prepared to talk about your research skills. As I have stated a few times, this chapter's raison d'être is to do just that. Whilst the focus is on research skills, however, you can be also thinking about some of the professional skills you could be preparing as these can also come up at interview. Chapter 8 is dedicated to developing your professional skills and so you can read that alongside this one. Chapter 5 focuses on being prepared for your first day and week, and much of the advice offered there is relevant to this section too.

Interview preparation requires you to be mentally ready. To do this you need to pre-empt some of the questions that you may be asked. The list below is a condensed version of what you need to think about prior to attending an interview for a work placement that will be focused on applied social research. This is followed by a case study from Zvi, who recalls how he used key people in his university to prepare for interview. Later in this chapter he talks about the interview experience itself.

Top tips

Preparing for an interview

- Use your university careers service if they offer mock interviews and/or ask a trusted academic if you can have a session with them
- Read through your CV, letter of application and the internship description to ensure all three align
- Read up about the company or organisation. Rehearse at least three facts about them that you could repeat if asked
- Think about *why* you want this position
- Think about *what **you** could bring* to this position, in particular what makes you different to other candidates
- Rehearse all of the things you can say about your research skills, interests and experience
- Employers often ask you to say where you imagine yourself in three or five or even ten years' time. Think about *how* this position could help you in your future. Try to avoid having no idea whatsoever
- Think about describing yourself in three words or short phrases (if asked)
- Read up on interview techniques, and especially the STAR (Situation, Task, Action, Result) methods often used
- Think about questions you have for the interviewers
- Finally, frame this as a positive experience and be determined to learn from it

---

The best way to help you understand how this preparation can work in practice is to draw upon the experience of others before you. Here's Zvi, one of our main characters. He is not that long out of finishing his first degree and so his memories are very fresh.

Case study 4.2

Zvi: How I prepare for an interview

I asked Zvi to tell me about his recollections of his preparation for his work placement interview, and then to expand upon that for interviews he has had since. Here is his recollection of the time he found out he had been called for interview with one of the organisations he had applied to do an internship with.

Even though I have always thought of myself as someone who is very confident especially when it comes to speaking, I find interviews a nerve-racking and, at times, quite anxiety-inducing experience. I see anxiety as a response to the fact that I really care about the position I am applying for and the fact I am worried/thinking about it shows how much it really means to me. I think it is important to allow these feelings of worry, anxiety, apprehension – whatever they may be – to come and go because they are human emotions and you should listen to them. After all, anxiety is only a defence mechanism and we only really protect things worth saving.

To handle this I use my friends and professionals. When I got my first interview for a summer internship I prepared by having a mock interview with the careers service, speaking to my academic advisor for tips and support, and doing everything I could to help me deal with the anxiety I was feeling. Because I cared about the result this effort was my way of coping and preparing.

Just a short note here to acknowledge that dealing with vulnerability and anxiety about interviews is normal. At the end of this chapter I include some further pointers for how to do this.

Get through an interview

To start this section I once again refer you to excellent careers guidance materials for a full set of pointers for how to deal with nerves before an interview, what to wear, planning to get there in good time and so on. My contribution here is to help you see that many others before you have trodden this path and come through an interview for a work placement. They were not all successful the first time (as you have already seen) and this is absolutely commonplace. In the next section I will guide you through using an interview as an opportunity to reflect. Here though, providing you have practised articulating your research skills as explained above, and given some thought to the interview from the employer's perspective as well as your own, I think you are in a good place to do well in the interview. You might also like to go back to Chapter 3 and recall what Sam (an employer) was looking for when he shortlisted candidates to interview.

Interview questions

I'm going to revisit Sam now, and list some of the questions he asked students when he interviewed them. To add context, it turns out that the position that his unit offers each year is actually one of the most popular with interns, perhaps because it's about social educational research, and often about differential outcomes. However, there is only one position and so they look for the best applicant. Shortlisted candidates are invited to a face-to-face interview.

Imagine you are the candidate. You're in the interview room, you have done your preparation and you really want this internship. There are three people on the panel: the person chairing it, Sam and one of his colleagues from the team you hope to be working in. You've sat down, been asked a couple of starter-for-ten questions by the chair of the panel: your name, the degree you're studying for and why you have applied for this internship position. And Sam tells you he is going ask you some questions to help him understand what type of applied research you have done. You feel good, as you know you have prepared well for this.

Here goes – these are the questions Sam asks. Could you answer them?

1   Can you describe a piece of social research you have undertaken? Perhaps you could take me through this starting with what your research question was and how you set about exploring it.

2   Thank you. Can you go into a bit more detail about the methods, and the software tools you used?

3   That's good. What did you find? Were the findings what you expected?

4   And how did you present the findings of your research?

5   Finally, what research questions were raised for you that you would like to consider if you were able to go back to this work?

Sam is guiding the interviewee through a series of questions designed to probe into the approach that was taken, the methods and tools used, the findings from the research, the ways these were presented and whether the research led to further unanswered investigations. At each stage he had the opportunity to probe a little further – which indeed he did. I was in this interview with Sam (and indeed with all the students interviewed for this position) and the first time he used this approach I was shocked at the perfunctory responses. It was really hard for me because I knew all of those interviewed could answer each part of the question, but many gave short answers that belied how much they knew, and how much they could bring to the position. For example, when asked to talk about the methods and software many students just said 'I did a regression analysis in SPSS'. What they needed to say was 'I developed a hypothesis to test whether my dependent variable was correlated with my independent variable. I used SPSS to test this and looked at the various statistical measures (like chi-square and the *p*-values) to see what the model was telling me.' Can you see the difference? The first is too short; the second explains that you have understood what you did, and this sets you up for discussing the findings. On the basis of this experience I started to give students coaching for how to answer questions like this, and this part of the book is a direct response to that.

Doing an interview is a little like doing an exam. It's anxiety-inducing (this is the phrase Zvi used earlier) because you don't know what is going to be asked of you. Just like an exam though, if you have studied hard, understood your learning and rehearsed it in a way that can restate it for the assessment, *and you focus on answering the question*, there is no reason why you cannot perform well. I promise you, I have sat through hundreds of interviews and it's so easy to spot the people who are prepared, can think clearly and focus on the questions asked, compared to those who struggle, not just because they are nervous but because lack of preparation has let them down.

Before wrapping up this section let me just list a few other possible question-types that you may be asked that will help you demonstrate your research skills.

Competency-based questions

I introduced competency-based questions in Chapter 3 in the section on preparing your CV. Interviewers often use them to elicit your prior experiences. There is a nice resource at TotalJobs that provides a lot more information about these types of questions (www.totaljobs.com/insidejob/how-to-handle-competency-based-interview-questions/).

Sam's questions above were largely competency based (around technical and analytical skills). These types of questions often start with phrases like 'Tell me about a time when …' or 'Can you give an example of when you …' or 'Describe a situation when you …' and they are designed to get you to talk about how you performed a task or dealt with a situation you found yourself in. They are not designed to catch you out, but rather to allow you to help the interviewer(s) understand your prior experience, and the way you approach problem solving and working relationships. It is helpful to reintroduce the STAR method here (also see Chapter 3) as interviewers may use this to assess your answer. STAR stands for Situation, Task, Action and Result. By practising this method of answering you will give yourself a framework to respond to questions. Taking a competency-based question – for example, if I asked you to give me a situation where you had worked in a team on a research project and encountered frustration with one of the team members, you could answer along the following lines:

> That's hard because I don't really like conflict [this gives the interviewer some insight into your way of working] but in the second year on a research group project [SITUATION] I had to be in charge of ensuring the team had all the data to analyse [TASK]. When we came to meet up as a group it was clear

that one of the team had not prepared the data so that we could analyse it. I could have done this myself but I decided to work with that person as he was struggling with the software and together we developed the model we wanted to test [ACTION – and to boot you have showed you decided to help someone improve]. The result was we finished the project on time and collectively got a good mark – as it was a group project it was in our interest to work together as only a single mark was awarded. Although this was hard it helped me to see that sometimes my peers need help [RESULT].

See how this goes? This would be an excellent response and far better than saying that one of the team let the side down and you all suffered as a consequence. I base this example on many students I have interacted with, especially those who find helping others challenging. Your university education can be a solitary experience, and the predominant form of assessment is to test your individual learning. In contrast, the world of work seeks and rewards collaboration and teamwork. Showing that you have the attitude for this is a good thing to do. Don't believe me? I was once turned down for a position with the feedback that I was too much of an independent thinker and had not shown in the interview scenario that I was given a capacity to work with others. I was in my late twenties but I learned a very valuable lesson from that feedback. Organisations value people who can think independently *and* work in teams.

Strength-based questions

Another type of questioning framework for interviewers is to focus on an applicant's strengths and development needs. Recruiters interested in what an individual can bring to their team and workplace use these strength-based questions. I say more about organisations that use this approach, rather than a competency-based approach, in Chapter 9 so you can look at that too. Although these types of questions are harder to prepare for – and far less formulaic than competency-based questions – a good way to plan for answering them is to learn to practise reflection. That is another reason why this book is full of opportunities for you to do so. If you reflect on your strengths – as well as your development needs – you will be much better positioned to be able to answer these questions if asked. You must, however, be able to back up your claims with evidence. There is no point claiming you are organised and analytical if you cannot give examples of this. Similarly these questions provide an opportunity to both share with the interviewer what energises you as well as help identify which areas you may be less interested in. Articles in careers and organisation psychology publications often use the term 'being in flow', which was introduced by Csikszentmihalyi in his 1998 book *Finding Flow*. In careers and coaching circles the term 'flow' is very much in vogue. All jobs have parts that we find tedious or less creative or interesting than we might like, and we do them as we know they are a necessary part of work, but to find a position that really motivates you it is important for employers to acknowledge your strengths and try to find ways for you to use to them. For that reason if you get to work for an organisation that does this, that's excellent.

By way of an example then, let's ask Zvi what he feels he could share with us about his interview experience given that he was successful in securing a work placement. We revisit Zvi in a later chapter where he talks more about how he has honed his interview skills and been successful in securing graduate roles. His contribution here is quite long, but I hope you agree with me that it is incredibly useful. Note that he uses his own version of STAR – which he calls Point, Evidence and Explain. I've included this to indicate that there are always other ways to do things, and you must find your own. The main thing is to choose one that works for you.

Case study 4.3

Zvi: How preparation helps me get through interviews

There is really one main way I prepare for an interview, which helps me get through it. I download all the job documentation (including the job role, person specification, experience/qualifications). For every point on the job description, I write in a different colour using the Point, Evidence, Explain method. You need to state a point, provide evidence/an example and explain what you learned and why it is significant. Before interview, I read over all the points, to refresh my memory of how exactly I meet the spec.

Before the interview you really have to think why you believe you are the most ideal candidate for the job. What makes you unique? In social research there is disparity between those who are very highly trained in data science and statistics and those who are educated within the social sciences more broadly. In my own case, I know how to critically look at social issues through a sociological lens, and my degree also really helped me understand how to use data and numbers and quantitative research methods to answer socio-logical enquiry. I emphasise this when I answer questions in the interview to show what I can bring to the role. For example, in my first internship inter-view, as an undergraduate I knew that I had less experience with quantitative research than others might have. But when I thought about it I knew I had a lot to offer, and drew strength from this.

It's vital to prepare well in advance and also to think reflectively in the interview. And you must have some questions up your sleeve – they will expect this and it's your chance to show your inquisitiveness in the position.

He gives a very honest appraisal of his approach to his internship applications and interviews. Zvi was such a thoughtful, interested and motivated student it did not surprise me that he landed the work placement he did. What I did not appreciate though, until he shared the above with me, was how hard he worked to prepare for success. Students who seem on the surface confident and capable are often putting in a lot of work behind the scenes.

Prepare your questions

Zvi's last point was about asking questions. This is so important. At the end of most, indeed probably all, interviews you should be invited to ask if you have any questions of the panel. If you say no it sends a very negative signal that you are not interested, or you have not thought about this. Always have *at least one* question you can ask and make it count. Probably best to avoid questions about payment, or anything practical that will have been covered in the documentation, but instead think of something you can ask that will make them remember you. Here are some examples – but get creative and make up your own, there really is no such thing as a bad question.

- Can you talk me through a typical working day please?
- What on-the-job training opportunities might be made available?
- Will I be able to learn any new software packages?
- I'm really interested in doing my third-year dissertation using data from your organisation – is there any prospect of this?
- What sorts of graduates do you recruit?
- How will this research project inform the organisation?
- How many people are in the team?
- Is there any prospect of presenting the work at the end of the placement?

Hopefully you can see that asking ambitious questions is what you are aiming for.

Reflecting on the interview

Finally then, this section introduces a tool to help you reflect on the interview. My strong advice to you is, after the interview is over, try not to be too hard on yourself. If it went well, give yourself permission to feel good about it. If you were successful and you were given the work placement position, celebrate. And bottle that feeling. If you were unsuccessful try not to be too self-critical. It's a learning experience. You need to allow yourself to let the news sink in, but also to think about what did go well, and what perhaps you could have done differently. It is incredibly likely that you performed well but were just unlucky that someone else was there on the day who was slightly better suited to the position. This happens all the time. It's happened to me and to nearly everyone I have ever spoken to about a job they have gone for. I even wrote a LinkedIn article about it when I got disappointing news from a position I really, really wanted, and was overseas when I got the news. I called the article 'Bouncing back in 24 hours' and wish I had learned how to do this years ago. Truth is I can barely even remember now what the position I had applied for was, and my career took a different turn. Yours will too, even if you think it feels like the end of the world. It's not.

I have had so many students over the years come to me in tears thinking they were terrible and they embarrassed themselves and they made a complete mess of the interview. We have talked about how it went and it becomes clear very quickly that there is a lot of catastrophising going on in people's heads. My job is to calm them down and help them see that actually most of what they did was good, but they really could have been better prepared for the question on their research project in year two, and they failed to answer the question well on why this internship would fit well with their future plans (which they hadn't really thought about), and they mumbled about their research results when in actual fact if they had practised they would not have done so. This is fine, it gives them something to go away and think about. I reassure them that failing to get something on your first interview for a professional position is normal. As long as they don't make the same mistake again, and learn from their experience, I think it's actually a good thing to deal with some failure. Maybe they could even use this as an opportunity to answer a question on 'Have you ever failed at anything?' Nothing is ever wasted. Nothing is ever unsalvageable. You might be the person who sails through the interview and gets that first appointment you apply for. On the other hand, if you are, you are probably the outlier in the pack. Most of us have to fail at something to improve at it next time. Most of you reading this will be in the second category – and that is just fine.

Your wellbeing

A final but really important note. A great LinkedIn post by the founder of Gradconsult raises the issue of the need to look after your wellbeing (Fielding, 2020). Her article is written for graduates seeking recruitment opportunities. Take a read of this extract:

> I really want us – students, parents, career professionals and graduate recruiters – to start talking about … rejection and perceived 'failure' much more openly. Not only because it is rational to do so (getting a job offer should be perceived as the exception, not the norm – rejection is much more normal) but because … there is a relationship between the number of applications students/graduates are submitting for jobs and a negative impact on their mental wellbeing.

She cites work from the Graduate Wellbeing report (Reino and Byrom, 2017) which provides empirical research to substantiate her plea. A nice aside is that the first author of the Graduate Wellbeing report was a Master's student at the time she co-authored it, and she is now an emerging talent coordinator. I would want to add an extra group in Fielding's opening sentence – educators. My attempt here is to give you the tools to be prepared, and to help you develop an open and positive mindset. Later in the book I talk about developing resilience too. By giving you real examples of students like Anna and Zvi I hope you can appreciate that they too got through this. And used their support networks to do that. You can do this too. Learning how to reflect is part of equipping you to be successful.

To finish this chapter then, I provide another checklist to help you reflect, together with a suggestions column on what you might want to do to improve your chances next time (Table 4.2). Because you owe it to yourself for there to be a next time. I hope I have helped to make this particular beast – the interview – beautiful enough for you to try to succeed.

Table 4.2 Checklist – reflecting on your research skills, interview preparation and experience

Question	Answer: Yes/No/N/A	Action: What you need to do and when
Did I spend time evidencing my research skills?		
Did I practise articulating my research skills in advance of the interview?		
Did I think about the different skills I have acquired through my lectures, classes and assignments?		
Did I prepare thoroughly for the interview?		
Did I use the STAR method for competency-based questions that were asked?		
Did I listen carefully to the questions that I was asked at interview?		
Did I prepare my own questions to ask?		
If I got the position have I allowed myself to celebrate and bottle the feeling?		
If I did not get the position, how can I learn from the interview to enable me to try again and have another interview that could lead to a successful outcome?		

Summary

This chapter has helped guide you through the steps to how you can show your research skills in a way that can help you get an interview, has prepared you to think about what you would say if interviewed, focusing on the research you have undertaken already, and particularly how you could apply this learning in the workplace. Anna and Zvi's experiences were used to show you how they both got, and got through, their interviews. Example questions from Sam, an employer, were included to help you prepare your own answers. Checklists are introduced which help you get organised and stay on track with possible and actual interviews, and I have stressed the need to recognise that interviews are a learning experience. The chapter began by acknowledging that interviews can produce anxiety for many, but I hope the Top tips and examples provided have boosted your confidence and will help you prepare for, get through and even perhaps enjoy an interview.

Three things you can do next

1   Create a LinkedIn account. Use this to start to develop your professional identity. Don't worry if you don't have a lot to put on there yet. Look at the LinkedIn articles by Rebecca Fielding, 'The shame, guilt and disappointment of graduate job hunting': www.linkedin.com/pulse/shame-guilt-disappointment-graduate-job-hunting-rebecca-fielding/ and by me, 'Bouncing back in 24 hours': www.linkedin.com/pulse/bouncing-back-24-hours-jackie-carter

2   This chapter focused on your research skills. Jump forward to Chapter 8 to start to think about capturing and developing your professional skills.

3   The GraduateJob podcast provides short 30–40 minute podcasts about all things related to getting a job. You can find it at https://subscribe.acast.com/graduatejobpodcast or on iTunes and other podcast channels. Episode 55 features Steve Rook, whose book was referenced in Chapters 2 and 3. The clip between 12:00 and 14:00 minutes talks about finding work placement opportunities to develop your skills. Listen to this and further explore this podcast series. The transcript for the podcast is at www.graduatejobpodcast.com/workexperience

5

HOW TO GET THROUGH YOUR FIRST DAY

---Learning objectives---

In this chapter you will learn how to:

- Set goals for your work placement
- Develop a positive and growth mindset from Day One
- Manage expectations
- Prepare for your first day
- Start to develop your professional support network and find a mentor
- Reflect at the start of your work placement

'Fortune favours the brave.'

Latin proverb

Overview

The chapter gives a taster of that all-important first day. Because your first day turns into your first week I have extended this chapter to cover that too. I believe they deserve a chapter all of their own as it's the part most new starters worry about. To address and allay concerns that many students have about the first day of their placement, this chapter will demonstrate how you can prepare for, get through and reflect on your first day, and week, and use it to set up the foundations for a valuable applied work experience, no matter the duration. Most importantly I aim to encourage you to do all of this with a positive outlook that will carry you through, from Day One into Week One and then the rest of your work placement.

Students' and employers' stories will be shared to illustrate how you can get started, ask for help, manage your and the host organisation's expectations, and enjoy the placement. Examples included reflect a range of experiences, and emotions, varying from feeling confused and overwhelmed to feeling very happy. There is no typical first day, or week, but the voices included here show you that creating a good impression right at the start of your placement is a wise strategy. Tips and techniques are provided to help you cope with this new experience, and to move you from the interview into the research project smoothly and with confidence. Doing a placement can be both daunting and exhilarating, and so the experiences of former interns serve to encourage you, like them, to grasp opportunities as they arise, and learn from them.

This chapter aims to whet your appetite for the start of your placement and give you the tools to make a good impression. It will help you manage expectations from Day One. Importantly it sets the scene for keeping a journal or log from the start as a way to get into the habit of reflecting on your practical experience. Students' reflections will pepper this chapter to help you see that many others have been through this already, and emerged from the other side wiser, more confident and experienced.

In this chapter you will hear predominantly from Julija (who provided so much material that I wanted you to read) and be reintroduced to Marcus. I introduced Marcus in Chapter 2, but Julija – who interned at the BBC – is a new voice. I also include some vignettes and quotes from other students to share some additional relevant insights.

Set goals for your placement

By the end of your work placement or internship you want to feel a sense of achievement, that you have learned new skills and knowledge and that you have made a contribution. In Chapters 7 and 8 I take you through the steps of how to capture and monitor your analytical and research skills and professional skills development. Here I want to introduce you to the idea of goal setting.

> Why is goal-setting important? Because a wealth of scientific evidence says that having a goal is so much better for performance than not having one. Why? Because it focuses the mind and gives us something to shoot for.
>
> Price (2018: 65)

My goal was to write this book. To do that I had to break it down into achievable tasks. First I had to have a proposal accepted by a book publisher, and so whilst I was studying for my Postgraduate Certificate in Higher Education I used the opportunity to use one of the modules on 'The Changing Culture of Higher Education' to learn about experiential learning, and that laid the foundation for the book proposal. Next I had to research how books of this type are written, so I looked at a lot of books, with the help of my publisher, and came up with this format. I then had to decide what was going to be in each chapter, and for each one, which case studies and vignettes I was going to use. And finally, I had to write it! My main goal – writing the book – was divided into sub-goals – as described above – and each one of those was broken down into a series of tasks.

No doubt you are well-versed in using this technique for writing assessments, so you need to now apply that to set your goals for your work placement or internship. Much of the goal-setting work I have come across in the literature, particularly in coaching and professional development literature, draws on examples from the world of sport. The idea and practice of goal setting can be incredibly helpful, and worth cultivating as a habit.

Duckworth (2017), in her chapter entitled 'How gritty are you?', introduces a very simple description of setting goals, coupled with a diagrammatic way of doing this. As grit (or resilience or stamina) is a central tenet of my book, I draw on her work here. She introduces the notion of top-, middle- and low-level goals, and describes goal setting as a hierarchy. Her approach is similar to developing a mind-map, for those of you who are used to those, and can be a helpful tool to plan what you need to focus on.

Here is an example, to get you started (Figure 5.1). It uses Carol Dweck's (2017) approach and draws on Julija's experience. Julija is a new voice and provides the main student case study in this chapter. She was a second-year Politics student when she was offered her placement at the BBC. I have used her example retrospectively to show what her goal-setting could have looked like if she had done this at the start of her placement.

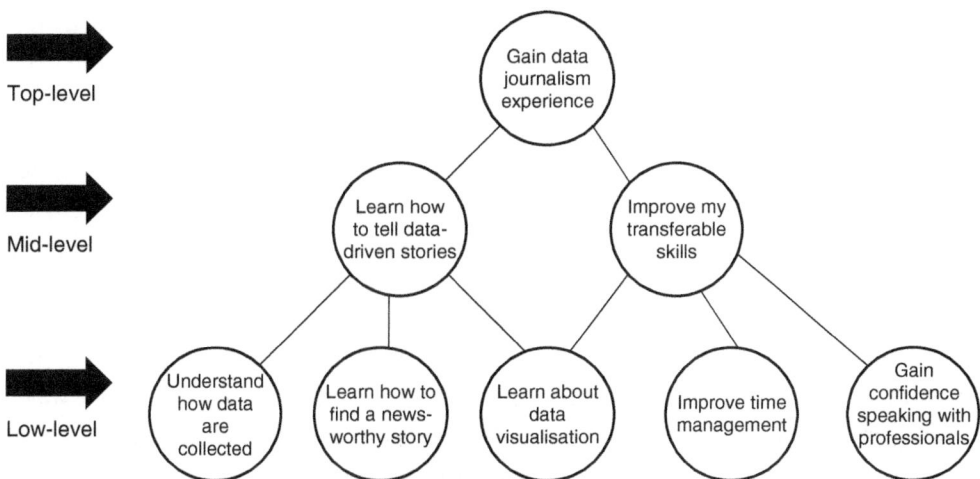

Figure 5.1   An example of hierarchical goal setting for an internship

Source: Adapted from Dweck (2017: 73)

Hopefully you can start to get the picture. Setting your top-, mid- and low-level goals at the start of your work experience can help shine a light for you on the way ahead. It gives you a sense of clear purpose and direction, and you begin your placement with a stated intention; in Julija's case this was 'to gain data journalism experience', which she could have broken down into smaller goals. You can of course change these goals as you progress, especially at the middle and low level, as you cannot possibly anticipate at the start everything that might come up. Being flexible and open is a good approach. The goals set your direction of travel, the tasks that enable you to reach your goals will then be a case of keeping a regular log, which we come to in Chapter 6 on reflection, and then in Chapters 7 and 8 as you monitor your skills learning during your placement.

Develop a positive and growth mindset from Day One

The positive and open mindset that runs through this book, like writing through a stick of rock, can start on your first day. I introduce it because I have observed repeatedly that those students who approach their work placement with a positive and open mind tend to get more out of it, and so do their organisations. I am not the only one to advocate that an optimistic approach is good for you, and those you work alongside, and leads to better outcomes for all.

Carol Dweck has written a book on what she terms a *growth mindset* (Dweck, 2017). I have earlier in this chapter drawn on the work of Duckworth (2017) and Price (2018). All of these authors speak enthusiastically about how framing challenges in a positive light, setting clear goals, being realistic about your potential, and using a feedback loop to help you become self-aware are important traits to develop. They also challenge the negativity biases that can creep into our everyday lives, encouraging us to avoid falling into the trap of believing we cannot do something if we fail at it (especially the first time). Whilst it is important not to be blasé or over-optimistic about your capabilities, especially when starting out towards your career, it is certainly worth cultivating a mindset that has been shown by all of these authors to be helpful. The subtitle of Dweck's book is 'Changing the way you think to fulfil your potential', so if you are inclined towards negative thinking, I challenge you to start to change that as you take your first steps into the workplace. In summary, then, when I use the term 'positive mindset' in this book I mean for you to find a way of framing challenges that enables you to be open-minded, self-reflective, optimistic that you will rise to the challenge, and determined to develop resilience in the face of adversity, and celebrate in the event of success. And to challenge yourself to learn and grow.

Top tips

Developing a positive and growth mindset from Day One

- Think and act positively
- Notice behaviours in the workplace but try not to be tempted to be judgemental
- Don't take things too seriously, try to relax
- Be kind to yourself – in particular don't expect to remember everything you are told on your first day
- Make notes – and use them to think about what else you need to know
- Be open to learning and taking yourself out of your comfort zone
- Be true to yourself – no need to pretend to be someone else
- Ensure you have some downtime and look after your wellbeing
- Try to identify someone you think would make a good mentor

The following student case study, which draws on an internship with the BBC, illustrates how to get off to a flying start. Below, Julija talks about how she felt about Day One, how she prepared for it, as well as what she did during it. It pulls together most of the advice I go through in this chapter. Her positive outlook comes across loud and clear. She also recalls how her first week had a few hiccups but they did not stop her staying upbeat. You'll hear more about Julija in later chapters, and see what a great time she had whilst on placement. And to add here, Julija did not get the first internship she interviewed for either – and used all the support at her disposal to get this one. By the time she walked through the doors of the BBC studios in Salford on her first day she had already dealt with a few setbacks.

Case study 5.1

Julija: My first day of the placement

I had looked forward to my internship since finding out I was successful at interview. I was nervous but excited about what it was going to be like working in a prestigious media company as a researcher.

On the first day I woke up far too early, and set off in haste. When I arrived I realised this was it – this was my summer. Was this a good move? I need not have worried. By the end of the day all my fears were allayed; I'd had coffee with my supervisor, understood better what they expected of me, told them I was excited and a bit anxious, and started to believe that I could do this. On

(Continued)

> Day One I started to take notes, and thank goodness I did as I referred to this book-of-my-internship throughout the first week, to remind myself who was who, what I needed to do, and where I needed to be. I could never have committed all of that to memory.
>
> Most importantly I started to realize I was going to like this. Regardless of some minor administration hiccups in the first week, I got a real sense of this mattering – to me, the organisation and especially the journalists and to the general public who were to be the consumers of the research. I determined to give this my all.

I know that she was anxious before starting, but when I read her first reflection (from which the above extract is taken) I was delighted. Her positive outlook and self-belief jumped off the page and I knew she was going to be fine.

A reason I believe so wholeheartedly in seeing reflections from interns (which I expand upon in Chapter 6) is because if things are not going well, I can pick this up early. There has been only a handful of times when this has happened, and I have intervened to set things back on course. This is also why we nominate an academic mentor to all our interns, so that we can offer support if they need it and provide a safety net. We hardly ever need to use this, but it is good to have in place just in case.

Manage expectations

As we saw in Chapter 3 (Table 3.1) there are different types of work placement experiences for undertaking applied research, which will be established and run in different ways. Regardless of which type of placement you undertake the host organisation will have expectations of you. In addition, you will have your own expectations of the placement opportunity and the organisation that takes you.

In my own work I am always careful to manage expectations from the start, for everything I undertake. In managing people I start by asking them what they need from me to perform their role, and at the same time make it clear what I need from them to deliver on my work. Similarly, in a placement role you need to know what is expected of you, and be told what you can expect by way of support and help. Being upfront about this from Day One will save valuable time, and potential misunderstandings. Whatever you do don't think you need to be psychic to understand what you are expected to do. Use your voice.

In this section we look at your own expectations and those of the host organisation. You need to acknowledge and be aware of both in order to have a good experience. And you need to do this before your first day.

Your expectations

You made it. You got through the interview and have been offered the opportunity to work in your chosen organisation. You're all set to put that classroom learning to use and start acquiring some real-world experience. First though you have to turn up for, and get through, the first day.

Some people love that excitement, a new challenge, getting to meet new people, finding out what it's all going to entail. Others do not. You most probably lie somewhere between these extremes, like most of us, and exhibit some apprehension as well as some curiosity, about the upcoming experience. It is completely natural to feel some nerves and for your mind to race concerning what's expected of you, and experience some worry about whether you can deliver. After all it's one thing answering questions in an interview and convincing people you have the right skills and attitude to do this; it's quite another to actually deliver on that. And in any case you did those research methods classes last semester – how can you remember what you learned and how do you apply it in practical terms?

Fear not, this book is here to help guide you, with the wisdom, experience and support of others who have already been through this. And this chapter will help you focus on that first day, and week, by showing how others got through it too.

I got through the interview, now what?

Let's start on a positive note by convincing you that there's a first day for everything new, by definition, and being conflicted is a normal part of starting a new work experience. The vignette below is an example of a student's experience. She was a little nervous about her first day, but was quickly reassured that help was at hand as her host supervisors had planned a good induction day. She and I had chatted prior to her starting the internship, and like most of her peers she had had reservations about her first day. She need not have worried. Her placement was at the university, in a research team attached to the department where she was studying, and her role was to assist them with some research on the role of fathers in children's upbringing.

Student vignette

On my first day I was shown around the office and I had a start-up meeting with my supervisors. We discussed practicalities and together we went through an action plan that I will be working through to achieve the agreed end goals. As well as creating a professional poster, these include contributing to a blog and briefing paper summarising the project findings.

(Continued)

> We discussed the goals I hope to achieve by the end of the placement which are to improve my research skills and to put them into practice, to learn new skills to improve my own data interpretation and analysis skills. I also aim to improve my confidence and use what I learn over the next 8 weeks to help me prepare for my dissertation. By the end of the placement I also hope to have a better idea about whether or not I want to do a Master's degree in social research and potentially pursue a research career in future.

This example illustrates wonderfully how you can start out on the right footing from Day One. Set goals, find out what your host organisation wants to achieve and think carefully about what you want to get out of the experience. Take charge of this and become a co-producer of the knowledge and skills you will develop. You know what you have learned in the classroom, and here is an opportunity to stretch yourself and apply this learning, even if you're not yet sure how this will pan out in practice.

This student was fortunate in that she was familiar with her surroundings, but still the prospect of becoming, to all intents and purposes, a research fellow with your lecturers is a quite scary one. She need not have worried. Her placement had been set up with this in mind and her supervisor was completely on board with the need to provide structure and support. This is one of the advantages of doing a research work placement run by your university; they have your interests at heart and so should have already considered the need to provide a good experience for you.

This highlights another important point, how to manage your and your organisation's expectations. After all, how can you plan for success if you don't know what's expected of you, and what support you will receive?

Organisation's expectations

The best experiences occur when there are clear goals and outputs articulated at the outset, and where there is a well thought through outcome designed into the activity. Without these the opportunity could feel aimless, and it will be difficult to achieve a satisfactory outcome for both sides. Much better to have a piece of work or research well-described so that all parties are clear what the expectations are for the duration of the placement. Chapter 6 deals in depth with how you can build in reflection to your experience, but before you can do that you need to know precisely what it is you might be reflecting on.

Recall we are dealing with *applied research skills in the workplace*. A successful way of describing such a piece of work to enable all involved to be clear about what is required is to frame this as a 'research project'. This articulation has the advantage of bounding the work, and describing the skills required for, and to be developed in, the role.

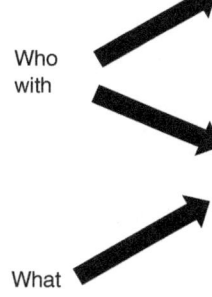

Who with

Organisation Name and Information: AudienceNet is an innovative market research consultancy built upon the application of connected technologies to profile and engage with specific target markets across the globe. As part of a wider organisation AudienceNet US has access to a rich database comprising 250 million US residents.

Team / Department: Social & Political Research

What

Title for project: AudienceNet USA

Short abstract of what the project will involve, and any data to be used
This internship will take place in AudienceNet's new Washington DC office and will involve the successful applicant using their statistical analysis skills to compile detailed consumer profiles in relation to key demographics or to dig for insights on behalf of our clients in music, technology and political circles.

Keywords (up to 12)

Quantitative Analysis, Qualitative Analysis, Data Visualisation Politics, Youth Engagement, Music, Online Communities

Essential and desirable skills and attributes that the student would need to have
Essential:

Confidence; Keen Interest in working with data; Attention to detail; Analytically minded; Ability to work independently

Desirable:

Experience of working with quantitative and qualitative data Basic Excel/SPSS skills

Where

Where the work would be carried out:

1250 Eye St NW, Suite 200, Washington, DC 20005

Preferred selection method (interview or other meeting)

Interview

Support and training offered by the organisation
Analytical:

How

Introduction to political research; Hands on supervision in working with quantitative data; An introduction to distinct online qualitative and quantitative research; Introduction to segmentation analysis; Encouragement with individual thinking and ideas; Support with quantitative dissertations

Practical: Help with finding accommodation in Washington DC

Any issues of data confidentiality and/or IPR that would need to be resolved

Non-disclosure agreement (NDA) for certain, commercially sensitive projects.

Figure 5.2   Example research project outline

Adapted from the University of Manchester Q-Step website. Original source: www.manchester.ac.uk/q-step/internships/internships-2018/

It also specifies any outputs that might be produced. An example *research project outline* is shown in Figure 5.2 to illustrate the way in which this can be achieved in a fairly light touch way. This is just one approach to describing a piece of research that can be conducted in the workplace, and the example given is just one of many you may encounter to describe the *where, what, when, why, who with* and *how* of an applied research project.

The example in Figure 5.2 is a shortened version of a research project outline used by my university internship scheme. Only the main parts relevant to this section are shown.

I have used an international example here, which introduces a whole new set of considerations, like getting to the US from the UK (in this example), finding accommodation, sorting out visas and so on. These are non-trivial tasks and I implore you once again to get organised, and get help, if you take up an international placement. Chapter 7 in Rook (2016) is a good source of information, and some of the websites listed in Chapters 2 and 3 have programmes dedicated to supporting internships abroad.

It is likely that a project outline similar to this one has been used to advertise the internship that you will undertake. Therefore you already know a certain amount about what is expected of you, at least a description of the work to be undertaken. Nonetheless as this chapter deals with Day and Week One you need to refer back to this outline to help you understand what you might need by way of clarification when you turn up. This will enable you to arrive at the host organisation on the first day, at the right place and right time, as well as assist in clarifying questions you may need to ask at the start of the placement.

The project outline helps you understand the expectations placed upon you from the perspective of the host, but also acts to help you understand the placement from your perspective. It is important to take both into account when thinking about your first day and week, as after all a work placement is designed to benefit all parties involved. Whilst the organisation expects to get something out of this, so do you. Park that thought for now. Let's deconstruct this in a little more detail below. Hopefully, after earlier chapters, you are starting to become familiar with stepping into the shoes of the host organisation.

Organisation's perspective

Using the AudienceNet example in Figure 5.2, the *where, what, when, why, who with* and *how* are either made clear, or provide a starting point for further questions:

- *Where* – practicalities about location are given
- *What* – the research to be undertaken is described in the abstract but you might wish to enquire further about expected outputs

- *When* – this is not provided, so you need to ensure you have already found out the start and end dates, and expected hours of work. You most likely know the first but may need to establish the second on your first day
- *Why* – this is also not given explicitly but should have been explored at interview stage and prior to that through desk research
- *Who with* – names of personnel are also not stated in the description, although the team this internship is placed with is evident
- *How* – although prerequisite skills are stated, it is not evident how these will be used in the research. The section on support offered by the organisation hints at methods that will be used, but they need to be clarified.

Your perspective

As there are some gaps in the information these need to be queried, to answer the question of 'What are your expectations of me?' You might want to do this in advance of Day One if you have been given a contact; otherwise write them down (as Julija did) so this can form part of your initial meeting with your supervisor. Consider the following bulleted list for further information you might need.

- *Where* – You know where to go but do you know how to access the building, which room to ask for, etc?
- *What* – What are the potential outputs from this research? What will I be doing on a typical day?
- *When* – What are the core working hours? What happens for lunch and breaks? What about holiday entitlement?
- *Why* – What are the reasons for doing this research? Who will benefit from it? To what purpose will the results be put?
- *Who with* – Who will be involved in the research? What do they need from me to do their job? Who can I ask for support?
- *How* – Which data and methods will be used to undertake the research? How will the prerequisite skills demanded feed into the research?

Now with a clear description of the research to be undertaken, the value this will add to the organisation, skills to be developed, and understanding of likely outputs to be produced, let's turn our attention to how you can prepare for the first day.

Prepare for the first day

I hope the content so far has reassured you that you're going to be fine. Understanding what you are expected to do when you arrive is good preparation. Let us now delve a little more deeply into getting ready for that first day. Some of what is included in this section is self-evident, but it does no harm to state it clearly here. We've all had moments where we'd wished 'If only ...' so I make no apology for including some obvious tips here. Follow these and you will not go too far wrong.

Know where you're going

It's an obvious thing to state, but as well as knowing what your work placement host expects of you, you need to know where they are. Geographically, obviously, but also it helps to research the sector, the position of the company or organisation within that sector, and the contribution the team that you'll be part of makes to the business or sector.

Check out the location

We've all had times when we think we know where we are going only to end up at the wrong location. Anyway, learn from my errors. Check, check and check again. You really do not want to get to the wrong place on Day One, or at the wrong time come to that. You may be fortunate in being placed somewhere where they are relaxed about time keeping, but you don't know that yet. If necessary do a practice-run, check out the commute in advance. Plan for a possible delay and build in a contingency for this. Have a phone number you can contact in the event of unanticipated circumstances on the day. And don't forget to ask for details such as what you need to do when you arrive at the location (i.e. where is the office?). Much better to turn up early and create a good impression than late and people thinking punctuality is not your strong point.

Check out the business

On the matter of what the team and company are contributing to the organisation's goals, if you haven't gleaned this before Day One then do some research prior to starting, though you really ought to have done this at the interview stage. Know where they fit (if a university – what are their core goals, a company – which sector do they occupy and what is their strategy, a voluntary organisation – what's their income source and their core mission?). In other words, know the *context* in which your work-situated learning sits. And how does the team you will join contribute to this? As it is research focused the chances are that your work will contribute to much broader goals; within academic research this could be a small part of a larger project, or a contribution to an academic's personal research agenda; a company or business will have a wide range of research they undertake – and in respect of your role it makes sense to understand where this fits; and in an NGO (non-governmental organisation) or charity, you would do well to find out exactly how your research will contribute to their core mission.

Collectively this will show that you are thinking more broadly about the work you are contributing. When studying it is fairly transparent how your next essay, exam or piece of coursework contributes to your degree. You will know which subjects you are studying, and have clear instructions about the contribution of the assessed work to your overall mark. With work-situated learning this is likely to be much less clear, unless your work is assessed as part of your course, but even then it's smart to know how your input, within your group or team, helps the wider aims of the place hosting you. We all need to know how our work contributes to the larger picture, and it helps us stay motivated if our values align with the organisation we work for. Conversely, if our values are at odds with our employer then it is a good learning opportunity to find out where we don't want to pursue our career.

Another way to put this is – be curious (remember, Chapter 2 talked about being curious, connected and courageous). Show an interest, do your homework, and be prepared. Also make sure that when you get to the workplace you make it clear that you want to be there. Recall the one-year long YouGov internship opportunity in Chapter 3? I was told that 500 people apply for that every year. For one position. The person they select has absolutely got to show that they are interested when they turn up on the first day. Employers are discouraged by people who appear to be uninterested or disorganised. To rephrase that more positively, host organisations like people who are motivated and well-prepared, and you have to show this. Aim to be that person, and to show this from Day One.

Marcus (who also featured in Chapter 2) provides the next case study.

Case study 5.2

Marcus: Understanding the context of the research

This extract, taken from Marcus's end-of-week-one reflective piece, shows how he got started on his work placement. The context of his research was extremely important to him, and he understood from the outset who the audience for his report was to be, for the think-tank he was interning at.

> On the first day I arrived at the IPPR North offices, met the team and started the day in a relaxed way over coffee. There was a lot to take in but I was excited at the thought of contributing to their State of the North flagship report. I was given a previous report to read so that I could understand the context of the research.
>
> I read the report then had a further meeting with the senior researcher who is leading on this work. It's important, as the results will inform the nation about how devolution is working in the north. Whilst a bit scary, I'm actually

(Continued)

> really looking forward to the work placement as it's an honour to be part of a research team that are so committed to making a difference to the lives of those who live here, and asking difficult questions.
>
> At the end of the first week I was clear about what I was going to focus on, if not entirely how I was going to achieve this.

Note how, like the vignette used earlier, the first day was paced well, he was supported by his host organisation and the context for, and purpose of, his placement work was made clear. He was given a task he was perfectly capable of undertaking – reading a background report – and although he exhibited some nerves, he got on with it. Also see how motivated he was by the purpose of the research. By the end of the first week he was already clear about what his research would entail. These are very typical comments from first days (and weeks) and in all my time of running the internship programme I have not had a single student who has left after their first day. Take comfort from this – you too can get through that first day and week.

Brushing up your skills

In Chapters 7 and 8 we spend time looking at the analytical, research and professional skills you can acquire whilst on placement. Prior to Day One you should not need to do too much, but a refresher of some of the technical skills you might need to know would be a wise way to prepare.

The research project outline (Figure 5.2 above) provides an indication of the expected skillset, under the Essential and Desirable listed criteria. Note that they asked for some knowledge of two software packages, Excel and SPSS (the latter is used frequently in statistical analysis) in the Desirables section. It may be some time since you used these packages, and you may not have used them at all (which is fine, as they are desirable, not essential, in this example). If you have been successfully appointed to a role where you do not have some or all of the desirable criteria, then use the placement as an opportunity to learn some of them as they are clearly on offer. However, as they are listed in the requirements for the project it would be good to have some familiarity with them before Day One. No one expects you to be an expert; after all, the purpose of the placement is to enable you to practise and develop your skills in the workplace. Nonetheless, consider going back over some exercises you have done previously in class, or find a YouTube video comparable to the level you are at or need, or even better avail yourself of training opportunities at your institution. Many internship schemes will run refresher days to induct you into the programme. Take advantage of these and show up, even if they are not compulsory. At my institution we spend a day-and-a-half getting our students ready to go out on placement, and alongside dealing with the practical issues of what to wear and how to get paid, we deal with the skills training too, which I say more about below.

Student vignette

To motivate you to think about brushing up your technical skills, here's a selection of feedback from students who valued the opportunity to undertake refresher courses:

I'd definitely recommend brushing up on your skills.

It was a while since I had done any analysis. So I was really glad to have the opportunity to take a couple of classes in SPSS (the statistical software we used in the first semester) over the two days training prior to starting my work placement.

By the end of the hands-on sessions I felt much more confident and it gave me a much-needed boost to think that I was going to be OK when I started.

I even went to the GIS (Geographic Information Systems) session – I had never done any mapping before. So by the time I was ready to set off for my first day I felt OK about having a bit more of a grasp on what I might have to do whilst on placement.

The nice thing about the training was that it gave me confidence to know I was going to start the internship having revisited some of the stuff we'd done previously.

So glad I made myself do the training. Now I have the notes I can use when on placement.

You can see from these comments that the students who attended these pre-placement training courses benefited enormously. Actually, one year we had a student request to have these courses run even though she was not undertaking a work placement. The student contacted me and we arranged a separate Excel training session for students who wanted to attend. Another year I brought a trainer from the UK Office for National Statistics (ONS) Data Science Campus team to the university to train a keen group of students how to programme in Python. We know that there is a demand for skills training, and I encourage you to seek this out at your institution, or online. There are so many excellent materials online nowadays that it is quite easy to find good training resources. Whether you choose to use online materials, or ask your lecturers to arrange some additional training, or do this collectively as a student group, the preparation will assist you in your internship.

Example training courses

To illustrate the sorts of face-to-face courses we run during our pre-placement training, Figure 5.3 shows a timetable covering what we provide to successful interns. It focuses on quantitative data analysis, reflecting our scheme, and the training students need based on an examination of the collective analytical needs of the organisations where they will be hosted. However, it could be useful to others who may wish to develop similar courses to prepare students to enter the workplace, or could be adapted for more qualitative research placements. Regard it as a flexible framework.

The training is a day-and-a-half long. The morning of the first day is taken up with practical matters relating to their starting. During this morning I cover administrative matters (getting them onto the university payroll, for instance), and all students are allocated an academic mentor to support them whilst on placement. These mentors are drawn from our lecturer team and it is important to us that the interns have a named point of contact back at the university should they need it. We manage expectations carefully though and tell the interns that their first point of contact is the supervisor or allocated mentor in their host organisation; we are here to support their analysis if they get stuck, or provide a sounding board if they feel they need one. The primary support has to come from the organisation where they are placed. By and large this works well.

Figure 5.3 illustrates the timetable for Day 1 and Day 2 for the short practical lab-based courses we put on.

Day 1 – each 90-minute session takes place in a computer lab			Day 2 – each 90-minute session takes place in a computer lab		
Training Session 1 (select one)			Training Session 3 (select one)		
Introductory Data Analysis with SPSS	Excel (Basic)	Excel (Advanced)	Intermediate Data Analysis (SPSS)	Excel (Basic)	Advanced Data Analysis (SPSS)
Break (tea and coffee)			Break (tea and coffee)		
Training Session 2 (select one)			Training Session 4 (select one)		
Intermediate Data Analysis (SPSS)	Excel (Advanced)	Intro to Mapping (QGIS)	Advanced Data Analysis (SPSS)	Excel (Advanced) (Will)	Intro to Mapping (QGIS)

Figure 5.3 Example timetable

Students can take different pathways through the courses depending on their prior knowledge. For example, those who have never done any SPSS but need this for the placement can start on Day 1 with an introduction to SPSS, proceed to do intermediate SPSS and then extend this on Day 2. Each course builds on the preceding one. Others prefer to go through the suite of Excel courses perhaps adding the Intro to Mapping course.

Mostly we manage to cover the needs of our host organisations, although we are finding that their requirements develop year on year. For example, Tableau is becoming more widely used in industry for data visualisation and we do not have in-house expertise on this. We expect host organisations to train students themselves where this is the case. For quantitative analysis Python, R and SQL are also increasingly in demand, and we have witnessed students learn these very successfully whilst on placement. The lesson for you to take from this is that you can learn new skills in the workplace and should take every opportunity to do so. There's possibly never going to be another period when you have a block of time to dedicate yourself to this, so throw yourself into a new software package and go for it.

Start to develop your networks

In Chapter 3 I developed a section on how to develop your support networks. Throughout this chapter you have seen through the case study students, and vignettes from other interns, how you will start to develop professional networks. This becomes even more apparent in Chapters 7 and 8 when you will learn how to develop your research and analytical and your professional skills, and how others can help you in doing so. The power of networks in your professional career cannot be understated. On Day One and in Week One, however, you have a lot to think about so rather than view this as a humungous task, I will break it down into two smaller and achievable goals. The first is to start to become a valuable member of the team. The second is to find yourself a mentor.

Learning to be a valuable member of the team

The testimonials included in this chapter so far have indicated how important first impressions are. It's not enough though to just show up; you need to do all of the above and ensure those you are working with can appreciate the value you bring to the team or organisation. I've said before that this is something of an alien concept to a university education, which largely rewards you for individual rather than team work. The world of work, in contrast, thrives on the need for teams to work towards joint goals, by each member of the team contributing to the best of their ability and in keeping with their own strengths. I've no space to go into the theory and practice of how good teams form and operate here, though there are many books and websites that do this and if you become responsible for a team in the future you would be advised to research how good teams are formed and led. (You could start by looking at the MindTools website: www.mindtools.com/.) However, I do offer thoughts, insights and evidence from those who have undertaken work placements, and show why being a good team player matters. This will aid you in developing an appreciation for what it means to be a valuable team member, and provide you with practical tips on how you can achieve this.

You might be a quiet person who prefers to work alone, an introvert by nature. Introverts have been written about quite extensively in recent times. A book you might be interested in if you think you incline towards introversion is *Quiet: The Power of Introverts in a World That Can't Stop Talking* (Cain, 2013), which has cornered the market in showing how introverts can add enormous value in the workplace. A couple of quotes which capture this and provoke us all to think is 'the next time you see a person with a composed face and a soft voice, remember that inside her mind she might be solving an equation. ... She might be deploying the powers of quiet' (Cain, 2013: 266) and 'we put too much of a premium on presenting and not enough on substance and critical thinking' (Cain, 2013: 52). Understanding how introverts process information and work could be extremely helpful if you encounter a colleague who may fall into this category.

You might on the other hand be a person who loves the opportunity to engage with others, always happy to present and contribute vigorously to class discussions, willing to help your fellow students to understand work they might struggle to follow, and collaborate in study groups to draw on each other's shared knowledge and perspectives. Probably most of us fall some way between the two extremes, or have different preferences in different situations.

Whichever type you lean towards, your modus operandi, supported through your school and university education to date, has been very focused around you studying with others, then submitting work as an individual, and having this returned with a single mark. Your contribution has therefore most likely been predominantly rewarded with an individual mark or grade or through feedback on your own performance.

Enter the world of work and you will find that success is often not measured this way at all. Although there is sometimes a single person accountable for the output of the task, which might be a research report or a presentation to a policy maker, many people are likely to have contributed to this and have shared responsibility in developing and delivering this. Teamwork is so important in industry, and in research. The traditional academic model does not reflect the external world so well, although there will be examples of courses where teamwork is incorporated, and if you are on such a course then do embrace this.

The need to be and show you are a good team player is important, and fortunately the work-integrated learning experience will provide you with the opportunity to do this in a practical, applied setting in a way that would be difficult to simulate in a classroom. Take it and use it to best effect. On graduating, this will set you apart from your peers, and if developed well, will provide a great way to evidence this skill and experience at future interviews. You can develop your capacity to become a valuable, if not invaluable, member of the team through your work placement. Time and time again host organisations tell us how valuable a particular intern was during their time in role, and this was often framed in terms of how well they contributed to the team. Set this as an intended goal at the start of your placement and you are more likely to achieve it.

I offer a short note here on late starters – those who take a while to find their strengths and achieve their potential. I include this here, as I want to help you manage your expectations. Different people bring different strengths to teams and I have introduced introverts and extroverts above. What is often not discussed is that we all develop at different rates. This is true in the workplace too. I recommend a book to you – *Late Bloomers: The Power of Patience in a World Obsessed with Early Achievement* (Karlgaard, 2019) – that might give you some comfort. I rate this book highly, not least because it resonates with my own experience. I introduce it here, in a chapter on the first day and week, to reassure you that you can get through this, and nothing can go so disastrously wrong that you can't have a second day, or week. We all had a first day once. Some of you will use your work placement as a springboard to great things, others may not realise the importance it has immediately, but it may come back to help you in years to come.

My own first day in my first professional job was traumatic. I used to be a schoolteacher in a secondary school. I started my first day with high hopes, had prepared thoroughly, was enthusiastic in the staffroom and commanding enough with the pupils. At lunchtime I went to the school office to use the photocopier (Google it if you don't know what that is!) and somehow managed to break it. This was the first day of the new term. Every single teacher in the school probably needed to use it that week. And I had unwittingly broken it. The shame was unbelievable. I had to confess to the office manager, who had to communicate this to the entire school. I became known as the 'newbie who broke the photocopier'. I am telling you this because if I could get through that first day, and survive, whatever you have to handle you will do so. Do it with good grace, and some humour and humility, if you can, and try to see that this will soon be behind you. Nothing quite matched that first-day experience in subsequent roles, and so getting it over and done with in my first graduate job was probably a good thing.

Hopefully your first day will be less traumatic.

Find a mentor

One of the characteristics that helps set people apart from others is to model the behaviour of successful people. The self-help sections of business bookshelves and websites abound with titles including phrases like 'Seven steps' or 'Ten habits of …' or 'Five pitfalls in …'. Next time you are in a railway station look around and see how many of these dominate the shelves of book stores. Essentially these all take examples of behaviours deemed to be worth copying, and teach you how to do this or avoid doing so in the case of unwanted behaviours. The idea of modelling yourself on a good example of a person in the workplace is not new, but it is certainly one worth considering throughout your time in a work environment. The two books I recommended in the previous section will help you model yourself on introverts (Cain, 2013) or late bloomers (Karlgaard, 2019) if you identify with those characteristics, for example.

Reading about role models is one way to do this, but a more powerful and practical way is to try to find a mentor early in your work placement. I try to be to my students the person I wish I had had in my life when I was at their stage in the educational process. If you can find someone who can do this for you, please do start now. You might already have role models in life – teachers, family members, people you admire from afar for whatever reason, but the chance for you to learn from someone on the job in a relatively short space of time is an opportunity to be embraced.

How do you find a mentor? There are different ways. You can silently observe someone but that will have limited impact, or you can ask someone outright. However you decide to approach this, be clear what you are hoping to get out of this. Your mentor might be your supervisor, or the manager at work. A good mentoring relationship will use a framework that makes it clear to each person what is expected (see, expectations again) and what the 'rules of the game' are.

I have both been mentored and been a mentor. I achieved both through a structured programme in the workplace, initially, but now I have adapted that to be a mentor to those people who ask me to. You probably want to know how you can find a mentor if there is no structured way to do this, and for short-term work placements this is unlikely.

Here is what I suggest you do to have a good experience, on the first day, and then week, in keeping with the focus of this chapter. Observe. Be mindful. Look around you and get a sense of who is likely to be a support for you. Try to identify someone who is going to help you learn – so if it is the most junior member on the team who you think you will learn the most from go for them; if you prefer to have someone more senior then find out people's job roles and ask to meet with them in your first week. Being the newbie in the team can be used to your advantage if you do this with grace and a positive attitude. Flattery can go a long way too – people like to be asked to support novices by and large, but try not to choose the most senior person in the organisation as you are unlikely to get much input from them due to their busy schedule. That said, in small companies the CEO has been known to take an interest in an intern and make it their business to support them throughout their placement.

Whoever you choose, and for whatever reason, your first day is an opportunity to spot them or ask around for one that would meet your requirements. If you cannot find one on Day or Week One, keep this task of looking for a mentor on your list of things-to-do at the start of your placement.

Your mentor will become a very valuable asset to you both during and after the internship so cultivate this connection and relationship carefully, be aware that you are doing this with purpose, and be prepared to listen to their contribution to your development.

Ask relevant questions

You have been given a golden opportunity to learn from people who are doing applied research in the workplace. One sure-fire way to find information quickly is to ask questions but take some care with the questions you ask. Try whenever you can to pre-empt the outcome – for example if someone on the reception desk can help you find various rooms or give you an organisational structure chart so you can determine who is who, make it your business to ask them rather than someone more senior. The most important point in asking questions is always to check whether the answer is easily obtainable. If it is – then don't ask the question but find the answer yourself. You can always ask for your answer to be verified (showing that you have at least tried).

Generally your colleagues will be happy to answer your questions at the beginning, but part of becoming a professional in a research environment is to cultivate a sense of when you can find out the answer to questions yourself, and when you really do need to ask for guidance. Therefore at the start of your work placement it would be acceptable to ask broad questions about the research, the approach, any theoretical work underpinning this and the context of the research, but as time develops (and in the space of a matter of days) you need to be working towards showing understanding and exercising good judgement. The questions then become more nuanced and insightful, reflecting that you are thinking about the research you are undertaking, and developing deeper questions that show your progression. Your team will start to appreciate that you are assisting them in the research, and as they acknowledge the value of developing the relationship it will become one of mutual benefit. Win-win. They will also be happy to be probed on their approach; as we heard in Chapter 2 this is one of the aspects of having new blood that organisations value. They welcome being asked 'Why do you do it like that?' and in time might even embrace your suggestions to do things differently. An internship is and should be a two-way learning experience.

Be proactive

Finally, strive to be proactive from Day One. Making yourself a valuable member of the team, asking relevant questions and finding a mentor are all ways in which you can show you are motivated by the research and the experience, but there are a multitude of other things you can do to show people that you are bringing something new to the organisation. These will be expanded in subsequent chapters but what can you do on the first day to show you have an approach and a positive attitude that will be of value to the team?

Case study 5.3

Julija: Learning to push myself in the first week

Julija describes how she set about cultivating a good working relationship with her host organisation.

> The news organisation I worked in was large and complex but I made myself speak to all the data journalists over the first few days. It was tough but I'm so glad I put myself out there. Actually I had to do it as my supervisor was called away at short notice so I took the opportunity to use that as a personal test – to push myself out of my comfort zone. It paid off as not only did I get to know more journalists, and them me, but it started the idea for several news stories that developed during the time I was there. That might not have happened if I hadn't been proactive in that first week. I'm glad I took the plunge. Also when they sent me to an investigative journalism conference in the first week I had enough information to participate. If I had not been proactive I would have been a bit of a spare part, but as it was I made some great contacts and felt much more confident to speak to people.

Reflect

Chapter 6 is dedicated completely to reflection and I believe there is no better time to start than on Day One. The student quotes in this chapter have all arisen from their reflecting from the start of the placement. If you get into the habit of writing down what you learn, and how you learn, it helps enormously later on when you come to look back on the experience and remember how you felt, and how you approached developing your skills and knowledge to make the most of the opportunity. It also helps you put things in perspective, and realise that what may have felt an insurmountable problem at the start of the work experience was actually far from that.

You can see from the examples in this chapter that each student articulated some concern about what they were taking on. I included these examples purposefully, to show that it's absolutely normal to experience the first day like this. Most of our anxieties are a natural reaction to not knowing something, and that characterises the first day of anything new. All the students in this book had a first day. They all went on to complete second days, first weeks and then multiple weeks subsequently. They all reflected throughout their placements and most reported they were pleased that they had done so from Day One. I hope you will take encouragement from this and acknowledge the value in becoming a reflective researcher from the outset. I might not have written this book if I had not reflected on the need to share this learning, and developed a practice of sharing my own as well as my students' reflections. This is why I am championing this approach here.

If you follow the advice in this chapter, based on real students who have gone before you, good things may happen. Here are two interns' first-week experiences, and each contends that their positive experiences could not have happened without their being open to the opportunities, and having a positive, can-do attitude from Day One.

Case study 5.4

Julija: Reflecting on my first week

In my first week I had the opportunity to attend an all-day conference on data journalism, which proved to be very interesting and highly related to my internship. I learned a lot of tips on how to analyse data, use Excel and R, how to put an FOI (Freedom of Information) request and how to **do** data journalism. I learned so much during this week. But most importantly – I am happy. I am happy with what I do, with what I learn, with the challenges I face and it's hard to believe … but I am even happy to get up early every day.

I feel like a real employee having to rely on her own judgements and make independent decisions, with real implications. It is so much better than my previous internship experience, where basically I did work no one else wanted to. I feel at last that my critical thinking abilities have use in real life.

Even though my mentor was away for some of the week I have coped, and I've used this to help me develop my confidence and organisational skills.

Student vignette

After two days in the office I was asked to accompany the head of research to a conference. The conference theme was Crime and Interventions and so completely relevant to the work. It was pretty terrifying listening to the experts present on the research that I was contributing to, but also exhilarating. At the end of the day my head was spinning, but I managed to write down my thoughts and was able to use these to hone the research questions that the government department where I was placed were interested in. This experience helped me enormously in focusing on what I could do to help the team whilst I was with them, and without it I might still have been flailing around halfway through.

How to check your progress after Day or Week One

The checklist in Table 5.1 can be used to help you think constructively about how you can embrace the advice in this chapter. Consider using this to capture the learning you have undertaken, and use it as a tool to help you think about how you could be further developing yourself. I provide more detailed reflection tools in the following chapters. This is intended as a short and easy one to get you started in the art and practice of reflection.

Table 5.1   First day/week checklist on personal progress

	Date of completion:	
Question	Answer: Yes/ No/Unclear	Action: What I need to do and when
Have I set my goals?		
Do I know what is expected of me (for the remainder of the first week/placement)?		
Have I started a reflective log?		
Do I have a good understanding of what the research is?		
Do I know why this research is important for the organisation?		
Have I opened myself up to opportunities?		
Could I have been braver?		
Do I know who to ask for day-to-day help with the research?		
Have I started to develop a network?		
Have I been able to identify a mentor yet?		

Now go home and relax. Tomorrow is another day.

Summary

This chapter has guided you through your first day, and week, in the workplace. It has helped you focus from the word go on what you want to achieve from your time, by clearly specifying the expectations placed on you by the host organisation, as well as encouraging you to think about what you want from this. I have provided some examples of those who have ventured before you down this track, to show how everyone's first day is different, but there are many ways you can make yours a good experience. Being prepared prior to the first day is important, and brushing up your skills in anticipation of what's going to be asked of you will help calm you and increase your confidence. Most important of all I have tried to persuade you that a positive and growth mindset is an important characteristic to cultivate, and being open to opportunities provides an excellent way to get noticed, and make a difference, in the early days.

And so let us move on, put Day or Week One behind you, and build on that good start to create the skills and experience from that applied research project that forms the basis for the remainder of this book.

Three things you can do next

1   Do a goal-setting exercise. Use the model provided here (in Figure 5.1, adapted from Dweck, 2017: 73). Whether or not you have a work placement or internship this is incredibly helpful to get you to focus on what you want to achieve. Make it realistic and achievable by giving yourself a timeframe (e.g. the next six months).

2   Take a look at the article 'Carol Dweck revisits the growth mindset', at www.stem.org.uk/system/files/community-resources/2016/06/DweckEducation Week.pdf. This highlights the main points of Dweck's (2017) book. If it resonates, consider accessing a copy of her book and read Chapters 1 and 2.

3   Get creative. Imagine you have finished your first week in placement. What would you want to see yourself having done? There is a lot of work that shows that visualising a successful outcome helps us achieve one. What will your success look like at the end of Week One? Write it down. Then go back to it when you have started your work placement to see whether you achieved it.

6

HOW TO USE A FRAMEWORK FOR REFLECTION

Learning objectives

In this chapter you will learn how to:

- Use reflection as a way of learning
- Develop a growth mindset
- Systematically reflect on your placement or internship using a reflective framework
- Develop your resilience
- Further develop your positive and growth mindset through reflecting

'Learning without reflection is a waste. Reflection without learning is dangerous.'

Confucius (date unknown)

Overview

In this chapter I will guide you through why reflection matters and show you how you can do this systematically to help you understand, document and remember your learning as you progress through your work placement. You will see, based on others' experiences, how you and the work you undertake can change throughout a work placement, and how the use of reflection enables us to learn from our experiences, both good and bad. Students who have employed reflection successfully to guide them through different situated-learning activities will describe their experiences.

This chapter introduces you to systematic reflection and shows you how developing this as a habit can be an effective tool. I will show you how you can evidence your learning, building on early chapters that taught you how to evidence your research skills. Capturing this learning becomes important when you return to your studies, or start to apply for roles after you graduate. I hope this chapter will encourage you to think about how reflecting on your learning is a skill that will help you develop into a self-reflective researcher.

This chapter introduces two case study students, Alice and Mia, and uses a vignette from Natassia from a published paper.

Introducing reflection

Donald Rumsfeld's (2002) famous speech as Secretary of Defense to President George W. Bush (in making the case to invade Iraq) included this framework for thinking through options:

> ... there are known knowns; there are things we know we know. We also know there are known unknowns; that is to say we know there are some things we do not know. But there are also unknown unknowns – the ones we don't know we don't know. And ... it is the latter category that tend to be the difficult ones.

Entering the world of work provides the chance to develop new skills and knowledge, to learn about the known unknowns, but to uncover the unknown unknowns too. How though can you measure and monitor your learning from a work-based experience? You may be assessed at the end of it, in which case reflecting as you go has obvious benefits. Some accredited courses include reflection as a way of assessing work-placed learning, but without an underpinning reflection framework the student has to store up their learning to produce an assignment after many weeks. It is very easy to forget what you have done. On the other hand you may not be given a summative assessment of your learning. At my institution we 'celebrate rather than assess' our internship learning, which is not the usual academic model but the placements take place over the summer break and do not contribute towards the degree mark. Interns are required to produce a poster and if they have not captured their learning during the placement this can present a challenge for them several months later when they need to create the poster from memory. In our programme we are every bit as interested in *how* you learn as well as *what* you learn, and the reflective framework, and the poster that follows, helps us better understand that.

Here I introduce a framework I have developed for introducing a reflective learning component into the work placement. Starting from the premise that I want you to think about measuring your learning along the way (which I develop further in

Chapters 7 and 8), one way would be to start the placement, finish it and somehow measure vaguely the difference between your before and after states, perhaps by recounting what you know at the end that you didn't know at the start. You can do this, and you would end up with a bunch of statements along the lines of 'I can now produce pivot tables' or 'learned R' or 'understand the importance of cleaning data' or 'carried out focus groups' – but this is somewhat unstructured. A much more targeted way is to do this systematically. By putting into practice the tips in this chapter you will develop good habits that will enable you to do, and reflect on doing, research. More importantly you will be able to look back at your skills and knowledge at the beginning of the placement, and compare them with your skills and knowledge at the end, and not only measure the attainment gap you have covered, but recount how you covered this in a structured way that monitored your progress *during and after* the experience.

This chapter will take you through a series of practical steps to help you get the most out of the opportunity you have chosen, or are required, to undertake. I will start by explaining why it matters to reflect – especially given this is an opportunity to develop good habits that will last you a lifetime. The common theme – having a positive attitude to learning which I have introduced elsewhere – will be revisited here and I will show how failure, and learning from it, can also take us a long way in research. I will introduce practical tips for how to reflect and how often, and finish with a checklist to help get you started on your own reflection. The Three Things You Can Do Next section provides practical exercises building on the research introduced in this chapter, to take your learning further.

Reflection is a way of learning

I start by considering why learning to reflect is a valuable endeavour.

In health sciences self-reflection has long been part of the practice of becoming a health professional. Medical professionals, as part of their training and ongoing practice, are taught to document their patients' cases, how they handled them, and the consequences of the treatment they prescribed. Likewise in teacher education, social work and vocational training, reflective practice is encouraged and usually forms part of the assessment framework for the qualification. More recently in higher education and curriculum design, problem-based or enquiry-led learning has been enhanced by the practice of developing a reflective mindset, especially when the learning happens in the workplace. Practice, and reflecting on it, is a valuable pursuit in many applied settings. Developing good reflective skills in order to critically assess the experience of what has been learned through practical application of knowledge is at the heart of this chapter. The following section presents a brief history of reflective learning and practice. It is helpful for you to know where this comes from and the areas in which it is mature. My aim in doing so is to encourage you to think about the application of reflective practice to *applied social research*.

Research on reflection in experiential learning

One of the most useful books on reflective learning in educational contexts is *Reflection in Learning and Professional Development* by Jenny Moon (2008). Moon is an educational developer, and the book is a must-read for anyone wanting to understand where reflective practice has come from, and the theory on which it is based. Her book provides multiple activities for how to become a reflective learner, and she writes about three types of reflection: *learning, writing* and *practice*. She points out that in the professional context:

> There is no one behaviour or one consistent set of behaviours that is reflective practice. ... reflective practice [is] characterized by listing behaviours that have been associated with reflective practice.
>
> The outcome of reflection is reflective practice including learning and action, empowerment and emancipation.

Moon (2008: 65)

The second of these two sentences is powerful and concurs with why I place so much value in developing a reflective practice that works for you. Her first sentence is a tad circular, but essentially says that you need to reflect to develop a reflective practice. Whilst this is completely obvious her emphasis on what this achieves – learning and action, empowerment and emancipation – offers motivation for developing this set of behaviours.

Because I want you to consider developing tools for *reflective practice*, I focus here on this aspect. The founding work of reflective practice in a professional sense was undertaken by Donald Schön and published in his book *The Reflective Practitioner* (1983). Schön drew on the work of earlier authors, including John Dewey (1933), who wrote about reflection as it relates to personal learning. Dewey described reflection as a purposeful and active process enabling us to think about learning, make sense of events through which we have learned by recalling them and considering alternatives to the outcome achieved. Schön developed this further by applying this thinking to the integration of theory and practice in the professional environment. His work focused on how professionals address the challenges of their work by iteratively learning and adapting their practice, and applying new learning to their current practice. Two important concepts that he proposed to enable this were 'reflection-on-action' and 'reflection-in-action'. The latter refers to what professionals do as they are encountering challenges in their role – so reacting to scenarios; the former describes looking back at what they learned – so considering the learning in a retrospective manner. Moon observed that this work was largely theory driven and not empirically tested and in her own work she goes on to address this. However, whilst the notion of reflecting-in-the-moment and reflecting-after-the-event both have value, this chapter focuses on refection-on-action.

As discussions of reflective learning and reflective practice have continued to advance since Schön, others have attempted to make sense of the theories proposed, within their own educational and professional contexts. This chapter aims not to provide you with a full history of how reflective practice has developed – the above provides merely a précis – but rather a reason to develop this, and practical suggestions for how to do so. In researching the history of the theory and the practice, the nexus, of reflective practice I have drawn several conclusions that are worth noting. First is that the literature is predominantly located in health and social care (e.g. nursing, general practice, social work) and education (e.g. teaching). Second, that until recently the literature has lacked a social or political dimension, that is to say that it focuses solely on the individual, rather than the individual within the context of complex organisational structures. And third, in accordance with Moon, the literature is predominantly theory based, with some, but limited, empirical findings. This book is full of empirical findings, and as I have said elsewhere, adopting reflective practice as a way of empirically exploring how this can develop good applied social researchers, is an area ripe for future research.

This book is full of examples taken from gathering *reflective writing* from emerging professionals in applied social research. This chapter draws on reflections by two of our main characters, Alice and Mia, who undertook their work placements in a charity organisation working on domestic violence, and the BBC respectively (Julija, who provided the main case study in Chapter 5, was also at the BBC, but she and Mia were in different teams). The sections in this chapter will help you understand how you, as they did, can apply a reflective framework to assist you in becoming a social researcher. In Chapters 7 and 8 I build on the typology of early career learning that was introduced in Chapter 2 (Table 2.1), and in order to be able to assess yourself against that the sooner you start reflecting on your experiential learning the better. Thomson and Pascal (2012) summarise here the need not only to reflect, but to reflect critically:

> … reflective refers to the process of thinking about the work we undertake – that is, we reflect on our actions either at the time (reflection-in-action) or at a suitable opportunity thereafter (reflection-on-action). In this regard, the hallmark of reflective practice is *informed* practice … [and] reflective practice needs to be *critically* reflective practice.
>
> Thomson and Pascal (2012: 319)

Before moving on to practical tips for how to be critically reflective, and case studies of students who have done this to give you models to follow, I return to one of the central themes of this book.

Develop a growth mindset

This, you will have gathered, is a central tenet of the book, and in doing research generally. I have been building this in gradually, but consistently, including a 'positive mindset' as one of the learning objectives at the start each chapter. In the previous chapter I challenged you to develop a positive mindset from Day One, providing some tips on how to do so, and showing how a former intern succeeded in doing so.

What is a growth mindset?

In this section I build on the notion of a positive mindset by returning to the term 'growth mindset' after Dweck (2017), who introduces the term to describe people and companies that do not believe that there is a limited capacity for learning, as opposed to a fixed-mindset, which renders a person or organisation self-limiting. I like this term because it helps you think about learning not just as an individual, but as an individual in the wider context of an organisation. And in keeping with my introduction to experiential learning in Chapter 2 it focuses on growth, and learning as an emerging practice. I especially like this finding from her research in examining growth- versus fixed-mindset approaches in organisations:

> What we found was fascinating. People who work in growth-mindset organizations have far more trust in their company and a much greater sense of empowerment, ownership and commitment. … employees in growth-mindset companies also reported that they were much more committed to their company and willing to go the extra mile for it. Those who worked for fixed-mindset companies, however, expressed greater interest in leaving their company for another.
>
> So employees in growth-mindset companies have more positive views of their organisations, but is that admiration reciprocated? Yes it is. … Supervisors in growth-mindset companies rated their employees as more collaborative and more committed to learning and growing. And are more innovative. These are all things that make a company more agile and more likely to stay in the vanguard.
>
> Dweck (2017: 143–4)

Education is essentially about giving students the knowledge, skills and attributes to empower them. As we saw above, Moon talks about how empowerment and emancipation can result from learning and action that follows reflection. Dweck's work challenges us to think about how our attitude to learning, individually and organisationally, can make a difference. Getting a handle on this is also important for helping you understand the type of organisation you might prefer to work for, by understanding the mindset culture and practices of the workplace.

In order to learn we have to be open to learning. We also have to be open to failing and learning from our mistakes. Becoming a self-reflective researcher will give you the opportunity to show how far you can travel and look back over that distance travelled. My students, and many others I speak to when I present at conferences, often exclaim, 'Oh, I can't do that' or 'No, that's way too hard' or 'But I haven't learned how to do that'. Of course they do. It's completely natural to think that, once we have managed to get to university or college, we have already learned so much. We are aware that our future learning has to build on our prior learning, but it can be scary and sometimes overwhelming to acknowledge that there is so much still to learn. We don't know where to start, or how to apply our previous knowledge. I've lost count of the number of students who come to see me thinking they can't do an essay, or won't be able to succeed in their studies. It helps to be able to tell them what I am writing about in this chapter.

Scaffolded learning

Most learning needs to be scaffolded (i.e. each concept or skill builds on a previous one) and we need to be able to draw on prior learning to advance our knowledge and skills, not just in formal education. Scaffolding theory comes from a psychologist named Jerome Bruner writing in the 1960s and building on prior work by Lev Vygotsky. Vygotsky proposed that novices (students) learn through appropriately guided activities supplied by the expert (teacher) and to explain this he introduced the concept of the zone of proximal development (ZPD). We don't need to get too deep into the theory here but note that in experiential learning, the ZPD describes where you are with respect to your current knowledge and skills (what you have learned in the classroom), and the role of the expert (in the workplace) is to enable you to develop and build on that learning. Doing this in a scaffolded way is the aim of a good work-placed learning experience. Vygotsky and Bruner represent two important twentieth-century educational theorists and many academics, educators and practitioners have expanded upon the theories they introduced.

Importantly they both proposed that new learning requires us to build on top of existing learning. If we are in the right frame of mind to do this we are far more likely to be successful than if we consider new learning to be a chore. If we regard new and potentially difficult tasks as surmountable rather than impossible we will be more likely to succeed at mastering them.

Research requires logical thinking and analytical skills. It may require you to use parts of your brain that are rusty. For example you may have left maths behind you when you were in school or you may have forgotten, or need to learn, how to write compelling arguments. You will have been honing and developing your critical thinking skills during your studies, and you need to adapt and apply these to new forms of work, new challenges and new questions. The sooner you vow to push yourself to learn something new, the sooner you will have the right mindset to face the challenges. Chapter 7 deals with developing your analytical and research skills in more detail.

The marvellous thing about undertaking applied research in the workplace is that you can expect to be surrounded by a group of colleagues who want you to succeed; this may be in contrast to being up against your peers intellectually in your studies, which is often a competitive situation. Your work team is willing you to help them with the research that matters to them and the organisation; after all this is a mutually beneficial arrangement. Hence, adopting a growth mindset is not just a personal thing, it's a cultural matter that will benefit the organisation. In my many years of working with external host organisations I have never met a team that does not want the intern to succeed. What a wonderful start to your professional experience, to have the team who have chosen you or with whom you have been placed rooting for you. Surely you owe it to them and yourself to be that force for good, and to bring your positive attitude to the workplace to make this a good experience for all. Host organisations often comment on the 'breath of fresh air' new students bring with them as they enter the workplace. You can be that student.

In a case study based paper entitled 'From the classroom to the workplace: How social science students are learning to do data analysis for real' (Carter et al., 2017) I introduced Natassia, a second-year sociology student, as one of the three case studies. I include an extract from that paper here to illustrate how her attitude to her work placement, at a prestigious research organisation, contributed to her success. Here she reflects on how she approached learning a new piece of software (Stata) on her internship, having previously been taught using a different one (SPSS).

Student vignette

I wasn't trained to use Stata at university, I was trained to use SPSS. [Here] they only use Stata. Stata is not visual whereas SPSS is, so I had to learn how to type a series of commands, which seems scary but actually it's not and it took me a couple of days to get my head around it ... but I wasn't frightened because I just assumed that they would tell me how to use it. I understood the basic foundations of that [why surveys are conducted and why people are going to use that data and how people interpret the results] before I went into the internship so on that level I was pretty confident.

This response shows a sophisticated and mature level of appreciation of her prior learning and ability to build on it. The student acknowledges that she was trained to use another software tool at university, but recognises that this provides a scaffold for her to learn other tools, albeit through a different approach (command line rather than through a visual graphical user interface). She has faith that the support of her colleagues will be forthcoming and this belief enables her to open up to learning new methods and tools. Her willingness to learn and appetite to be challenged is evident – an attitude that in fact continued to serve her well throughout the placement, and indeed beyond it.

A growth mindset will carry you an awfully long way – if it's not your natural habitat at least try it out; you might be surprised what a difference it makes.

How to reflect and how often

The *Oxford English Dictionary* defines the verb 'reflect' [usually on or upon] as 'to think carefully about' and the noun 'reflection' as 'an idea about something, especially one that is written down or expressed'. I use these definitions here, the first to describe the act of reflecting, the second to articulate the output as a result of reflecting. This section is to help you think about how you can get into the habit of thinking hard about what you learn in the workplace and write it down or capture it in a way you can subsequently look back upon. Moon devotes a full chapter of her book to reflecting through learning journals and you may wish to read this if you are inclined towards including this in your own practice (Moon, 2008: 186–202).

Here is a relevant personal example of reflection, and how I learned from it. When I first introduced work-placed experiences with my students undertaking internships I was lax about introducing structured reflection, although as a self-reflective practitioner I knew from experience that this was important, for the reasons given above. Wanting to improve this, and keen to evaluate the programme, I employed a research assistant who interviewed all of the interns in our first cohort at the end of their placements, and some of the hosts from the organisations where our interns had been placed. The interviews, which were based around a series of open-ended questions, were richer than I could have imagined. I co-authored an academic paper (cited above) drawing on some of these, describing the experiences of sociology students undertaking applied social research in the workplace. It was apparent that learning was taking place, in leaps and bounds, but also that this was quickly being forgotten. More accurately, this learning was not being capitalised on, as the students were simply not capturing it in any systematic way. I determined then that in subsequent years of running the programme I would introduce a structured framework for self-reflection and monitor how this helped capture the interns' learning. I wanted them to acknowledge the technical and research skills they were acquiring and help them to also notice and document the development of their professional – sometimes called softer – skills. Chapters 7 and 8 deal with both these aspects. In this section I introduce a self-reflective framework that has assisted interns to see the distance travelled from the start to the end and beyond of a work placement. I also include the questions I asked them to consider, in order that this might help you to think about this for your own reflections.

Reflecting with purpose

Working from the above dictionary definition of *thinking hard about* and *expressing* that thinking in some way, let's consider here the reflection you might wish to do, identifying particular aspects of your applied learning, and outlining why it helps to think about them so that you can reflect *purposefully*.

Focus on research skills

To reiterate, this book focuses on identifying how a work placement can support development of your research skills. For that reason we need to identify the types of skills you might have opportunity to acquire *in the workplace* to enable you to undertake research. By identifying different research skills, we can start to think about how we can reflect on these – thinking hard about and expressing them – in a way that helps you move beyond what you knew when you started. We saw from Natassia's example above how she had learned a particular software package in her studies, and had the opportunity to learn a new one on her placement. Whilst software is not a research skill as such, it certainly features in terms of you needing to capture this, as we saw previously when we listed your skills in Chapter 3, and itemised these on your CV. In this chapter I focus on your research skills generally. In Chapter 7 I unpack this to consider your analytical and research skills, then in Chapter 8 I focus on developing your professional skills. In all cases I will show you how you can adopt the same reflective framework and hone it to fit the skillset you are interested in developing.

In the interests of keeping things simple to start with, the following list covers the main research skills you might expect and hope to acquire through undertaking an applied research project, together with associated activities you might undertake in the workplace to acquire these:

- Literature review
- Research design
- Data skills
- Analysis skills
- Report writing
- Communication to different audiences

The purpose here is to imagine how you might *acquire and reflect on* each of these opportunities as they arise. Again, these are just for examples – you may prefer to use a tried and trusted (for you) technique that has worked in your learning to date. There are many texts to support you in *study skills and research skills*; the aim here is not to repeat these but to help you apply the tools you already have – after all you are on a research project so you've got this far – to the application of your learning in the workplace. Table 6.1 identifies a set of skills and provides suggestions for how these can be acquired during the course of undertaking your work placement and introduces ideas for how you can start to reflect on these systematically.

Before introducing Table 6.1 I provide a list of Top tips for you to consider, all of which are taken directly from the table and will make a handy note for you to refer back to. I have grouped them so that you can quickly see the sorts of activities that you can put into practice during your placement. Some sound very obvious but my intention is that you can use this as a list to prompt you into action.

Top tips

- Observe/observe common practices
- Record/make notes/take careful notes/document
- Ask for feedback/probe/ask questions
- Research data management practices
- Figure out your own good practice/keep a learning log or notebook or e-portfolio/develop a method for reflecting
- Learn to focus
- Ask to look at an example/find examples
- Know your audience

Table 6.1 How to reflect on research skills acquired in the workplace

Research skillset	Develop and reflect on skills
Literature review	**Observe** how colleagues make reference to related bodies of research. **Record** these in a journal or notebook. Use your academic skills on developing a literature review to keep a bibliography or set of references (ideally using reference software) to maintain a record. Undertake desk research – websites, grey literature – maintain a digital record of websites and date searched. **Make notes** on the most relevant literature and websites found. Develop a system (e.g. colour coding) for highlighting the important ones. **Ask** a trusted work colleague **for feedback** on whether this aligns with their thinking on the issue.

(Continued)

Table 6.1 (Continued)

Research skillset	Develop and reflect on skills
Research design	Research design is important, especially for the validity of the results. Make it your job to ensure you capture as much information about this as possible. **Observe and document** how the research is conducted. Is the research design clear? Have choices been made to take account of the research question, data availability, skills in the team, etc? Real-world research is often done under very different conditions to academic research. **Probe** your colleagues as to how decisions have been made to do the research, and how choices have been taken due to practical issues such as timescales/resources available/expertise. Has the research design been documented? Research should be reproducible.
Data skills	This could be challenging to observe as colleagues often have their own ways of undertaking analysis. A systematic approach to data analysis is critical. **Observe common practices** and **ask questions**. Do your own **research** on **data management practices** (e.g. Corti et al., 2014: Chapter 9) and commit to being scrupulous about developing a methodical approach. Develop a naming system for folders and files; keep a record of the version of data you are using; note the method and parameters employed to analyse the data (e.g. which software menu options you selected); always make a copy of your original dataset so you can recover it should you need to; familiarise yourself with your data structure before attempting to analyse; pay careful attention to missing values; save files regularly; you might also want to note the software version used. Work out a system that works for you – this could be keeping a written notebook on how you perform a data analysis, or keeping a digital log of commands and naming conventions used, or creating a tagging mechanism to ensure you can find your 'working out' subsequent to the analysis. The important factor is to **figure out your own good practice** so that, should you need to, you could repeat the data analysis.
Analysis skills	**Learn to focus** on how you *do* analysis (i.e. research methods). **Document** all the methods that the organisation uses and contemplate whether you could suggest new ones. Also think about how *you* do the analysis. Are you better at thinking in the morning or afternoon? Does your office environment make a difference? Do you need complete quiet or work better to music or the office hubbub? Do you process numerical information differently to textual? Do you have a preference? Whatever your preferences, note them down. **Keep a learning log or notebook or e-portfolio** – a way that you can capture how you do your best (and worst) analysis. Read this back frequently – look out for common themes that will help you identify how you work to your optimum capacity. Be systematic, and be honest, include how you felt at the time – were you hungry, happy, upset, anxious, distracted, and if any of these how did this affect you? Use this to consider how you might develop habits that will enable you to be a good analyst, and help you realise what you might need to change about yourself if you want to be a better researcher.

Research skillset	Develop and reflect on skills
Report writing	This is one of the major skills that can be developed in the workplace. Often university essays do not lend themselves well to report writing in the workplace. Feedback to interns is often that they need to 'leave the essay behind'.
	Ask to look at an example of a report if you are asked to write one. Use this as a template for anything you are expected to contribute content to.
	As above, **develop a method for reflecting** on how you write a report. Note the difference between a research report for work and a university essay. Think about the purpose of the report, the structure, the relative split between background/introduction/methodology/analysis/results/conclusion and note that often a Recommendations section is required, and sometimes an Executive Summary.
	A report is also likely to require you to work with colleagues, taking responsibility for different sections – write about how this worked for you – did you enjoy this? Or want to be sole author? What was difficult for you and how might you improve on this in future?
Communication to different audiences	In the workplace this is incredibly important. At university or in your studies you are generally communicating to your academic instructors, and usually to be assessed towards your degree qualification. In the workplace your peers are your guide, and your work will either be communicated to them, or stakeholder groups who are interested in the findings, who could be paying clients or senior government ministers. The workplace will give you an unrivalled opportunity to develop your skills in this area.
	First you need to **know** who **your audience** is. Your mentor or manager is best placed to advise you here but be sure to ask before any presentation or report you write, who the intended recipient(s) is/are. Many client groups and research organisations are tasked with undertaking complex analyses and then charged with communicating the findings in direct and straightforward ways. How does the organisation achieve this? If your host organisation could improve in this regard can you **find examples** of how this could be done to improve their communication? Visualisations and infographics are often held up as the holy grail of communication tools, but these are only ever as good as the research underpinning, and the designers developing, them.
	Take careful notes on what works well for your organisation but also consider the competition and see where others excel in this space. Of all the skillsets, this is the one you are most likely to have most to learn – unless you are studying a course involving graphical design. Try not to expect too much from yourself here but be aware of what you might be able to do in your future career to develop this skillset.

The list (see Top tips) could go on. It does not include professional skills, as we cover these in a later chapter, but as you are reflecting you will see that you start to include these. For example you may use LinkedIn or other networking sites to consider how others are communicating their findings to non-academic audiences. You may have opportunities to attend conferences or meetings where you will start to see how the organisation works, and how you need to adapt to this in order to be accepted and for your role to add value. One of the first things you will be introduced to is 'how we do things here' through communication channels involving emails, phone etiquette, workplace intranets and online communication tools such as Slack – watch, listen and learn. All of these lend themselves well to developing and practising reflection.

Frequency of reflection

Having suggested how you can reflect and document your work-placed learning, you might be wondering how often you need to do this. There are no hard and fast rules for this, but this section is based on my experiences of helping students develop a framework that has enough flexibility to satisfy personal preferences, but is structured enough to be useful. It also ensures that the expectation for a student to reflect is established at the start of the internship or work placement. This is important. Reflection might be optional, but it would be strange for you to be in a scenario where your situated learning does not matter, and so I advocate strongly for you to develop this as a regular practice from the start. In Chapter 3, Table 3.1, I introduced different types of work-integrated learning, noting that not all of these would be assessed. Regardless of whether your experience in the workplace is or is not formally assessed, the following framework can be applied, and adapted.

Suggested framework for reflection

As a general rule you should try to capture your reflection at the beginning, middle and end of your work experience, as a minimum. For a two-month long placement we have found this is a good frequency. It allows you to think and write impressionistically after the first week, consolidate the thinking in the middle (end of the first month) and reflect more deeply at the end (within two weeks of completing the placement). For different length experiences you can adapt this general rule, so if your work placement is a year long you would be advised to reflect at least monthly, and if only a fortnight long you may want to write on days 1, 7 and 14. The reflection needs to be useful, and you will be in a position to determine what is most useful for you. The absence of any reflection means you will miss a trick, whereas too much reflection may become tedious. The goal is to find a happy medium – where reflecting becomes a regular habit that benefits your learning, but not a chore that detracts from the return on investment of your time. You may choose to reflect intermittently, and only when you think you have something worth capturing. In some ways reflecting is most useful when you have a light bulb moment, or you made a huge error, or you learned something you previously thought was completely out of reach to you – so capture those moments rather than being a slave to regular reflection for the sake of it.

Within this general (and adaptable) beginning – middle (may be several stages) – end framework I advise you to keep a record or log of your learning (see Top tips and Table 6.1 above). As noted above a learning log or journal could be the way to do this, or you may prefer to record this in some other way. In 2019 I experimented with filming some of my interns and inviting them to talk to camera about their work placements at the end of weeks 1, 4 and 8 of their two-month placements. This was to explore whether this could be a useful method in future. The short films are available on our Q-Step website under a section called Student Stories (www.manchester.ac.uk/q-step/student-stories/).

The two case studies below will illustrate how a regular reflection framework can work in practice. To frame these, the instructions given to the students are provided here.

You are going to be on placement for two months. You are required to produce three written reflective pieces (1, 2 and 3) within that period, as follows.

BE HONEST – it is important to share your experience with us, warts and all. We will use these to observe your progress, and you can use them to reflect on and capture your learning.

Reflective piece 1

- On your **first day or end of your first week** send an email to [email address] with the **Subject line: Reflection 1**.
- Write anything you like about your experience. No more than the equivalent of one side of A4 on anything that has happened so far e.g. orienting yourself, your experience compared to your expectations, the 'reality' of being an intern, etc.

Reflective piece 2

- **Half-way through your internship** send an email to [email address] with the **Subject line: Reflection 2**. Equivalent of 1–2 sides of A4.
- Write about your experience focusing on what you are learning (data analysis, analytical methods, stats), and how you are experiencing this (challenges, successes, frustrations, highlights).
- Think about how this is impacting you – not just from the point of view of research and analytical skills. What about your professional skills?

Reflective piece 3

- **Within two weeks of finishing your internship** send an email to [email address] with the **Subject line: Reflection 3**.
- We will write to you towards the end of your internship with what is required. So check emails and the closed online support group.
- You will expand on the earlier two reflections and help us understand what you have learned and how you have developed.

Having been told what they were required to do – and having had the pre-placement training through which we covered the reflective framework – students submitted their three reflective written pieces.

In order that you gain a sense of the sorts of things they wrote about, and I can draw your attention to some of the main points in support of reflective practice, I introduce the voices of Alice and Mia. I will begin with Alice and take you through three extracts from her beginning, middle and final reflections. Alice's case study is longer than all the others in the book, but I include it in this format so you can understand and see for yourself the journey she went on in just six weeks.

Case study 6.1

Alice: Reflecting on my placement experience

Alice was a highly motivated student. She had not done any work-placed learning previously but embraced the need to capture her learning in a way that she could revisit. After the placement, so enthusiastic and convinced was she that this worked for her that she shared her story with a cohort of new interns, imploring them to think carefully about how they could learn, drawing on her own experience. More on this later.

She undertook a six-week research project at a London-based not-for-profit organisation working to end domestic abuse. She joined a small team that had limited capacity for undertaking social research, but had taken a student on work placement the previous year and were very impressed and pleased with the research that had been undertaken. Alice was their second intern. She had to relocate to London for the internship, and was aware that she would need to navigate a steep learning curve.

The project was designed to use data collected through the phone helpline, and to explore demographic factors collected by the callers. Her brief was to help explore patterns of users who accessed the helpline. The extracts from her three reflective pieces are included in this case study.

Reflection 1 – end of week 1

My first week has been very interesting, due to the nature of the work I've been a part of. I spent a lot of time listening in as advisors took calls, which was fascinating but also quite heavy … [but] the calls gave context to the numbers and reminded me that each statistic is a person. It's also fascinating as I can hear the advisors collecting data that will be anonymised and I will be analysing. This is frustrating sometimes however, as people can cut off calls before asking demographic questions! We discussed the opportunity for some possible qualitative analysis, as well as the chance for me to take some [calls] (though to professionals only, not those calling for help).

I've really enjoyed working in the office with everyone, and it's been nowhere near as awkward as I thought it would be. They were all really excited to have me there and I've had lots of requests, beyond the original aims set, to help different parts of the team analyse their work. I feel I'm being quite ambitious with some of my ideas (we discussed mapping and I've also thought about using webometrics) but the team are aware of this and excited to see what I come up with.

Here we see Alice reflecting already on how the data are collected, to what purpose they are used, and starting to develop ideas about the research she can undertake. Although it may feel like a difficult task to suggest the direction of the research in Week One, she is brave enough to start to develop co-ownership of this project by sharing her ideas with her peers. This sets out the direction of travel for her, and her new colleagues, in a way that helps everyone. By setting clear expectations at the beginning of the internship Alice has established that she is willing to work collaboratively, and bring her ideas to the table. She also evidences here how important it is to her to understand the way the data are collected, and anonymisation is ensured, and that she understands they represent cases that she will be working with. Finally she shows how she is open-minded and happy to join in with her new colleagues, as well as be adaptable regarding the original aims of the project changing, both traits that will take her a long way. Her written reflection allowed her to capture all of this in a single page, and she might not have done this had she not been asked to produce a written piece. Her enthusiasm for the project is palpable.

Reflection 2 – end of week 3

This work has taught me an incredibly important lesson about the reality of data. In university courses we work with faceless data sets and it's so easy to disconnect and just write them off as numbers. However here, I spend every day listening to the data being collected. It is fascinating to know the source of the data, as well as important. When it came to formulating my own questions (encouraged by the team) it was invaluable. I knew the problems and issues that the team had been facing as well as the questions they were curious about. Initially I did find it quite challenging to propose my ideas, as I felt they were experts who knew the topic better than I did, but I'm getting more confident with it and quite enjoy the discussions now about what the data is telling us and what we should do next. I feel communication in a professional setting is something that takes a bit of adjustment but luckily my team are pretty relaxed and open to ideas and creative thinking.

(Continued)

I've also learnt a lot about what's involved in formulating a research question in the real world (which is very helpful considering dissertations and such), as well as the need for both qualitative and quantitate data. I now fully realise the importance of qualitative research to give a deeper understanding of the data.

In the middle of her work placement Alice reflects further on the value she places on understanding the data and its collection methods. She has started to think more deeply about the research questions needed and how the data might in their previous form not be able to answer those – and she has been able to influence the questions asked of helpline callers. Her writing here also highlights that she is beginning to value herself and the contribution she is able to make to the organisation – and acknowledges that even as a relative newcomer her ideas are welcomed. Through the mere process of articulating this for her reflective exercise, she has identified herself as part of the team, and the work she is involved with as being important to assisting her organisation to gain insight. Crucially she has also been made aware of the need to have an appreciation of both qualitative and quantitative methods to undertake and understand social research. This is a really important part of her learning experience, and she uses this throughout the remainder of her time. Her comments about finding things challenging initially also indicate how she adopted a growth mindset – she could have chosen to accept the work she was given and use only the tools that the organisation was familiar with. Instead she chose to push herself, to engage with them through sharing her ideas, and stretch herself through learning new skills because she could see the potential to present some of the findings in maps. This was really taking her out of her comfort zone, but as we shall see below it was worth it.

Reflection 3 – two weeks after completing the internship

At this stage the interns were asked for a much fuller reflection on what they had learned, how it matched their expectations, what the barriers and successes were, how they learned from their mistakes and what they would tell themselves now if they could go back and offer advice. I supplied them with a list of directed questions and asked them to either answer these one by one or use them as a guide. I framed this as enabling me and my team to learn about what the students had done, as well as for them to think back on what they had learned.

Here are two extracts from Alice's final reflective piece.

I realised after two weeks into the project (and after completing most of my analysis for the phoneline data) that I had downloaded and completed the analysis using the wrong data. … this was exceptionally frustrating but taught me an important lesson about not panicking and being honest. I was very nervous to tell my line manager about my mistakes, but he was very understanding about it and I assured him that I could fix the problem (relatively) easily. This has taught me to view my mistakes in a forgiving light and not be hard on myself when I am still learning. I also feel that I must've developed my interpersonal skills as the conversations we had about my mistakes went smoothly and I was able to stay calm and admit my mistakes in a professional way.

In terms of success, producing the maps was certainly a highlight. It took so much work and attempt after attempt, making mistakes and learning from them, that when I finally managed it I was ecstatic. It was a challenge I'd set myself without having any idea whether it was really possible. My success was certainly helped by how supportive the team were, they shared my curiosity and encouraged my further exploration of the data. They also trusted me, trusted that I knew what to do with the data. We taught each other and worked together – I really felt like part of the team. [My manager] was also really wonderful constantly telling me not to feel stressed or pressured and to let him know if what he'd asked me to do was too much, he is a very creative thinker and I think was worried that he'd sometimes asked me to do something beyond my skill set. But, it's surprising how much you can learn on the job. It was actually really nice to have the team observe my work, realise what the [mapping] software could do and come up with their own suggestions of research they wanted completed.

At the end of her internship Alice was able to look back and discern how far she had come. From her early nervousness in contributing ideas, she had gone on to co-design her research project, get her colleagues on board with her ideas, learn how to produce maps and even persuade her team to learn new mapping skills themselves. In six weeks she had developed a good professional relationship with her manager, and was able to use this to deal with a difficult situation when she realised she had made a mistake. He supported her by acknowledging her situation, and in the event she was able to reproduce the research with the correct datasets, in part because she had developed a systematic way of working and was able to reduce the amount of time it took her to run the analysis. Her sense of accomplishment in achieving a goal she had set herself at the outset, even though she had not mastered the tools at that stage to produce maps, is perhaps the best way to see how her reflection captures her learning. Her growth mindset throughout her placement was delightful to see. Without her reflective pieces all I would have had from Alice was her poster (we post all of these online at: www.manchester. ac.uk/q-step/student-stories). None of the richness of her experience would have been evident. Instead I have a case study I can share with you, and an understanding of what Alice did, what she learned, and then how she was able to use that to progress her studies. Moreover I was able to tap into her enthusiasm for work-placed learning and ask her to give back to the programme, which she did with passion and energy. Above all of that I spotted that Alice was an incredibly accomplished novice social researcher, and I was able to connect with her throughout her final year to make sure that she knew about career options, and further study opportunities, that she was more than capable of applying for. This is a positive by-product of asking for reflection; it really helps lecturers have a much deeper appreciation of our learners.

Sharing the value of reflection with peers

Alice was kind enough to come back one year after undertaking her placement to speak with a new cohort of work placement students who were undertaking their pre-workplace training. Her advice to them, based on her own experiences and how she had continued to reflect in her final year of her degree, is captured as follows.

Alice had learned that reflection gave her a way of dealing with her academic work that she had not had previously. She was at pains to point out that when doing research now, she keeps a notebook with her at all times, and is constantly scribbling in this, capturing what she is doing, recording how she changes her analysis, and keeping short notes on her progress (what works as well as what does not). She is systematic in recording the date of everything she does and learned this from the internship. She was adamant that this saves her so much time and makes her more effective. It also helps Alice organise her thoughts. Sometimes she will summarise her work, to capture where she is at a particular timepoint, helping her see what she might not yet understand or where she might have more work to undertake. Synthesising her research in this way has proven to be hugely beneficial. It enables her to stand back and take stock and remember what she is trying to do and provides an opportunity to process her thoughts. She concluded by saying the placement reflection helped her with her third-year research dissertation, and she would highly recommend others get into the habit of reflecting and systematically capturing their learning. She was glad that she had experienced this during her internship.

There is a lovely ending to Alice's story. Whilst writing this chapter I was lucky enough to meet her just before her graduation for her Master's degree in Social Research Methods and Statistics. We had kept in touch and I had continued to encourage her to pursue a career in applied social research. On the day after her graduation she was interviewed for a research associate position in a university. See Chapter 10 for what Alice is doing now.

I hope this section has helped you to understand that developing reflective practice, together with a growth mindset, can be a winning combination. Although on the surface Alice's extracts make her internship look like a very straightforward one, I know there were periods that were challenging for her. One of the ways our students are supported whilst they are on work placement is to provide them with an academic mentor (as discussed in Chapter 5), as well as a closed social media group where they can communicate with each other and with me. This means at all stages of the placement they have a support network, and along with the reflective pieces I can pick up if anything is going awry and provide advice. It also means that I have a mechanism to encourage our interns to develop resilience, which I talk about next. Wellbeing and good mental health are so important to learning and by creating a nurturing environment for interns, from start to finish, everyone can have an optimal experience.

Develop resilience

I have already introduced you to the notion of developing a growth mindset. This will, by definition, mean that you sometimes have to take some risks, and risks sometimes result in failure. Dweck (2017: 263) identified the five characteristics of people who develop and maintain a growth mindset as those who:

- Embrace challenges
- Persist in the face of setbacks
- See effort as the path to mastery
- Learn from criticism
- Find lessons and inspiration in the success of others

She argued that it is not simply a case of developing a growth mindset, but that this needs to be accompanied by the development of a resilient approach in order to achieve our goals.

There is indeed a lot to be said for developing a thick skin in the workplace. Or grit. Or resilience. Or a way of coping. Whatever you choose to call it, how can you develop your own way of learning from setbacks and ensuring you don't make the same mistakes time and time again if you don't cultivate the practice of reflection? Over the years I have witnessed many students encountering pitfalls they could avoid if only they had developed the practice of reflection sooner, and cultivated their resilience alongside a growth mindset. Those with a sensitive disposition can suffer more than those with a hardier approach to setbacks and disappointments. However thick our natural skin, we owe it to ourselves to develop a coping mechanism for dealing with adversity. Life after all is full of setbacks.

Not long ago I went to Japan, a country I had never previously visited, for a conference. I flew in two days before the conference started, to orientate myself. Everything I was experiencing was new – the language, culture, people, travel and currency. I felt very challenged. On the first day of the conference I rose early, navigated the transport network and arrived at the venue in plenty of time. On the second day I made myself take a different journey – I wanted to experience an alternative and trial a new route.

The result? I got lost, had to ask for directions (tough when you know no Japanese), and the journey took twice as long. But – and here is the important part – I learned a new route. I made myself vulnerable, not in a foolhardy way but in a way that opened me up to learning, in order that I could build my own resilience. And I did this by design. The outcome was that by the third day I had learned a new and quicker route to the venue, some Japanese words, and had an appreciation of the city that I could not have had had I stuck to my first-day experience. To build our resilience we need to be open to taking ourselves outside of our comfort zones, and learning from what does not work.

If I had continued to traipse the inefficient transport route I had taken on day 1 throughout my time in Japan I would have missed out on a shorter route, with more interesting cityscapes, and the opportunity to learn some new phrases. My (forced) learning to cope with being in a new country brought rewards. I shared this with my students via our closed online group, to demonstrate (1) an open and growth mindset, (2) the practice and value of reflection and (3) the result of being willing to be a reflective learner and push myself. I hope this small example persuades you to open up your learning too.

To show that this practice of reflection actually does make a difference, and contributes to you being able to develop your own resilience, here is Mia, who learned how to reflect systematically whilst on placement, develop her resilience and become a better researcher as a result.

Case study 6.2

Mia: Learning resilience from making mistakes

Mia was hosted by a media organisation, the BBC, to help journalists undertake data-driven research. Amongst other tasks, this entailed discovery of relevant data sources and the application of appropriate research methods to elicit news stories. She had to work to tight timescales and with colleagues whose journalism training had equipped them to verify any facts their articles and news stories were based on, but not necessarily given them the statistical appreciation to help them critically evaluate the sources of the data, or interpret the data. Mia was able to support them in this endeavour through her role as a researcher for the data-journalism team. In her mid-point reflective piece she notes:

> One of the these [lessons learned] is to make sure that I note down the source for every bit of data that I collect, as it makes it much easier for the …
> team to then use it as they don't have to go back and do any research,
> or I don't have to go and search [the sources] all again. … I have always
> written bibliographies and references as I go but I think as I was collecting

> data from several sources I forgot to do this in my first few days. A lesson I quickly learnt and a mistake I didn't make again!
>
> Tracking sources as I go meant I didn't end up looking at the same database five times. This was particularly a problem when I first used a lot of open data, and ended up looking at the same ones several times. It's a small thing but making notes improved my efficiency and gave me confidence. And that helped develop my resilience too as it helped me realise that I could learn from my mistakes.

She continues:

> I think before [doing a work placement] I definitely took for granted how organised and easy to use data was. I didn't realise just how much organisations and companies are in need of data interns spending a summer organising their research data! I guess I was under an assumption that everything was neatly and automatically organised into Excel files which could just be sent when FOIs [Freedom of Information requests] came in or were uploaded to statistical websites.

Mia's personal reflections here serve to do two things. First, they enable her to recall how she needed to be systematic in noting the source of her data, and her rationale for doing this (as a time-saving device and to help her colleagues see the data source). At the same time she developed her resilience and her confidence as she was learning from her early mistake (of not being systematic). Second, the process of having to find her own data sources has opened her eyes to the difference between learning in the classroom and applied social research in the workplace. The former often uses pre-packaged data, or data developed for teaching use, whilst the latter requires the application of this learned skillset to data sets that are messy, dirty, often unstructured and frequently contain missing values. Such data are a hallmark of a researcher's life. Since Mia was able to express and read back over her learning, she is better placed to pass this knowledge onto others and in doing so become a better researcher herself. Again had she not been required to reflect on this it is not evident that her practice would have improved, and certainly I would not be sharing her experiences with you now to help you develop your own approaches to good data management. Developing resilience is really as straightforward as learning from your mistakes and ensuring you don't repeat them.

This section started with outlining the need to develop resilience. What has been presented so far is the *result* of developing that resilience. Mia kept in touch through-out her placement and used her support networks to help her over the days when things were not going so well. She reached out for help – and in doing so stretched herself and learned from her work experience. I have countless stories of students who found the placement provided challenges not just to start with, but throughout. They had to develop strategies for dealing with boredom, being in an office for eight hours a day, transport woes, having senior staff – their mentors – go on holiday, software failures, data cleaning tasks taking days and weeks, being the strongest in a weak team or the weakest in a strong one, and being told their reports were too essay-like. At every setback they were encouraged to reflect and learn. Thankfully they listened, persevered, and due to their required reflective logs were able to capture what was happening, and then look back and see how they overcame it. Reflecting on their learning, and the obstacles to it, helped develop their resilience in a multitude of ways.

To sum up this section, and to show you that I practise resilience myself, I refer you again to a piece I wrote in 2016 on LinkedIn, which I titled 'Bouncing back in 24 hours'. I've just re-read that article and see that even after the setback of hearing I had not got a job I really wanted, finding this news out on the other side of the world and at a time when personally things were not going well for me domestically (my house had flooded and I was dealing with the difficulties that brought with it), I decided to just get on with my day. There are a few sentences in that article that are worth including here:

> After the conference I met with an academic I have admired for a long time. She helped me re-engage with what it is I'm really passionate about – helping undergraduates get the most from their studies. … Talking to her helped me think carefully about my next steps. The first is to write my book.

You see – I'm giving you advice that I follow myself. And in my case I use platforms like LinkedIn to reflect. For now though I want to move on to the final section, on how you can evidence your work-placed learning, once again focusing predominantly on the applied research skills you develop whilst on placement.

Evidencing learning

Developing a systematic approach to reflection will aid you in evidencing what you have done during your work placement. As stated at the start of this chapter this is one of the primary reasons for reflecting along the way, to have a record of your learning and development to refer back to. You may be required to write about your learning for accreditation purposes, or the placement could be non-assessed. Whatever the reason, the outputs you have developed whilst reflecting (see examples below) will be of great use to you when you come to describing to others what you have done.

For example, you may be required to produce a summary of your internship. This could be a report, a blog post, a news article, a communication piece for a think-tank or a government department, a poster for a student conference, and so on. The list really is endless. If you're like many of us you will have already forgotten what you did in the middle of your placement, never mind during the first week. A regular record of your time spent with the research organisation will act as an aide-memoire, a prompt to remind you that you really did spend a fortnight finding data sources, another month cleaning your data and undertaking exploratory analysis, and actually only two weeks writing up that report for the organisation. Nonetheless, along the way you have captured a trail of what you did, how you did it, and hopefully also how you felt about it during the process.

Both Mia and Alice's case studies show how they learned whilst doing their internships. The process of writing this down helped each of them look back over their learning, and in both these cases they went on to use the technique of reflecting on returning to their studies. Mia took this into her workplace and Alice used it in her Master's course. Later chapters will give multiple examples from work-integrated learning to show how this helps in the development of research skills that employers value, and will also provide examples of professional skills that can be developed and captured through reflection.

Finally I provide a checklist to bring together the main themes from this chapter (Table 6.2). This can help you structure your own reflective practice. I break this down further in the next two chapters but for now this will get you started.

Start by imagining yourself at the end of your internship and think about what you would like to have captured, and how, so that you can recall what you learned. The following questions in the checklist are designed to get you to think about what you would like to know at the end of your applied learning experience. By encountering them beforehand, you can start to visualise a positive outcome. Your challenge is then to use this checklist to create a positive outcome. The next two chapters will show you in more detail how to do this.

Table 6.2   Checklist – reflective practice activities for a work placement or internship

Name:		Date of completion:
Reflective practice activity	Answer: Yes/No or statement	Action: What could I do to improve this?
Did I start to capture my learning from the start?		
How did I document my learning?		
How often did I reflect? Was it frequent enough?		
Are there any key lessons I learned? What were they?		
Did I also reflect on what did not go so well?		

(Continued)

Table 6.2 (Continued)

Name:		Date of completion:
Reflective practice activity	Answer: Yes/No or statement	Action: What could I do to improve this?
Is there any advice I would give myself if I were to undertake an internship again?		
What advice might I give to someone who is thinking about the value of reflecting on their applied learning?		
Did I maintain a growth mindset throughout the work placement?		
Did I develop resilience? Could I have improved how I dealt with difficult situations?		
Did I have a good support network to enable me to bounce ideas off during the work placement, and did I incorporate this into my reflective practice?		

Summary

In this chapter I focused on developing a framework for reflection. Starting with a section on why this is a valuable thing to do, and after introducing some of the theoretical background on reflective practices, the content throughout this chapter has been written to help support your work placement learning. I have suggested a growth mindset is also important to provide the best chance of getting the most out of the experience, and the development of resilience to accompany this. Suggestions were given for the frequency of reflection, making sure this is achievable and flexible enough to be personalised, and being clear about why you will do this. Real examples were provided to show what reflection might look like, what it can include, and the value of this to the learner. The two case studies from Alice and Mia were included to illustrate how this assisted them to capture their placement learning, develop a written record to which they could subsequently refer, and enable them to deal with pitfalls and celebrate their successes. Expressing the experience through the written form is only one way of doing this, and other means using multimedia could suit different people. An example of using film was included to show how this could be a valid way to record student learning (as we have done at my own institution), and an extract from my own article on LinkedIn demonstrated how I use a professional networking platform to share my reflective practice with others.

The main outcome of reflecting has to be the potential to look back over what you have learned, and to have a way of comparing that to the distance you have travelled. That is to say, not only can reflection assist you in evidencing your learning, it gives you a breadcrumb trail method for revisiting this to help you decide if you would do it the same way, or differently, next time. The self-reflective researcher ought never to stop reflecting if the aim is to strive to be a lifelong learner.

Hopefully this chapter has persuaded you to think about developing your own reflective framework and to put this into practice, tweaking and adapting so that it works for you.

Three things you can do next

1   Read Ruth Helyer's (2015) paper, 'Learning through reflection: The critical role of reflection in work-based learning (WBL)', *Journal of Work Applied Management*. Pay particular attention to the sections on Reflection as a development tool and support – peers and mentors. Available at: www.emerald.com/insight/content/doi/10.1108/JWAM-10-2015-003/full/html

2   Read the paper which I took Natassia's case study extract from to see how three sociology students used work placements to learn data analysis skills. From the classroom to the workplace, it shows how social science students are learning to do data analysis for real (Carter et al., 2017, available at: https://iase-web.org/documents/SERJ/SERJ16(1)_Carter.pdf). Note in particular how far students can travel on a short internship in terms of the data skills they can acquire, even with only a few introductory courses.

3   Read Chapter 2 'Inside the mindsets' in Dweck (2017) or Chapter 4 'How gritty are you?' in Duckworth (2017). Focus on the need to be able to deal with failure as well as success, and think about how the reflective framework I offer in this chapter can help.

7

HOW TO DEVELOP YOUR ANALYTICAL AND RESEARCH SKILLS

In this chapter you will learn how to:

- Think about your analytical and research skills and how you can develop them
- Develop a personal analytical and research skills audit to give you a baseline (MARS Audit Tool)
- Develop an analytical and research skills personal development plan (MARS PDP)
- Monitor your analytical and research skills development
- Document your analytical and research skills acquired in the workplace to help update your CV
- Use previous students' experiences to help you understand how a work placement can develop your analytical and research skills
- Do all of the above with a positive and growth mindset

'Research means to investigate something we do not know or understand.'

Neil Armstrong (2005)

Overview

Chapter 7 draws on the experiences of many who have already travelled the path you hope to embark upon, and builds on Chapter 4. It focuses on developing your analytical and research skills, drawing on work from the British Academy, which provides a helpful framework to think about skills that are relevant to humanities and social sciences careers. In order to help you measure and document your development the chapter starts by helping you assess your own analytical and research skills baseline (I call this a MARS – My Analytical and Research Skills – Audit Tool), drawing on work from earlier chapters. A personal development plan (I call this a MARS PDP) is introduced for you to take ownership of your learning through the work placement. A three-step approach takes you from the MARS Audit Tool to the MARS PDP. An example is provided to help you see what this looks like. You are encouraged to use these tools as you progress through your placement and document as you go, being adaptable and responsive to your own development throughout your placement.

The chapter includes examples from two former interns, whose outputs (a poster and a report) show the learning from their work placements. The research and analysis they undertook, the methods and data used, and research findings are shown with an illustration of how these were then recorded so that they could be used on their CVs.

The student case studies are used to show some typical work placements, and some common student concerns are also included together with examples from host organisations to illustrate how they value the interns' analytical and research contributions. Finally the chapter will reiterate how the best experiences are gained from undertaking the placement with a positive and growth mindset, and a proactive approach.

Ryan, who had very few applied research skills before undertaking his internship with the General Medical Council but has since gone on to use the internship to his advantage, provides the main case study for this chapter. I also include Natassia as an example of an intern whose research was published following her internship, Julija for her project with BBC journalists, Victoria for her poster, and Elena, whose contribution to research made it onto national radio. All examples included show how former interns developed their analytical and research skills, measured their progress whilst on placement, and used their learning when their placement ended.

Why develop your analytical and research skills?

A report published by the British Academy entitled *The Right Skills: Celebrating Skills in the Arts, Humanities and Social Sciences* provides a compelling lead (British Academy, 2017). The report, which analysed a number of disciplines in the arts, humanities and social sciences (AHSS), concluded that there were a set of core skills they shared, plus additional subject-specific skills, and argued that these core skills contribute to society in multiple ways. Three particularly relevant extracts to this, and the next, chapter follow:

- We have identified a common core of skills shared across AHSS.
- Our analysis has shown that this core of skills is shared by undergraduate students and early career researchers, although the level of proficiency changes as an individual becomes more advanced in their study.
- These can be divided under three broad headings:
  - communication and collaboration;
  - research and analysis and;
  - attitudes and behaviours characterised by independence and adaptability.

British Academy (2017: 9)

In addition to the set of core skills, which can be found across AHSS disciplines, there are other skills which are specific to individual disciplines or groups of disciplines. These include ... languages, high-level numeracy, qualitative analysis and data processing, geospatial skills. ... These subject-specific skills are described in detail in subject benchmark statements and the publications of learned societies, professional bodies and subject associations amongst others.

British Academy (2017: 21–2)

AHSS Graduates contribute to society in many ways: they are a highly-skilled workforce employed in sectors which underpin society's cohesiveness, such as social work, local government and the voluntary sector; they become the researchers that produce world-leading research which underwrite[s] the social and economic health, wealth and reputation of the UK; they are active and engaged citizens and responsible media professionals; they contribute to arts and culture and the wellbeing of the wider population.

British Academy (2017: 42)

This British Academy report provides a useful backdrop for the material covered in this book, and this chapter, and signals how research and analytical skills are given serious consideration for social science and humanities graduates. Specifically, it provides a framework for the analytical and research skills covered in this chapter. Note that 'research and analysis' is just one of three categories or groups of skills that the report identifies. Chapter 8 on developing your professional skills will make more reference to 'communication and collaboration'. The third category, 'attitudes and behaviours characterised by independence and adaptability', is represented in this book through the emphasis on a positive and growth mindset and reflective practice. The final extract (from page 42 of the report) also makes reference to the professions and sectors that AHSS graduates enter. The case study students and vignettes I include in this book reflect these sectors.

Developing your analytical and research skills

In Chapter 4 you were led through a series of tasks to help you identify and evidence your research skills. I want to help you build on that here. To frame this chapter, it is instructive to consider what employers look for in graduates. To do that let me first draw your attention to some authoritative sources that you might turn to as you start to look for a graduate career. Table 7.1 provides some links on information and support available for early career researchers. These show you the sorts of analytical and research skills that are in demand, and help you think about how you can use your work placement to gain these. The final section of this chapter returns to employers needs with a short example. Chapter 9 then gives more examples from early career researchers.

Table 7.1 Research support and research jobs websites

Website name/address	Information on website purpose
British Academy report on skills: www.thebritishacademy.ac.uk/publications/right-skills-celebrating-skills-arts-humanities-and-social-sciences-ahss	Report commissioned by the British Academy to develop a set of core skills across subjects in the arts, humanities and social sciences. Provides a comprehensive list of skills relevant to research and analysis.
VITAE: www.vitae.ac.uk	A comprehensive source for those undertaking doctoral research in UK.
SAGE Methods online: https://methods.sagepub.com/	A comprehensive website for research methods. May require you to login (you can get a trial login) but there is a series of podcasts that are open access.
University of Leeds Library Skills for Life: https://leedsforlife.leeds.ac.uk/skills.aspx	A university website that lists skills to help you succeed in your academic study and career. Has a section on analytical skills and another on research skills, and many case studies.
TARGETjobs: https://targetjobs.co.uk/careers-advice/skills-and-competencies/668281-analytical-skills-the-ability-to-make-sense-of-data	A website aimed at supporting future graduates to secure jobs. Provides information on research and analytical skills required for different careers in different sectors.
UK government careers website: https://nationalcareers.service.gov.uk/skills-assessment	A website that helps you determine the career path that might suit you in a UK government role.
RAND International: www.rand.org/international.html	RAND is an international organisation that aims to support policy makers with the best available information, supported through rigorous research. Their website provides a rich picture of the research and analysis they undertake globally. They have 12 research areas covering seven regions of the world.

A quick web search for 'support for researchers' will return a long hitlist of library resources. Your own university library will most likely have customised their pages to support you to undertake research, by making available sources and information that you will have access to. Use them. Information professionals are experts in supporting students and researchers.

Graduate attributes: analytical, research and critical thinking skills

In Figure 7.1 I have included the Skills for Life online resource from the University of Leeds (see also Table 7.1). I like this website as it collates a long list of what are deemed to be transferable skills for employability. These skills are often referred to as graduate attributes (a term I introduced in Chapter 2) and are included here to show you what are regarded as the types of transferable skills you should aim to develop in your studies. The Skills for Life resource enables you to select subsets in particular groups. Figure 7.1 is based on the Analytical Skills and Research Skills, which represent a subset of seven taken from all the skills listed under Critical Thinking.

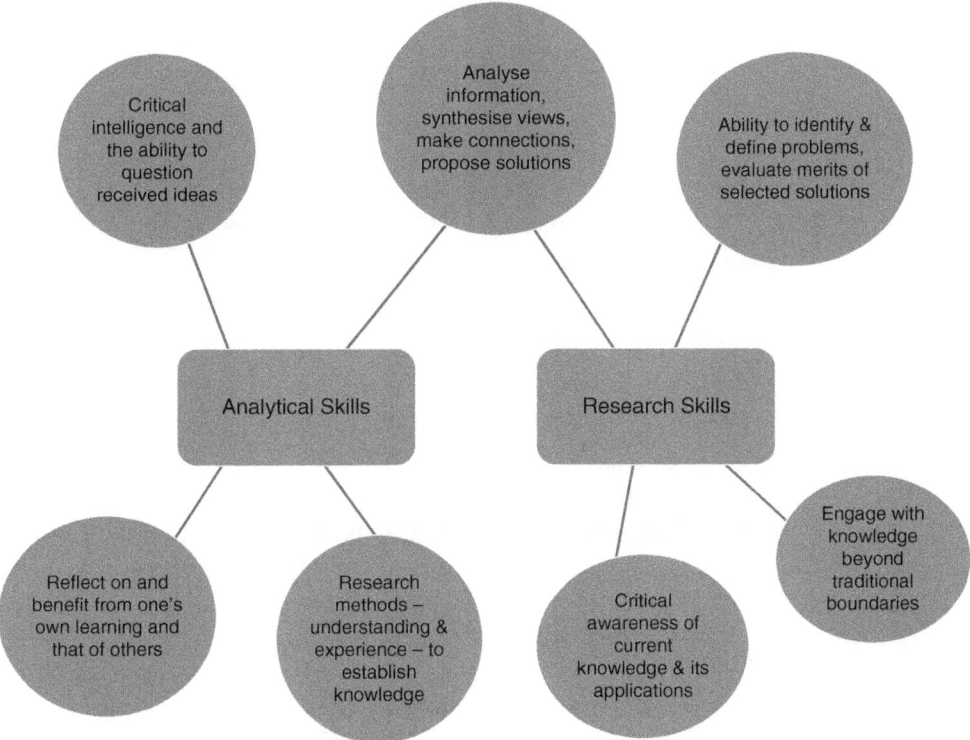

Figure 7.1 Analytical and research skills

Source: Skills for Life, University of Leeds

In addition to the seven skills in Figure 7.1, the eight additional critical thinking skills depicted in Figure 7.2 are needed to become a good researcher.

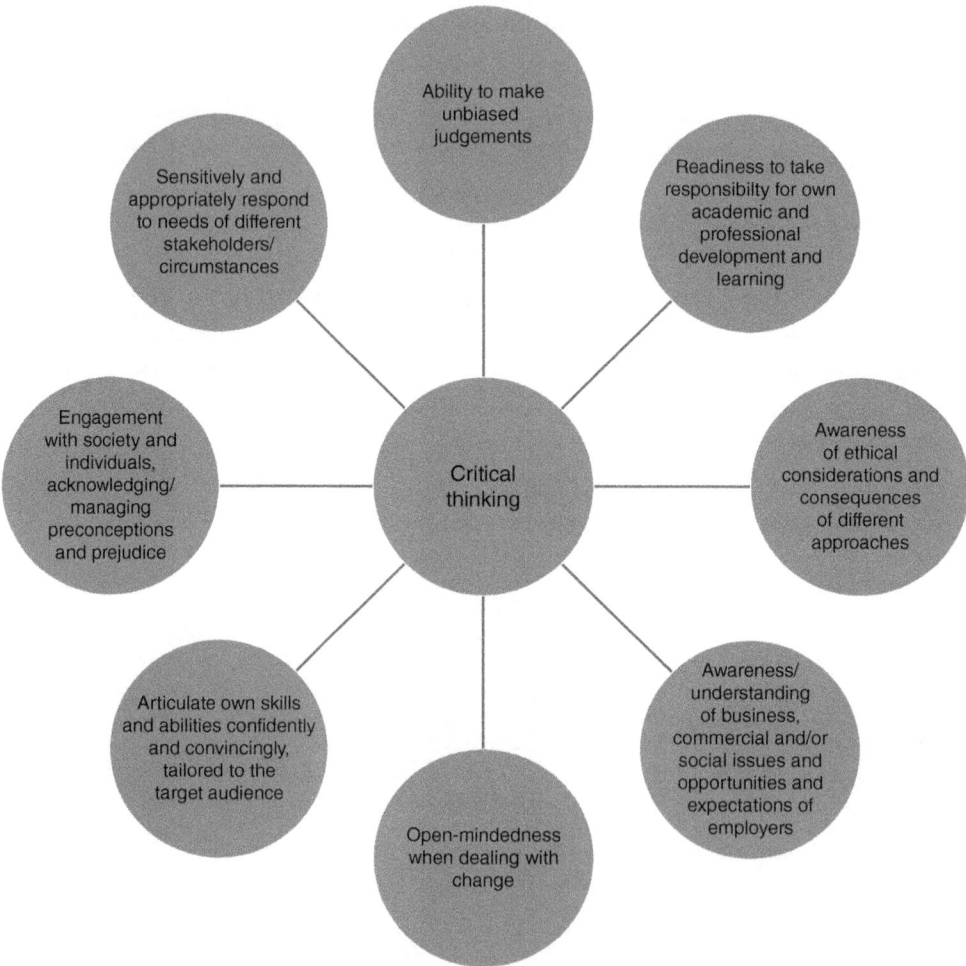

Figure 7.2   Critical thinking skills

Source: Skills for Life, University of Leeds

The broader set of graduate attributes (combining both Figures 7.1 and 7.2) is helpful to frame the wider context of why and how you are trying to develop these skills. Critical thinking is a core part of a university education and you will already have been taught many of these skills prior to starting a work placement.

Self-assess your skills to give you a baseline

To be able to develop your analytical and research skills it is important to capture your assessment of these at the start of your applied learning experience. This section will show you how you can do this, by getting you to self-assess your skills to provide you with a baseline (a point from which you can measure your progress). Assessing yourself at the start means you can see which skills you want or need to develop, and plan how to do this. Once again reflection plays a critical role in enabling you to do this. I start with this here by drawing on a skills audit tool that University of Exeter academics have been kind enough to share with me, and which I have adapted for you to use.

You have already documented your skills if you have followed the steps in Chapter 4, where you evidenced them for your CV. At that stage the aim was to get yourself an applied work placement. Now you have done this it is time to start thinking about the skills you have, but this time with a view to developing these further on placement. As this chapter focuses on analytical and research skills I provide a suggested skills audit below. We will extend this in Chapter 8 when we look at professional skills, and it provides a basis for Chapter 9 where we look at how you can apply these to your continued studies and career.

The British Academy report (2017) refers to a number of skills that social science and humanities students develop to enable them to make meaning from information. I have adapted the skills they list, to make them relevant to the context of acquiring these skills in the workplace whilst undertaking applied social research. For *designing research and collecting evidence*, I list five research skills, which I refer to here as group R (R1–R5). And for *undertaking the analysis*, I list six analytical skills, which I call group A (A1–A6). Table 7.2 captures these 11 skills, dividing them into the two categories used in the report. R 'Research Skills' and A 'Analytical Skills' are used to reflect the focus of this chapter.

Table 7.2 Research and analytical skills

Research skills		Analytical skills	
R: Designing research and collecting evidence		**A: Undertaking the analysis**	
R1	Formulating a research question	A1	Ability to manipulate, analyse and filter information
R2	Deciding what evidence is needed to answer the question	A2	Ability to interpret and synthesise information using qualitative and quantitative research methods, and appropriate technology
R3	Determining how evidence can be collected	A3	Detecting partial or ambiguous information by critically evaluating its source
R4	Understanding the ethics of undertaking the research	A4	Understanding the consequences of using unreliable data and information sources
R5	Organising the information, selecting relevant information and identifying gaps in the evidence	A5	Drawing conclusions based on critically assessing the evidence and findings
		A6	Appreciating the need to be open-minded and reflect on the evidence-base and conclusions drawn

Source: Skills R1–R5 and A1–A6 adapted from British Academy (2017: 10)

In order to make sense of this table and assess your own skills to baseline where you think you are for each of them, you need a personalised analytical and research skills audit tool (Table 7.3). Whilst completing this it will help you to start to think about the areas that you wish to extend your learning in during the course of your internship or placement. This will help you strategically plan how you aim to fill some of the gaps in your own CV. I move on to that in the second part of this section.

Table 7.3 My Analytical and Research Skills (MARS) Audit Tool

Date of completion:						
For each column tick the level that you feel you are currently at for each skill. Use the values from **1** (not started) to **5** (competent and could help others)	**1** (not started) **2** (started but need more practice) **3** (able to do this with some help) **4** (competent without help) **5** (competent and could help others)					
I feel at this level for each skill identified	**1**	**2**	**3**	**4**	**5**	**Justify my answer**
Research skills						
R: Designing research and collecting the evidence						
R1: Formulating a research question						
R2: Deciding what evidence is needed to answer the research question						
R3: Determining how evidence can be collected						
R4: Understanding the ethics of undertaking the research						
R5: Organising the information, selecting relevant information and identifying gaps in the evidence						
Analytical skills						
A: Undertaking the analysis						
A1: Ability to manipulate, analyse and filter information						
A2: Ability to interpret and synthesise information using qualitative and quantitative research methods, and appropriate technology						
A3: Detecting partial or ambiguous information by critically evaluating its source						

Date of completion:							
A4: Understanding the consequences of using unreliable data and information sources							
A5: Drawing conclusions based on critically assessing the evidence and findings							
A6: Appreciating the need to be open-minded and reflect on the evidence-base and conclusions drawn							

Adapted with permission from a student skills audit tool used by University of Exeter

As the aim of this chapter is to measure and document your acquisition of the skill-sets R and A (skills R1–R5 and A1–A6), you need a starting point, a line in the sand. By assigning a score of 1 to 5 (see Table 7.3) in each of the categories R1–R5 and A1–A6 you will give yourself a baseline self-assessed measure for where you feel your skill level is. The tool will help you see your progress, as you can return to it during the placement, or after you finish. Adding the date is important, as it is likely that without this you will forget how you self-assessed at that point in time.

This is a high-level skills audit, by design. As we go through this section you will start to unpack each of these areas so that you can delve into the skills areas one by one. For example, A2 includes 'using qualitative and quantitative research methods' – that is a huge area. Whole books have been written about single methods, for instance. The idea here is not to ask you to itemise all the things you could do under each heading, but to help you appreciate where you already have *some* knowledge and experience, and where you might wish to focus on developing the gaps you have. This is part of being a researcher: as we develop our skills and expertise we tend to gravitate towards a set of tools and techniques, but by being open to learning multiple methods and approaches we diversify our thinking, read critically and expand our knowledge. Undertaking a work-placed learning opportunity is a perfect time to observe how applied research is undertaken, and to expose yourself to new skills. Having or acquiring a growth mindset is a fundamental requirement to enable you to do this. As the British Academy report states, 'attitudes and behaviours characterised by independence and adaptability' is a core skillset (2017: 42).

Using reflection

Once again I propose that using a reflective framework will help you to baseline your own analytical and research skills, and in time to capture and measure your new skills as you develop them in the workplace. Later in the chapter I provide two example case studies of students' reflections after their placement learning. First, I introduce Ryan as he provides a good example of how reflection helped him during his work placement.

Case study 7.1

Ryan: Project objectives and reflection three years later

Ryan had a rapid trajectory through his early graduate career. For this chapter I asked him to reflect on where he felt he was several years on from his placement. Ryan was a PPE (Politics, Philosophy and Economics) second-year undergraduate when he was placed in the General Medical Council, London, UK. In the first part of this case study you see what his research project entailed. This description was captured on his poster at the end of the placement. In the second part he describes the placement from the vantage point of three years after doing it.

Project objectives from his poster

Objectives

The aim of the project was to compile a comprehensive database of all exam data from the Royal Colleges throughout the country that could be accessed by third parties in a clear to use way.

Various exams were used to assess which specialisms doctors were entering. The scores and frequency of these specialist exams and exam data from medical schools across the country were all entered into the UKMED database, to enable an anonymised sample of the medical profession with data on race, gender, age, background and test scores to be created.

Three years after his placement Ryan said:

> As an intern at the General Medical Council I was exposed to the whole process of deriving insights from data. This process began with identifying the problem to be solved, gathering the necessary data, cleaning it, structuring it, and then visualising the relationships. Most of my work was focussed on data preparation, the cleaning and structuring part, which I was not exposed to in my courses at university. Often university projects used data that was prepared for the assignment, and tested our ability to apply some model to it. In the real world, however, data rarely exists in such a clean format.

Ryan's project involved data collection, data linking, and developing tools to visualise and access the data.

In a few sentences, three years after doing the project, Ryan was able to recall it to memory easily. He sums up the research and analytical skills he acquired succinctly. He talks about 'deriving insights from data', goes on to say that he needed to identify the problem to be solved, giving a good example of formulating the research question. Thereafter he tells us how he had to collect the evidence and spend time preparing it for analysis. He notes the unstructured nature of data in the workplace, contrasting this to teaching data, which are invariably cleaned. Even several years after Ryan undertook the research he remembers the steps he took, describing his project concisely and with clarity. This itself is a skill worth acquiring. Before you can do this though you usually have to go the long way round.

Looking back at Ryan's reflection at the mid-point of his internship I see that he was already reflecting on his learning (in the year he did his work placement I had not introduced an end-of-week-one reflection). Although quite long, I include his mid-internship reflection here as several years after the placement his recollection is not too far away from the one he wrote several weeks in. If you use reflection as part of your learning journey you will have documentation along the way to remind yourself what you undertook, and what you learned. More on this in the next section on building a personal development plan (PDP).

Case study 7.2

Ryan: Mid-internship reflection

Here Ryan reflects halfway through his placement and shows how he is capturing his analytical and research skills.

My project at the General Medical Council has mainly involved work on education progression and coverage reports of all medical students across the UK. I have had to match exam data provided by medical schools to student information in the register to manipulate the data for future research.

The majority of my projects have been in SQL and Tableau, with SQL used to create the data output necessary and Tableau to visualise it in an accessible format. SPSS and Excel have also been used when tasks are more efficient in those software, such as altering data formats and concatenating data. The majority of the work within software is about joining data files so that the final output is organised and readable in other software, since the data provided from various sources is not always formatted identically. … one must do this [carefully] without greatly altering the data presentation, making sure that clarity is not lost when adding detail.

(Continued)

> I have learned a great deal of data analysis techniques, including how to use SQL, SPSS, and Tableau, having no familiarity with any of these previously. Various analysis methods and shortcuts in Excel have also made me a considerably more proficient user than when I began. Above data analysis, my work has given me a lot of insights into the Health Sector of the UK, learning about it not only through the work that I am doing, but also through conversations with co-workers, and meetings I attend. The internship has provided a thorough learning experience that has guided me through the work and made it easy for me to learn and pick up.
>
> I will certainly be taking the skills that I have learned here and applying them in my Economics dissertation.

Ryan provides an exemplar of what students can take from a work placement opportunity. Within the space of only four weeks he had learned to use two new pieces of software (SQL and Tableau) and become more expert in Excel. I recall talking to Ryan at the time and remember his being a little shocked at how unprepared he felt – indeed he commented that the training he had been given to date at university, and with the pre-placement training, was not adequate. He was partly right – for we had given him a primer in most of what he needed, and an opportunity to launch himself into his own learning trajectory. The pre-internship training he was given was as much about having the right attitude to learning new things as it was about getting reacquainted with or learning a software package.

In Ryan's case he embraced the opportunity, throwing himself into learning the software and data-linkage techniques required of him. His supervisor was supportive, but expected him to be a self-directed learner. Ryan's appearance as one of the case studies in this book is testament to his success.

Develop a personal development plan (PDP)

Careers service websites abound with helping you develop a personal development plan (PDP) for your career. Take a look at some careers websites, which are easily discoverable, if you are interested in this in a more general way.

I want to help you narrow this down to thinking about how a PDP could help you target your research and analytical skills more precisely, and apply this in the workplace. Ryan's case study showed how he used reflection to think about the skills he was developing, and wanted to further develop, as part of his work placement. I now present a way you can identify the skills you would like to develop during your internship to enhance your CV and open up careers in applied social research.

Five PDP skills groups for research and analysis

Building on the skills audit above (Table 7.3) I propose the following five groups of research and analytical skills to develop as part of your placement, and to help inform your personal development plan during that time. I could have included more than five, but these cover the main areas that will help you to become a good applied social researcher. All of the skills listed above in R1–R5 and A1–A6 are included in the five PDP groups, perhaps with the exception of understanding the ethics of undertaking research, which actually is a cross-cutting theme through all stages of research from development to communication. I will later show you in Table 7.5 how you can focus in on the area you most want to develop.

I call these skills groups PDP1–PDP5 and they form the basis of the My Analytical and Research Skills Personal Development Plan (MARS PDP), which I introduce below.

Table 7.4 shows the five PDP skills groups which you can develop.

Table 7.4 Five personal development plan skills groups to develop

	PDP skills group to develop
PDP1	Formulating the research question
PDP2	Data literacy
PDP3	Data analysis
PDP4	Synthesis and evaluation
PDP5	Report writing and presentation of findings

Here I describe what each of the PDP groups of skills is. I go on to develop a mapping between the PDP skills groups and the analytical and research skills I presented you with in Table 7.2. I then show you how you can develop your MARS PDP and finally give you an example of what this might look like. From here I will drop the word group for ease of reading (but remember that the PDPs refer to a number of skills).

The five PDP skills explained

PDP1: Formulating the research question

In a work placement setting it is likely, although not certain, that the research question has already been formulated for you by the organisation. For a post-graduate research placement it is possible that you will be asked to come up with your own research question, but at undergraduate level you will probably be given guidance with this. The research question is the starting point for doing applied social research.

In your studies you are likely to have had opportunity to already pose your own research question(s), and we touched on these back in Chapter 2. Developing a research question is not hard. Developing a good research question, however, takes skill. Where skill is needed is to develop a research question that can be investigated for the duration of your work placement, with the available resources (people, data, knowledge of methods and software) and in a way that you can hand over the work once you have completed it. Much of this will fall to the way you analyse the question, but you need to take all of these factors into account when formulating the question. Your host organisation will help so don't panic about this, but as you start to do the research you will become the expert and you need to own this. We saw in the last chapter how Alice started to offer her ideas right from the start and when she left her co-workers were asking her for advice on the research. She was able to do this as she had developed her own skills and knowledge and adapted the research question as she progressed through the placement. Remember that 'readiness to take responsibility for own academic and professional development and learning' is one of the critical thinking skills in Figure 7.2.

PDP2: Data literacy

A technical report produced in Canada (Ridsdale et al., 2015: 2) collated information from multiple sources to help understand the concept of data literacy, which the authors defined as:

> … the ability to collect, manage, evaluate, and apply data, in a critical manner. [Data literacy] is an essential ability required in the global knowledge-based economy; the manipulation of data occurs in daily processes across all sectors and disciplines.

They produced a word cloud based on the meta-analysis from the reports and articles they studied, which is shown in Figure 7.3. The most frequent words found in the literature on data literacy are shown by the size of the larger text.

Critical data literacy is incredibly important. It is essential to be able to understand and critically evaluate your sources. Social media and news media have brought the need for the skill to the fore and UK organisations such as Full Fact (https://fullfact.org) and the BBC's Reality Check (www.bbc.co.uk/news/reality_check) work hard to verify the facts behind stories in the media. The US-based Pew Research Center has introduced a fact tank (www.pewresearch.org). The Conversation (which originated in Australia), an online news and reviews website, works with academics to make research available to the public and has a robust fact-checking procedure in place (https://theconversation.com/how-we-do-factchecks-at-the-conversation-73134). Others are contributing to this hugely important area, and you absolutely need to have this skillset to be a competent

Figure 7.3   Meta-analysis word cloud

Source: Ridsdale et al. (2015: 42)

social analyst. The websites here mainly deal with quantitative data literacy, but it is equally important to be able to critically evaluate qualitative data sources too.

It's essential to know your data. Your critical data literacy skills will develop as you gain more practice with applied research. Any analysis should be preceded with the question 'whose data are they?' Bell et al. (2020) devote a chapter of their book *Making Sense of Data in the Media* to this topic (Chapter 3, 'Recognising which numbers you should trust: Where is data from?'). De Vries (2019), in his book *Critical Statistics*, titles Chapter 2, 'Where do numbers come from?' Being critical of and with data, qualitative and quantitative, is the first thing you must do before diving into any analysis.

PDP3: Data analysis

Data analysis requires you to identify methods used to analyse research questions, and software to do so. Ryan documented his new learning (SQL, Tableau) and extended his existing learning (Excel and SPSS). He did not specify new research methods that he used, but did comment upon analytical techniques deployed to link data sources, and recorded that he was contributing to the creation of a database that could be used after his internship.

Methods and techniques such as this should be documented as the work placement progresses in order that you can monitor your progress. This also introduces an important principle of being able to develop a reproducible research or analytical pipeline. This is becoming a must-have in government data science practice (Upson, 2017) and scholars are publishing on the need for reproducible research in the social sciences to be able to verify and build on others' work (Playford et al., 2016).

PDP4: Synthesis and evaluation

Synthesis and evaluation are skills that you will have opportunity to acquire through the workplace. Often research produces multiple findings, sometimes using different methods, and the role of the researcher is to ensure there is a set of findings that can communicate the relevant research undertaken. Some of your findings will be more important than others, given the research question, and you need to ensure these take centre stage in reporting to your target audience. Synthesis and evaluation together require a refined, higher order skillset. You will already have had opportunity to practise these through your university education, but with an applied research project you have the chance to extend this further.

PDP5: Report writing and presentation of findings

You are probably already accomplished in writing essays, and answering academic questions. Report writing is a different skill altogether and is one of the main gaps in students' skills that work placement organisations often comment on. That's to be expected given the nature of most universities' assessment practices. Nonetheless a work-situated learning experience provides an ideal opportunity to learn how to do this in a way that is likely to help you stand out from the crowd when you start applying for graduate jobs. Recall Anna, our first intern we introduced back in Chapter 1? She had the opportunity to develop an industry report on the voice of the business traveller, which was then presented to a conference of 250 companies by the director of her host company. The prestigious think-tank where Marcus interned credits their intern each year with the analytical and written contribution they have made to their annual flagship report whilst on placement. Writing reports is definitely one of the areas you should seek to gain confidence and experience in, through your work placement.

An associated skill is in presenting research findings, conclusions and sometimes recommendations. Posters can be an effective way to achieve this as I will demonstrate below, but there are many other ways too and again you should try to get experience of this if you can.

Case study 7.3

Ryan: PDP skills developed through an internship

To see how Ryan used his placement to develop these transferable analytical and research skills, I have inserted the PDP skill he developed in square brackets to show you how these can be evidenced through the work placement. This extract is taken from speaking to Ryan three years after he undertook his internship.

> The experience of data preparation benefitted me in numerous ways [PDP2]. First, the frequent use of SQL throughout my internship gave me an understanding of a new analytics tool, one that I have continued to use on projects that require multiple data sources [PDP3]. Secondly, the understanding of the data analysis pipeline, and the importance of preparation provided me with an approach on how to structure the various projects I have worked on since, even when they are in applications not related to health care, such as forecasting house prices or analysing the impact of policy changes [PDP3; PDP4]. Finally, the experience of data preparation made me more aware of the limits of analytical tools, as the plethora of data that exists does not automatically translate into something usable [PDP4]. A lot of domain expertise is still required to understand what can and cannot be used and for what objectives.

The extract from Ryan's reflection shows how he can acknowledge the acquisition of some of the skills. PDP1 and PDP5 do not register in the reflective piece here but there is certainly evidence elsewhere in this chapter of both those skills. Finally, Ryan mentions the need to have domain expertise.

Whilst domain expertise is not included in the PDP framework I have developed, it is fundamentally important that the researcher knows the context in which the applied social research is being undertaken. This was highlighted in the British Academy report referenced at the start of this chapter. Good applied social research requires domain expertise in order to have real-world meaning and relevance.

Be proactive

The work placement will provide opportunities for you to develop your competencies (more on competencies and capabilities in Chapter 8) across a range of skills. In order to get the most out of your project you need to be as proactive as possible. Without doubt all of the students I have seen across the years who excel in their internships are the ones who use it to gain experience, and take a lead in their own learning. Sometimes this comes as a shock to students, who have been used to being told what to do for class, the next assignment and so on. It can be empowering for them to see that they can control and direct their own learning, but once they embrace this they learn to fly. The best interns are proactive in ensuring they consider where they are at the start, and plan what they want to get out of their time in the host organisation. This is exactly how a personal development plan should work, and here we focus on the analytical and research skills, whilst in Chapter 8 this approach can be adapted to professional skills development.

All of the PDP skills listed are important, but I am going to suppose here for the purposes of illustration that the one you may wish to focus on is data analysis, PDP3. Evidencing that you have applied your research and analytical skills in the workplace, as shown throughout this book, differentiates you from your peers. To help you record these skills and competencies as you progress through your placement I introduce the following tool.

MARS PDP: My Analytical and Research Skills (MARS) Personal Development Plan (PDP)

I now show you how you can develop your own PDP to focus on your analytical and research skills development. I call this My Analytical and Research Skills (MARS) Personal Development Plan (PDP). All the building blocks have been introduced already and now, in three steps, you will bring them together to create your MARS PDP.

Step 1: Understand the skills mapping

Remember the 11 analytical and research skills I introduced earlier in the chapter? If not, take a look back at Table 7.2 as a reminder, as this next section makes reference to them. Figure 7.4 shows you how the research (R1–R5) and analytical (A1–A6) skills map onto the PDP skills (PDP1–PDP5). (Note that some appear in more than one place).

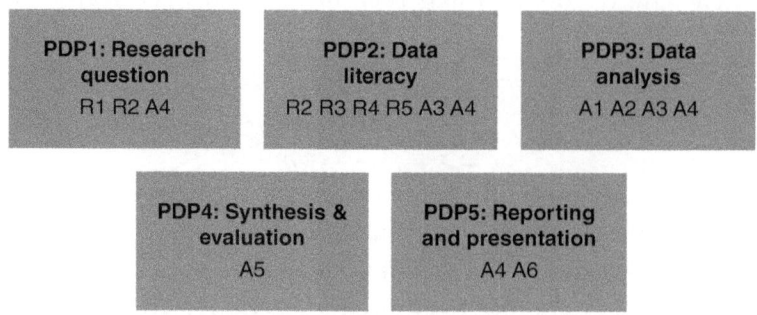

Figure 7.4 Mapping the PDP skill groups to the British Academy analytical and research skills

Step 2: Decide which skills to focus on

For this step you need to refer to your self-assessed scores in your MARS Audit Tool (Table 7.3) and see how they map to the five PDP skills (in Table 7.4). This will help you decide which skills (or skills areas) you want to develop.

The planning tool in Table 7.5 enables you to do this.

Table 7.5 MARS Personal Development Plan – planning tool

PDP skills 1–5 (Table 7.4)	Research & analytical skills R1–R5 and A1–A6 (Table 7.2)	My score (Table 7.3)	Decide which PDP skill I want to develop and say how I will do this
PDP1 Research question	R1		
	R2		
	A4		
PDP2 Data literacy	R2		
	R3		
	R4		
	R5		
	A3		
	A4		
PDP3 Data analysis	A1		
	A2		
	A3		
	A4		
PDP4 Synthesis and evaluation	A5		
PDP5 Reporting and presentation	A4		
	A6		

The planning tool in Table 7.5 helps you quickly see and decide which of the PDP skills groups you want to develop. When you fill this table in you might have lower self-assessed scores in Data Analysis for example. You can then see that you need to focus on skills A1, A2, A3 and A4 whilst on placement.

Alternatively you could use this tool to look across a range of PDP skills groups and use it to develop your skills across a range of areas. For the sake of this introductory example I will continue to focus on a single PDP skill (PDP3 Data Analysis).

Step 3: Create your MARS PDP for one of the chosen PDP skills

Following on from the above step, let's suppose you decide that you want to focus on PDP3 Data Analysis during your placement. Perhaps your self-assessment from your skills audit shows you are unconfident, or you just decide you want more practice. You would then take the PDP3 Data Analysis row, with analytical skills A1, A2, A3 and A4, and decide how you are going to fill in these blanks in the MARS PDP checklist. Table 7.6 shows this row, and these skills, extracted into a table to help you do this. This simple design will enable you to have a record of your priorities and how you intend to achieve them. Two things to note:

- The date is important as it captures where you are at that point in time (so you can look back and see yourself at the start of the plan).
- I have included a row for you to write in your goal so that you are clear from the outset what you wish to achieve and why. For example, the goal here could read *My Goal: I want to improve my Data Analysis skills whilst on placement so that I have more career options open to me when I graduate.*

Table 7.6   Checklist for MARS PDP for Data Analysis (PDP3)

Date of completion:		
MARS PDP for **PDP3 Data Analysis**	My score	How I will improve my score during the work placement
My Goal		
A1: Ability to manipulate, analyse and filter information		
A2: Ability to interpret and synthesise information using qualitative and quantitative research methods, and appropriate technology		
A3: Detecting partial or ambiguous information by critically evaluating its source		
A4: Understanding the consequences of using unreliable data and information sources		

You might feel you don't know at the start of your placement how you can improve, as you may not know how the project or work placement will develop. This is an important part of using the tool. You could show it to your work placement supervisor to ask them to help you understand how you can develop your skills.

Here is an example. Natassia featured in Chapter 6. Table 7.7 shows how we could have used this tool for her. When she did the placement, her supervisor, Natassia and I spoke about what she wanted to develop her expertise in during her placement. What she discussed with us is captured in a MARS PDP for Data Analysis.

Table 7.7   An example MARS PDP for PDP3 (Data Analysis)

Date of completion:		
MARS PDP for PDP3 Data Analysis	*My score*	*How to improve my score during the work placement*
My Goal: To learn new software and methods to answer the research questions for my internship project		
A1: Ability to manipulate, analyse and filter information	2	The survey I have been given is a cross-sectional probability sample of the population of Great Britain. In university I learned SPSS, but the research team here uses Stata so I need to learn this in order to undertake the analysis.

Date of completion:		
A2: Ability to interpret and synthesise information using qualitative and quantitative research methods, and appropriate technology	2	I have learned simple linear regression in my university courses and this project will enable me to learn logistic regression. This will advance my quantitative research skills.
A3: Detecting partial or ambiguous information by critically evaluating its source	2	I need to explore the data to ensure that we have sufficient data points to be able to conduct a rigorous analysis for the research question we are trying to answer. I am conscious I may need a lot of help with this. The Natsal survey we are using is an authoritative data source but I need to better understand if the data are fit for purpose for answering the research question.
A4: Understanding the consequences of using unreliable data and information sources	2	This follows directly from above but I think with the survey we are using, and the expertise in the team, I will be able to learn a lot about using a well-respected nationally representative survey. That said it depends on how many data points satisfy the criteria we are considering.

Hopefully you can see how this starts to work for each set of skills. You can easily create these tables for yourself and fill in the blanks. The aim obviously is to use the work placement to improve your score from whatever you give yourself at the beginning in your MARS Audit Tool.

This brings us onto the final part of a PDP, and that is to ensure you measure your progress. In a work-situated learning experience you might not be assessed in the same way as you are in college or university. Whether or not you are assessed, your aim is to improve your skills and knowledge, and creating a PDP will help you become familiar with assessing your own abilities, and improve your self-rated score at the end of your work placement. That is why the date at the top of the MARS PDP tool is important; the end of a placement should show improvement in your self-assessment of your skills.

In Natassia's case she knew she had progressed at the end of her work experience as her supervisor told her so, and indeed we made a short film to this effect, to celebrate her learning (https://youtu.be/pLBdJeFjZFI). She also used the placement learning to help inform her third-year dissertation topic and then her choice of a postgraduate course. In her own words she said, 'the project had everything to do with me choosing to do a Master's in statistics and social research methods'. Finally, her research helped inform an academic research paper which was published, with her as co-author, two years after her project finished (Black et al., 2016). It is clear from our ongoing contact that her work placement was instrumental in helping inform her career. The important message for you is how she documented her work-placed learning (on her CV, LinkedIn, and through her published paper) and how she used it to plan her next steps. She went on to become a market researcher in a prestigious organisation, and she has continued to extend her analytical and research skills.

Measure your progress

This chapter so far has introduced you to ways of assessing where your analytical and research skills baseline is at the start of an applied social research placement, and provided you with a framework for identifying the group of, and the individual skills you would like to develop, and a tool for doing this. Ryan (one of the case study students) and Natassia (who provided a vignette in Chapter 6) have been introduced to inspire you on your way, and they have both progressed into careers in which their placement learning played a part.

I will now list some examples of analytical and research skills you can capture, and then use on your CV.

Document as you go

Document as you go, and grow. Don't wait until the end of your placement to do this. By using the reflective framework introduced in Chapter 6 you can start to capture the new skills you learn, the challenges you faced, and how you overcame them. Employers are always looking for evidence of application of your learning. By documenting as you go you will stay ahead of the curve. And by using the MARS PDP you will also have a record of your analytical and research skills development.

Try to capture everything you do under categories that map onto your CV. I suggest five, which have worked for my students, and made it easy for them to insert these new skills into their CV, and add to what they documented before starting the work placement. They were asked to capture these skills in their reflective pieces written during the placement. You'd be surprised at how quickly these skills expand and mark you out from the crowd.

Top tips
_____

How to classify skills acquired through your work placement

Document your analytical and research skills using the following five categories:

- Software
- Data
- Methods
- Outputs
- Presentations

Two students' project outputs

Here are two examples of outputs from internships. The first is a student poster; the second is a report that an intern contributed to whilst she was on placement. Below each I show how the interns documented their newly acquired skills.

Posters provide a simple and effective way of evidencing learning through the work-place. In my own internship programme this is the standard way of asking students to share their learning at the end of the work placements, and we have a research half-day where all students present a poster as part of a celebration event.

Victoria, who will feature again later in the book when we see how she went on to use her placement learning, produced a poster. Figure 7.5 presents her poster summary together with a map she produced at the end of her eight weeks spent analysing crime data around vehicle thefts.

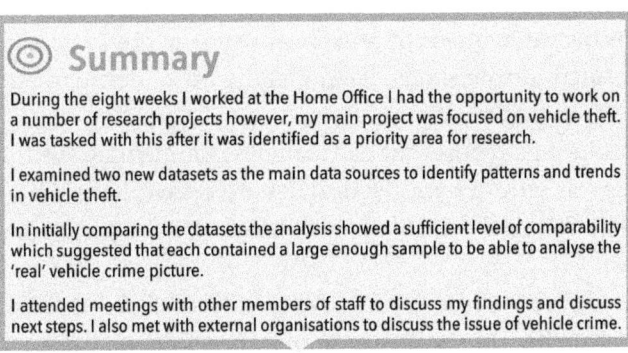

◎ Summary

During the eight weeks I worked at the Home Office I had the opportunity to work on a number of research projects however, my main project was focused on vehicle theft. I was tasked with this after it was identified as a priority area for research.

I examined two new datasets as the main data sources to identify patterns and trends in vehicle theft.

In initially comparing the datasets the analysis showed a sufficient level of comparability which suggested that each contained a large enough sample to be able to analyse the 'real' vehicle crime picture.

I attended meetings with other members of staff to discuss my findings and discuss next steps. I also met with external organisations to discuss the issue of vehicle crime.

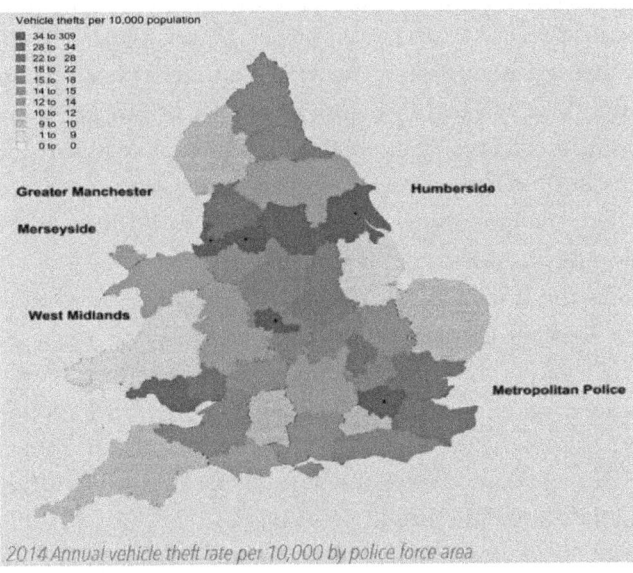

Figure 7.5 Victoria's project output

Source: https://hummedia.manchester.ac.uk/faculty/qstep/student-stories-2015/Smith.pdf

Here are the analytical and research skills she acquired through her placement:

- **Software:** Excel – developed skills in using formulae, including nested-if statements, V-lookup and index/match functions, and countif, sumif functions. MapInfo used for mapping data.
- **Data:** Used official data at police force area level to undertake the analysis. Understood the ethical issues surrounding the officially sensitive and non-disclosive nature of the data used. For the annual vehicle theft rate in 2014 I used driver licence statistics from the Department for Transport and police recorded data for vehicle thefts in England and Wales.
- **Methods:** Created summary statistics in Excel. Used time-series techniques including indexing, moving averages, secondary axes, month-on-month and year-on-year comparisons. Developed scatterplots and correlation coefficients to explore patterns of association between variables. Developed charts and visualisations including maps of hotspots of vehicle theft rate at police force area. Analysis informed further statistical modelling. Also looked at sensitivity analysis and learned when this can be useful.
- **Outputs:** Produced a report that contained recommendations for further research. This was sent to senior colleagues after the internship concluded, and circulated to all relevant vehicle crime colleagues. Poster of research undertaken also produced.
- **Presentations:** Presented results to the Crime and Policing Analysis Unit team whilst on placement. This unit aims to provide evidence and analysis to ministers and policy makers to support decisions on crime and policing topics and policies.

Elena, a student at the University of Warwick, conducted her one-month long work placement at NatCen (which features as an employer organisation in Chapter 9). She was one of the four researchers who worked on a project that NatCen had been commissioned by the BBC *Women's Hour* radio programme to undertake. The research topic was to find out the best and worst places (local authorities) for women to live in Britain, by developing an index to measure this.

Figure 7.6 shows the front page of the report she contributed to and a table from that report which looks at three age groups for the best and worst places for women to live in Britain. Elena pointed out that this was a team effort.

Here are the analytical and research skills she acquired through her placement:

- **Software:** PDF to Excel conversion – developed skills in identifying data sources, web-scraping data and data format conversion.
- **Data:** Used data from multiple sources including Office for National Statistics (ONS), Scotland's 2011 Census, Department for Food and Rural Affairs, Understanding Society and Annual Survey of Hours and Earnings. Pre-processed data in Excel, including extracting relevant variables, ready for uploading into Stata.

Table 1 The best and worst local authorities for women in Great Britain				
Rank	Core	Younger	Middle	Older
Best				
1st	East Dunbartonshire, Scotland	West Oxfordshire, South East	East Dunbartonshire, Scotland	South Oxfordshire, South East
2nd	East Renfrewshire, Scotland	East Dunbartonshire, Scotland	East Renfrewshire, Scotland	West Oxfordshire, South East
3rd	West Oxfordshire, South East	Wycombe, South East	West Berkshire, South East	Winchester, South East
Worst				
1st	Islington, London	Kingston upon Hull, Yorkshire	Nottingham, East Midlands	Islington, London
2nd	Blackpool, North West	Islington, London	Blackpool, North West	Manchester, North West
3rd	Corby, East Midlands	Blaenau Gwent, Wales	Kingston upon Hull, Yorkshire	Hackney, London

Figure 7.6   Elena's project output

- *Methods:* Assisted in development of an index for analysis. Used experts' judgement to weight different variables appropriately (for instance negative items had a reduced ranking). Variables were then transformed using a formula from the literature and informed by expert opinion. Through this method we deduced a best and worst (high to low) index to answer the research question of 'which is the best/worst Local Authority for women to live in in the UK?'
- *Outputs:* Various. Included a report that was used on BBC Radio 4's *Women's Hour* (www.bbc.co.uk/news/uk-41203240).
- *Presentations:* Presented results at event at the University of Warwick and awarded 'best poster presentation' in 2017.

Update your analytical and research skills on your CV

I have introduced the two examples above to illustrate how posters and reports are excellent ways of capturing your learning. The bulleted sub-headings accompanying each of the examples given help capture skills acquired through the work placement. Your aim should be to try to develop all of these skills, or as many as possible.

These examples show how you can evidence your learning. Of course work placements are not the only opportunity you will have to develop these skills, and you can certainly acquire them through other means, but I would encourage you to use every opportunity you do have prior to graduating to develop your research and analytical skills. Likewise, posters and reports are not the only outputs from applied learning, and other outputs including blog posts, news stories in the media, short films, presentations and academic papers. I propose you try to create some of these as they provide tangible examples to include on your CV.

Whether you acquire these analytical and research skills through a work placement or through other means, I list here the main skills that you should try to document. To miss out on capturing new learning, skills and knowledge on your CV would be foolish. The checklist in Table 7.8 is based on the one I introduced in Chapter 4, when you were collating your research skills developed through your studies. Having an applied social research work placement under your belt takes this to a whole new level.

You now need to add your new or updated skills (like the ones listed by Elena and Victoria above) to your CV. You might want to refer back to your PDP here to ensure you have captured the finer detail of the skills development you were aiming for. You don't need to have all this detail on your CV, but documenting them so you have an aide-memoire of how you acquired the skills is useful. This could also provide excellent interview preparation material (back in Chapter 4 Zvi talked about how he does this in preparation for all interviews he attends).

Table 7.8 Checklist of analytical and research skills acquired through the workplace

Analytical and research skills I have acquired	How I acquired this skill	Evidence of this skill
Software		
Data		
Methods		
Outputs		
Presenting research		

Critical reflections on acquiring analytical and research skills

In Chapter 6 I introduced a reflective framework, and in this section I introduce two short case studies (7.4 and 7.5) to illustrate critical reflection on the experience of undertaking an internship. In presenting these case studies I summarise the learning from the two students' reflections, and in that sense they differ from the other case studies in the book which reflect the students' own voices. Case study 7.4 is taken from one of the ten students, and case study 7.5 from one who provided a vignette in Chapter 6.

There are three main types of work placements I have seen that reflect the types of data-driven research projects that many students will do whilst on placement (and which provide the main focus in this book). They tend to be characterised as follows:

- Data manipulation and visualisation
- Data literacy, exploratory analysis and mixed methods
- Data analysis involving statistical modelling

Whilst all internships are different they tend to cohere around these three types, at least those that entail research involving data analysis. Ryan's project could be described by the first of these. Here I include Julija and Natassia to show how their internships reflect the other two types, and how each of them embraced opportunities to make their work available through outputs other than the required poster.

Case study 7.4

Julija: Data literacy, exploratory analysis and mixed methods

During Julija's internship at the BBC, uncovering data-driven stories meant she quickly became a data-runner, and she was tasked with examining the underlying data to explore journalists' hypotheses (often expressed as hunches or questions). Julija spent time becoming data literate, undertaking some data manipulation tasks (mainly in Excel) and learning how to issue Freedom of Information (FOI) requests for data that could be used to explore the journalists' questions.

Her reflective pieces indicated enormous personal growth over eight weeks. Her reflections captured her appreciation of how useful the internship was, her satisfaction in becoming more expert with Excel and producing compelling visualisations, and her tenacity for uncovering a story. For instance, she probed into the relationship between private schools in northwest England that were closing, and free schools

(Continued)

that had opened, discovering a pattern in the data that she persuaded her colleagues was worth investigating. They conducted interviews, and uncovered a news story that was previously not on their radar. Julija's new found confidence and expertise in digging into data had emboldened her. She acknowledged that everything she had learned in the classroom gave her a strong foundation, and reflected on the opportunity to really stretch her analytical and research skills on placement. Although she slightly regretted she did not undertake complex analyses, this gave her an appetite for more.

Case study 7.5

Natassia: Data analysis involving statistical modelling

Natassia's post-placement interview highlights one of the key findings from work-placed learning – the opportunity to contribute to academic research, and to inform continuing study. Her placement supervisor said in a short film that was recorded that she 'blew them away'. Natassia described learning skills and methods (logistic regression in Stata) she never thought she would have an opportunity to do as an undergraduate sociologist, feeling enormously satisfied after spending weeks cleaning and merging the different waves of the survey she was using, and 'being made' to present the work to her colleagues. She was named as a co-author on an academic paper, which was published a year or so after her placement. Her reflection records her utter determination, and how she felt there was simply no barrier that she was unable to overcome. Her positive mindset was inspirational.

By the end of her work placement she had decided on her research topic for her undergraduate dissertation, and that she would apply for a statistical and research methods Master's degree, an option she had never previously considered. Natassia had her head turned and her future changed through the internship and she was self-aware enough to acknowledge this through her reflections.

Three common concerns

Drawing together the case studies and examples presented in this chapter my thoughts on analytical and research skills development through applied research are captured here. During my experience of placing hundreds of students into work placements, across all sectors, in over 60 organisations, and from interviewing and talking to others, there are a number of common concerns. My own reflection on these follows on from the short discussion on anxiety that I introduced back in Chapter 4, when I talked about interview concerns. It is this. I am absolutely convinced that by using the tools in this book, and reflecting on your experiences, you can overcome these worries and prove to yourself that you are a capable applied social researcher.

The top three student concerns that I have heard over and over again are:

'I don't know enough'

Nearly all students think they are inadequately prepared through their formal studies to undertake a work placement. Well, that is just plain wrong. Every student has something to offer, and the minute you are selected to undertake a placement or internship that is your chance to show what you can bring. Look back at the student voices in this chapter – not one of them thought they knew enough when they began. They all went on to complete successful research projects with their host organisations and in time to use that learning to build on it further. Their secret? They were prepared to open themselves up for learning, and proactively make the most of it. You can do this too.

'What if I get it wrong?'

So what? Learn from it. The wonderful thing about undertaking a work placement is that your professional peers will support you. And getting things wrong is part of learning. We learn so much from making mistakes, and providing we don't keep making them then that is just fine. In the last chapter we heard Alice talk about owning up to a mistake she had made and her supervisor was very supportive of that. I still make mistakes and get things wrong, but I reflect on and learn from them. Again this shows why reflection is so important – learn that skill through your work placement and make it a lifelong habit.

'But I'm just an intern – will they listen to me?'

No one is 'just an anything' in my book. Therein lies self-denigration and lack of respect for your own contribution. Time and time again the reflections I read and hear demonstrate how students grow in confidence within days of starting a placement. Because these have been designed to benefit the organisation (as we saw in Chapter 2 and elsewhere) the hosts are primed for you to succeed. Honestly in all my experience I have only seen one set of negative comments from a host and on inspection that turned out to be because their expectations were too high at the start (they were looking for a graduate rather than giving a student a chance to learn new skills), and there was a change of personnel within a week of the student starting. We nipped this in the bud within days of it becoming apparent, thereby rescuing the placement for everyone. And 'will they listen to me?' – well hopefully you have been convinced by the student voices in this book that the answer is a resounding yes. I will come back to this when we talk about developing your professional skills, of which speaking up convincingly and being persuasive are key characteristics you can practice whilst on placement.

My reflection on the many student reflections I have had the pleasure to read is that a work placement experience is absolutely an opportunity for students to confront their concerns about the work environment, and prove to themselves and their host organisation that they are more than capable of producing a valuable piece of applied social research. And the evidence that they can develop their own analytical and research skills capabilities in the workplace has been presented to you here.

What employers say

Employer perspective

Hopefully having assuaged your fears a little by dealing with the three top common concerns students have, I thought it would be a nice way to wrap up this chapter by including a short section on what employers say.

Here are a handful of quotes taken from organisations in different sectors that have previously hosted interns. Their comments reflect the hosts' expectations and the impressions of the analytical skills and competencies the students gained whilst on placement.

Central government department

Q: *Do you have any comments about how placements provide a pipeline into government research careers? And what you expect of interns on placement?*

A: *An applied social research work placement gives students a good insight into the language, competencies and culture that would be helpful for the application process. It also provides links to people within the department who would be able to provide information and advice on future roles in government. The interns are expected to get up to speed quickly on the subject matter, and work independently to meet deadlines.*

Voluntary and public sector

Q: *How valuable was the research and analysis undertaken by the intern(s) to your organisation?*

A: *She did some excellent analysis which we will take forward in future. She learned a new programming language to achieve this and whilst we helped her with the initial research question she became the expert in no time.*

A: *They worked incredibly hard, developing a large dataset to help our analysis, and engaged with the complex subject matter enthusiastically.*

A: *The interns analysed data that is invaluable to our learning outcomes and helping us to understand where a change management programme is needed.*

These abridged answers to questions asked of some host organisations, when seeking feedback on the internship programme, shows what is achievable through an applied social research work placement, and provides confirmation that the analysis and research that the interns undertook was of value. Later in this book I will include more examples to indicate how the work placement outputs led to opportunities that might otherwise not have come about.

Summary

This chapter is hopefully one of the most useful in the book. It has provided you with multiple examples of how you can assess your own baseline for your analytical and research skills and given you tools – MARS Audit Tool and MARS PDP – to support you to self-assess, plan and measure your skills development. These tools are derived from a British Academy report that reflects the skills that social science and humanities graduates acquire. I introduced you to several former interns who have undertaken applied social research placements and showed how their classroom learning was put into practice in the workplace. Using outputs from two students produced after a work placement I showed how you could capture your skills learned and update your CV. The examples in this chapter show that students already have research skills that workplaces value, and interns can and do undertake applied research projects that matter. Although the featured students faced some stumbling blocks, they overcame them and went on to develop valuable outputs both for themselves and their host organisations. The 'can do' attitude that these students adopted is an essential element of their success. I introduced some common concerns that students often express in wondering whether they are capable of doing an applied social research placement, and showed through multiple examples that they were (and so are you). The case studies used show that work placement research projects differ, but common factors for success are the motivation to learn, and the determination to improve analytical and research skills.

Finally, some short extracts from employers were included to indicate what types of analytical and research skills they are seeking, and their expectations of incoming interns. Chapter 9 will introduce some early career researchers whose experiences will help you understand what an applied social research role entails, and which skills they are developing.

The Neil Armstrong quote used at the start of this chapter is fitting. Undertaking an applied social research project through a work placement means you will investigate something that was previously unknown or not understood. Your analytical and research skills will be enhanced, and you will gain and then be able to share new knowledge.

Three things you can do next

1   Fill in Table 7.3 My Analytical and Research Skills (MARS) Audit Tool. Print it out or reproduce it in your chosen software. Completing it will immediately give you a handle on which skills areas you may need to focus on.

2   Go through Steps 1 to 3 in the section on MARS PDP: My Analytical and Research Skills (MARS) Personal Development Plan (PDP). Complete Table 7.6 Checklist for MARS PDP for the PDP skill that you choose to focus on. Focus on the skills you will develop on placement.

3   Dream a little. Read back over the two students' project outputs (Victoria and Elena). Make a note of the sorts of outputs you would like to produce from your placement. Resolve to make this happen and use this to spur you on to learning the skills to enable you to achieve this.

HOW TO DEVELOP YOUR PROFESSIONAL SKILLS

┌─ Learning objectives ─

In this chapter you will learn how to:

- Recognise what professional skills are and how you can develop them
- Develop a professional skills personal development plan (MPS PDP)
- Monitor your professional skills development
- Document your professional skills acquired in the workplace to help update your CV
- Get the most out of your supervision whilst on placement
- Use previous students' experiences to help you understand how a work placement can help you develop your professional skills
- Do all of the above with a positive and growth mindset

'Through my education, I didn't just develop skills, I didn't just develop the ability to learn, but I developed confidence.'

Michelle Obama (2016)

Overview

While Chapter 7 focused on your analytical and research skills, in the broader context of critical thinking, this chapter focuses on the set of professional skills that you can acquire in the workplace, in the broader context of graduate attributes. In this chapter

I extend your thinking to help you develop a broader range of transferable skills and attributes that will help you develop as an early career professional.

Once again I will introduce tools and frameworks that can help you self-assess and measure your progress. I use two main industry sources (McKinsey and LinkedIn) to provide the backdrop to this chapter, and the framework to the tools I present.

As well as student experiences throughout this chapter I will draw on the voices of the many employers who have helped me understand what types of skills they are looking for in students who undertake work-placed learning, and this will help you prepare to enter the labour market. A personal development plan will show you how you can document the professional skills you want to develop.

Like Chapter 7 this one covers a lot of content, and I try to capture the key points for you. Entire books have been written on developing transferable skills, and so this chapter homes in on the relevance of these skills to applied social research careers. Skills needs change year on year, and so this represents a snapshot at the time of writing.

This chapter draws on the experiences of five of our case study students: Marcus, Anna, Zvi, Julija and Sarah. The first four will be used to illustrate four of the professional skills covered, and show how they used their placement learning to demonstrate or build this skill. Sarah provides the professional skills personal development plan example.

What are professional skills?

In Chapter 2 I introduced the term professional skills when discussing benefits to students of undertaking a work placement, and some of these were listed in Table 2.1 (A typology of early career learning). I use the term 'professional skills', where others might use the terms 'transferable' or 'soft' skills or 'graduate attributes'. I choose this term as I place a lot of store on being professional, think professional skills are important, and I want to make you aware of them. However, just be mindful that you will come across different terms for what I cover in this chapter, as you can see below.

Peggy Klaus wrote a book entitled *The Hard Truth about Soft Skills: Workplace Lessons Smart People Wish They'd Learned Sooner* (2008). In her introduction Klaus says 'However you define them, soft skills still suffer from a fundamental lack of respect'. The following pragmatic definitions show how careers sites and services usually distinguish between 'soft' and 'hard' skills:

Hard skills – tend to be skills you acquire through education or training, such as a specific piece of software, or a technical skill, or a method for undertaking analysis, or your degree grade. They are relatively straightforward to evidence. Chapter 7 covered skills in this group.

Soft skills – usually refer to traits and characteristics such as creativity or leadership or communication or time management. These skills can be more difficult to evidence. This chapter deals with these skills.

In *The Oxford Handbook of Skills and Training*, Payne (2017) notes:

> New categories of 'generic', 'transferable', 'basic', 'employability', 'soft', and 'social' skills have emerged. Today, the 'skills' label is applied to everything from thinking, communication, reading, writing and numeracy, team working, problem solving, customer handling, leadership, motivation, initiative, a positive attitude, punctuality, personal appearance, stress management, and even plain obedience.
>
> Payne (2017: 55)

> 'Soft skills' is a broad umbrella term for ... attitudes, behaviours, dispositions, and personal characteristics.
>
> Payne (2017: 59)

It is debatable whether it is even useful to separate out skills required for the workplace, crudely referring to them as hard or soft (or equivalent). There is considerable overlap; for example critical thinking can be regarded as a soft skill. Payne goes on to say:

> ... soft skills and technical skills/knowledge are interdependent, with the latter adding depth and complexity to problem solving, communication, and relationship building with customers/clients.
>
> Payne (2017: 66–7)

Acknowledging this overlap between the skillsets is important; they are often a combination not just of acquiring new methods, tools and ways of doing research (Chapter 7 covered this), but also an approach to doing that research (Chapter 8 focuses on this). Both require subject knowledge expertise.

Klaus's book (2008) is based on her own interviews and experiences and backed up by empirical research undertaken by organisations including the Stanford Research Institute International and the Mellon Foundation. The latter reported that 75% of long-term job success depends on people skills, with only 25% being attributed to technical knowledge. Knowing what companies mean by soft skills is therefore worthwhile.

The professional social networking platform LinkedIn – whose 2019 *Global Talent Trends Report* I draw on in this chapter – identified soft skills as the first of four categories that organisations and employers should pay attention to (LinkedIn, 2019). Soft skills topped the survey responses at 91%, compared to 72% (work flexibility), 71% (anti-harassment practices) and 53% (pay transparency). Their news release for their 2019 Global Talent Trends Report stated:

Soft Skills – 92% of talent professionals and hiring managers agree that candidates with strong soft skills are increasingly important. In fact, it could make or break of hiring the perfect candidate as 89% feel that 'bad hires' typically have poor soft skills.

https://news.linkedin.com/2019/January/linkedin-releases-2019-global-talent-trends-report

Let's move on to see how industry identifies the skills covered in this chapter and show you by example how work placement students acquire them. The aim is to help you create your own professional skills personal development plan.

Why develop your professional skills?

The section above introduced you to professional skills. Here I demonstrate why you should consider developing them through your work placement. I draw on two reputable industry sources. First, LinkedIn's 2019 *Global Talent* report (see above) identified the top five skills industry professionals believe to be in short supply. And second, a McKinsey Featured Insights discussion paper in 2018 identified what they referred to as higher cognitive and social and emotional skills in high demand for the future workforce. I will combine the findings from these two reports to develop the framework for your own professional skills development.

I have seen many students graduate over the years and enter various professions in different sectors. I have worked with around 60 organisations across these sectors and professions. Demonstrating a professional approach to one's work is important. Whilst technology and the work environment may change the underlying skills and behaviours for success in how we do, and communicate, applied social research persists. In Chapter 7 I referenced a British Academy report, which identified three broad headings for core skills, two of which were *communication and collaboration* and *attitudes and behaviours characterised by independence and adaptability* (British Academy, 2017: 9). This chapter reaffirms the importance of these core skillsets.

I introduce here an example of when something as straightforward as writing an email can be done badly, but is easily remedied. Email is still widely used in the workplace as a communication tool. The continued ubiquity of email demands that you learn how to be professional in your use of it. In the box below I present an example of when a student got this wrong, so that you can learn from their mistake.

Student: 26 Dec	I'm really worried. I've just opened a letter saying I can't continue my studies. Will you contact the organisation to tell them this is a mistake? I look forward to hearing from you. Thankyou.
Me: 27 Dec	Dear Lee,
	Thankyou for your email and I'm sorry to hear you have received this letter.
	As it is the Christmas break I cannot resolve this. I will ask the University when it reopens to investigate this for you. Please send me a copy of the letter.
	Best wishes, Jackie
Student: 2 Jan	This is the letter I received (letter attached).
Me: 6 Jan	Dear Lee,
	Your course administrator is Jo Doe. Please contact Jo who will provide you with support. I'm sure we can resolve this. Here are Jo's contact details. Please keep me posted.
	Best wishes, Jackie
Student:	No response

Top tips

Dos and don'ts of sending an email

Don't send an email:

- On a public holiday/when the recipient is not working
- Without a proper form of address
- Without signing off with your name

Don't forget to close the loop:

- If you send an email that asks someone to do something remember to let them know when this has been resolved

Do the following:

- Imagine you are receiving the email. Is it courteous and informative?
- Ensure the email has a purpose and makes it clear what the recipient needs to do next

Why am I including this as an example? First, for you to understand that emails require you to be courteous, and to read and respond carefully. Lee failed to use any form of opening or closing address, did not respond in a timely fashion, and did not close the loop of communication that had been started. Communication is a two-way process and requires both sides to listen and respond. Lee's emails were terse and there is a lot to learn from this. Emails are not the same as text messages. Professional emails demand a certain etiquette and you are advised to learn this.

Perhaps Lee has never written an email of this nature before. The letter received was clearly distressing (it turned out to be a mistake) and Lee was reaching out for help to the right first-port-of-call person (me). With a few simple changes this could have been a different type of exchange for both of us. I should add that these types of emails do not offend me – I see them as a learning opportunity – but I know from conversations with a lot of colleagues that they do find communications of this nature irritating. And I also know from my discussions with employers that they expect good email etiquette.

The top professional skills sought by employers

I introduced LinkedIn's 2019 *Global Talent Trends Report* above. Because soft skills (their wording) are identified so prominently in the report, I introduce their top five categories for what they discovered companies said are in high demand but short supply. You may be planning to work in a non-commercial organisation, but these five categories of professional skills are useful regardless of the sector you plan to develop your career in. I add to these five later in this chapter.

Soft skills companies need but have a hard time finding (LinkedIn, 2019)

1. Creativity
2. Persuasion
3. Collaboration
4. Adaptability
5. Time management

I also draw on the McKinsey Featured Insights discussion paper (McKinsey, 2018). McKinsey researched the global shift in skills required for the workplace due to increased automation, drawing out five groups of skills. The two categories most relevant to this book are *higher cognitive skills* and *social and emotional skills*, the other three being *physical and manual, basic cognitive* and *technological skills*.

The report summarises the skills of the future, due to increased automation, as follows:

> Higher cognitive skills and social and emotional skills will also be more in demand, according to company executives.

McKinsey (2018: 15)

Figure 8.1 shows how higher cognitive skills and social and emotional skills are perceived by respondents to be increasingly needed in the next three years. For example, there is a positive difference of 8% of surveyed executives who say more creativity is needed in the workplace in the next three years. As you can see from Figure 8.1 all of the skills in these two categories shown are in demand.

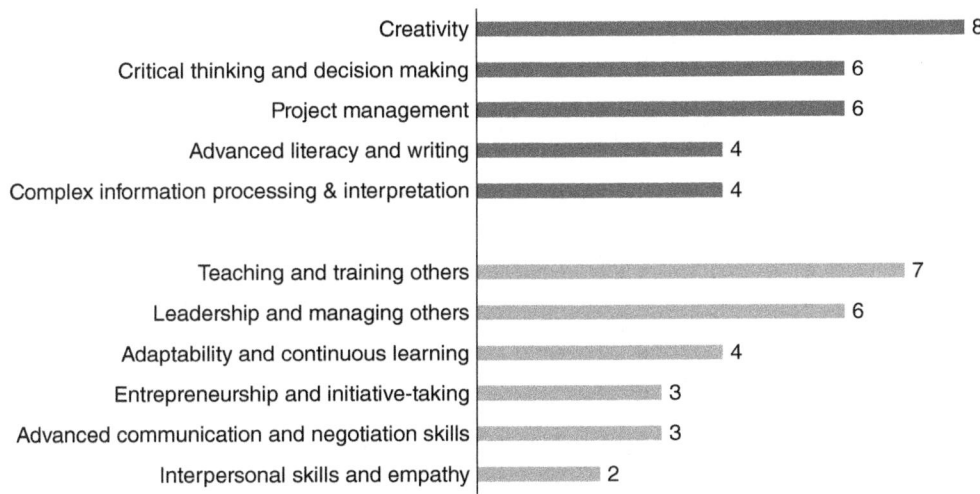

Figure 8.1 Percentage difference between respondents reporting needing less vs more of a skill in next three years; higher cognitive skills (top) and social and emotional skills (bottom) needs

Source: Adapted from McKinsey (2018: 16), https://www.mckinsey.com/~/media/McKinsey/Industries/Public%20and%20Social%20Sector/Our%20Insights/Skill%20shift%20Automation%20and%20the%20future%20of%20the%20workforce/MGI-Skill-Shift-Automation-and-future-of-the-workforce-May-2018.pdf

The McKinsey report goes on to show the most important and growing skills needs as perceived by the executives surveyed. Of importance to this chapter, and you in the early stages of your career, are the ones I have highlighted in Table 8.1.

Table 8.1 Most important and growing skills needs from McKinsey, 2018

Category	Skill
Social and emotional	Leadership
	Communication and negotiation
	Interpersonal and empathy
	Entrepreneurship
	Adaptability
	Teaching and training

(Continued)

Table 8.1 (Continued)

Category	Skill
Higher cognitive	Critical thinking
	Creativity
	Project management
	Advanced literacy
	Complex information processing

Both LinkedIn and McKinsey include Creativity and Adaptability. I highlight Communication in Table 8.1 as I think this is an essential skill for you to acquire and practise in the workplace, and as you saw from the example of how *not* to write an email, developing your communication skills is vital. The non-highlighted skills in Table 8.1 are important, but in order to help you focus in the early stage of your career I have been selective. Some of the skills under the higher cognitive category (e.g. critical thinking) were covered in Chapter 7.

Employers' perspectives

The LinkedIn and McKinsey reports are helpful for understanding what professional skills are being sought in the workplace, especially where there is a skills shortage. I conclude this section by including a few examples from host organisations I have worked with who have taken work placement students. This serves to show you the sorts of skills they look for on application and will help you see how, by showing that you have them, you can differentiate yourself. Your work placement is a golden opportunity to develop these skills further.

This example comes from a host organisation, a strategic think-tank that takes our students year on year. They had previously taken students and found success through doing so, but in this particular year they were less happy with the students' CVs and letters of application that we had passed on to them. They explain why:

Employer perspective

We are a small group, with limited time to supervise a student. We have looked through all the CVs you sent us and academically they look strong, but hand-on-heart we cannot interview these students as they show no evidence of having worked in an office environment, or having the sorts of exposure to professional work that we really need them to have in order to hit the ground running.

This reply was a wake-up call. It helped me understand the importance of capturing these professional skills on your CV. Your CV is your first communication with the organisation where you hope to be placed, and you need to aim to evidence your professional skills on it to convince them to invite you to interview. Of course it may be that you do not have office skills and the organisation, like the think-tank above, will see this as a gap and not invite you, but it may be that you actually do have some of these skills but simply have until now omitted them from your CV. You may plan to use the internship or work placement to acquire these skills if you don't have them and some places will take you to give you this opportunity; but you still need to be aware of what these skills are. You need to think about how you can include experiences you have had in a way that will assist organisations to see that you may be a good choice.

This particular story has a happy ending. We went back to the pool of students and did go on to match one with the organisation, and she went on to do a fantastic piece of work with them. Her CV happened to be full of examples of where she had gained previous experience, and this got her a foot through the door to this think-tank, and then a place with them. When I spoke to the host during the placement they were at pains to point out just how important it was to them that she had prior experience, and that she had been able to very quickly use this to contact clients and data providers, and to start the research they had prepared. Organisations, quite understandably, would prefer someone who already feels confident using the phone or sending professional emails to ones that they have to train to do this. After all, their reputation matters and they would prefer to avoid having to deal retrospectively with a mistake. The particular happy ending to this story is that the intern they chose then went on to produce a phenomenal piece of research which benefited the organisation, and appeared in their flagship annual report, but also helped her undertake her third-year dissertation. The result, as in so many placements, is that they got the right student to do what they needed, and she got a fantastic opportunity to extend her skills and experience. Another case of win-win.

Here is a final example in this section which sums up much of what employers are looking for. A central government department was asked what they wanted from the students who were to be placed there for a summer internship, and how they thought interns could develop their professional skills whilst on placement:

> It would be good for interns to bear in mind the development of skills around office etiquette, email dos and don'ts, communicating professionally with a wide range of people and presenting themselves professionally. They are expected to get up to speed quickly on the subject matter, work independently and meet deadlines. They are also expected to present their findings in a user-friendly format relevant to the audience.

Employer perspective

This example hopefully provides you with an insight into how you can start to think about these important attributes, know what is expected of you in the workplace, and plan to develop these skills. The next section uses the framework developed so far, and takes account of what employers say they need, and will help you establish a baseline and develop your professional skills.

Developing your professional skills

In this section I show you how you can start to recognise your professional skills. Taking each of the top five skills in the LinkedIn report I will first describe them in a way that will be more meaningful to you in the context of work-placed learning. I will show you, through case studies of Julija, Marcus, Anna and Zvi, and my own example, how to develop these professional skills. This will lead up to creating your self-assessed Professional Skills Personal Development Plan (MPS PDP). The aim here is to help you see how you can identify your own skills gaps and start to develop them on a work placement so that you can then speak convincingly if asked about any one of them at interview, and capture them on your CV.

I have added Communication and Networking to the top five LinkedIn skills and adapted one of them slightly (Collaboration and teamwork) to better address the needs you have at the start of your career (see Table 2.1). The list below provides the *seven professional skills* I will focus on through the remainder of this chapter. The ordering is deliberate and should help you think logically about the skills you can develop in the workplace.

Top seven professional skills (PS) to develop on your work placement

- PS1 Communication
- PS2 Collaboration and teamwork
- PS3 Time management
- PS4 Creativity
- PS5 Persuasion
- PS6 Adaptability
- PS7 Networking

In order to unpack these seven top professional skills, here I provide an explanation of the definitions and some examples from the case studies in this chapter and my own experience.

PS1: Communication

Good communication is a skill required by every professional position I have ever seen advertised. I have included it in the set of seven top professional skills as every organisation I have ever spoken to has been at pains to point out that this is in their high priority list. Communication comes in many forms and the workplace will be a place for you to understand how professional communication can differ dramatically from academic communication. By giving you the example of the Dos and Don'ts of email communication in the workplace I have already introduced you to styles and codes of practice for written communication. There is no single way of addressing all the different forms of communication other than to say you will learn how an organisation does this when you are there. Be alert to their way of writing, speaking, presenting and find out very early on what they expect of you. In your reflections ensure you think about this from Day One and please do not worry if you get anything wrong initially – you are there to learn. That said, if you are encouraged not to use your mobile in the office, for example, be sure you adhere to that code of practice.

Developing your communication skills whilst on placement is one of the most straightforward things you can aim to do. In order to do this to greatest effect, though, you have to develop a clear idea of what you can achieve, and be prepared to use the questions introduced in this chapter to stretch yourself. There's a quote often attributed to Albert Einstein that I see quite a lot in professional circles: 'if you can't explain it simply, you don't understand it well enough'. That is worth bearing in mind as a way of framing good communications, whatever the medium. The students in this chapter, and elsewhere in the book, have all been exposed to various methods of communication, and by thinking carefully about their before-during-and-after work placement experiences, using reflection as a development tool, and capturing their learning, they can provide clear examples for future job applications to demonstrate the skills learned.

I have not included a case study example for this professional skill as the book is full of them. Flick to any chapter and look at the student case studies, and you will find different styles, but take comfort in knowing that if they have made it into this book you can model your own communication on theirs. You will find your own style as you develop, and students are often nervous about this initially, but we all had to start somewhere. Be observant and listen carefully – this is how we all learn how workplace communications work.

PS2: Collaboration and teamwork

Collaboration is a cross-cutting function and depends heavily on developing rapport, trust and authority with colleagues. In other words, working as part of a team. I combine collaboration and teamwork together for the remainder of this chapter.

In Chapter 2 I introduced one of the core skills of experiential learning as being the opportunity to collaborate with professional colleagues and co-create new knowledge. Collaboration should be a lifelong pursuit, not one that lasts just whilst you are on placement. Indeed so important is this as a professional skillset that the McKinsey report (2018) makes repeated reference to this, talking about collaborative cross-function working environments, collaboration between human and computer interaction, and designing collaborative workspaces to encourage this. The LinkedIn report (2019) also pays attention to the need for collaboration for successful team working and recognises that this poses challenges for workers too.

In contrast to conventional formal education assessment methods, to succeed in the workplace you absolutely need to be able to demonstrate that you can collaborate and work with colleagues across a number of different roles and teams. Good communication is an essential part of being able to do this.

Here is an example from my own secondment, when I went to work in a national government department. As with anything new I was nervous about learning who was who, and working out how I was going to do the best piece of work in the time available. I knew that I was going to have to work across many government functions and departments, and master their communications channels quickly. I had limited time to get up to speed but was determined to make the most of the opportunity. I had never used their online communication channel – Slack – before but made sure that I learned how to use this tool quickly, worked out the key people I needed to know, not just in the immediate team I was in, but in the teams that I was going to be working with. This took effort, a systematic approach and courage. And I ensured I met people face to face, not just virtually. Shortly after I finished the secondment I was asked to attend a high-level meeting. I was introduced to a group of senior professionals and civil servants who I had never met before but because I had at least one point of contact with each of them through people I *had* worked with, they introduced me confidently and with authority. Developing a strong, collaborative way of working with a supportive and trusting network of colleagues ensured my reputation was good.

Collaboration is a highly prized skill. Your reputation can rest on the rapport and respect you build whilst working with colleagues, and even though you may work in a confined environment in your work experience, you never know how far the reports of you as a colleague, and your work, can travel. Below I will give you tips and tools for how you can get the most out of your experiential learning to acquire collaborative skills. And you have already seen examples throughout this book of former interns who have worked collaboratively during their placements.

PS3: Time management

Although the LinkedIn report (2018) does not specify exactly what it defines as time management, interpret this to mean good personal time management skills. The McKinsey report (2019) lists good project management skills, which can also be acquired in the workplace. Punctuality is an absolute given as far as professional behaviour and etiquette is concerned. No one likes to be kept waiting, and it's the height of rudeness to keep others waiting. If you are not a naturally punctual person you need to aim to cultivate this skill through your work placement.

In Chapters 4 and 5 I talked about the need to be organised and arrive on time for interviews and the first day of the work placement. Following up from that, you need to develop good time management skills to help you with your applied social research project.

O'Donnell et al. (2017) describe time management and organisational skills together:

> **Time management and organisational skills** – ability to create a plan of action (individually or with others) to achieve desired objectives. Setting and maintaining realistic and achievable plans and short-term/intermediate targets. Showing perseverance and resourcefulness when working to deadlines and having the ability to think ahead and overcome/manage potential obstacles to progress.

Time management is crucially important, especially where there is a set number of weeks to undertake a piece of work, such as in a time-limited internship or work placement. In Julija's case, she was with the BBC for just eight weeks, the first two of which her line manager was on leave. She therefore had to be a self-starter in order to get up to speed with her work, and although this did not always come naturally to her she persevered. Her host organisation had warned us that there would be busy, and much less busy, times whilst on placement and had selected Julija based on her impressive interview. The following extract from her final reflective piece shows how she exercised time management and organisational skills during her placement.

Case study 8.1

Julija: How my internship helped me become organised

A very typical outcome through a work placement is for students to improve their time management and organisational skills. Here Julija tells us how it helped her do both, and more.

> Through my internship I had to find different datasets all the time and do it quickly – this is why I now know the most efficient ways (and the best places) to find the data. By the second week, I became much more confident, talking to local authorities and other data providers, and could precisely formulate my requests in a couple of sentences. I am truly surprised how the internship has transformed my people skills and how much more assertive, sociable and organised I've become.

PS4: Creativity

What do employers mean by creativity? This is rather a difficult thing to describe. The following extract is taken from the McKinsey Featured Insights discussion paper:

> Demand for higher cognitive skills such as creativity, critical thinking and decision-making, and complex information processing will grow through 2030, at cumulative double-digit rates. The growing need for creativity is seen in many activities, including developing high-quality marketing strategies.
>
> McKinsey (2018: 11)

Creativity here is a catch-all category for a basket of skills. Here it relates to the need for employers to develop creative approaches to complex problem solving, and to nurture professionals who can think laterally about attacking business problems, and develop leadership in this area. The report explores the need for skills in a changing world, as automation plays a bigger role in companies and organisations.

An interestingly titled book by Scott Hartley (2017) – *The Fuzzy and the Techie: Why the Liberal Arts Will Rule the Digital World* – captures why creativity is arguably needed more than ever. The business, commercial, public and voluntary sectors need knowledge creators and translators. The results of rigorous analysis need creatives to communicate the findings to multiple audiences, and often the approaches to gaining insight require creative thinking.

Case study 8.2

Marcus: How I needed to think creatively

Here Marcus talks about his opportunity to work creatively in his internship. The case study starts with the host organisation discussing the task they set him, and how they expected him to investigate it.

Organisation:

> Marcus was asked to investigate different datasets that would help us gain insight into our research on the Northern Powerhouse, for a flagship report we publish annually. He trawled through many, many datasets and through his perseverance, and tenacity, found a figure that has come to be known as the early years' gap. This statistic was previously hidden, but his creative approach and sheer determination helped us uncover an incredibly important finding, which has since been picked up by national media and others.

> Marcus:
>
> [For the external report] I was just told to go and find the data and write it all up and send them what I had done so that we could all build on it. Whilst initially there was a very steep learning curve and at times I was worried I was floundering, it was great to be trusted from the start and for the team to have faith in me to do what was required. I think that the freedom of doing what was required in my own direction, choosing my own priorities, really allowed me to flourish and succeed during my internship.

You can see in these two extracts how Marcus, and his host organisation, operated on a basis of mutual trust and he was *expected to be* creative in his approach. These statements provide evidence of creativity. Marcus was given somewhat of an open-ended task. I order to deliver on that he had to be open-minded in thinking about the activity – indeed in his reflective pieces he wrote about how he spent the first few weeks just finding data sources, and then tools for combining these, and it was not until later into the placement that he was able to have a clear idea of what the data were showing him. This largely refers to the analytical and research skills he employed, but his *approach* was creative.

This is the difference between the skills covered in the previous chapter and those covered here, and illustrates the somewhat less tangible nature of these professional skills.

PS5: Persuasion

Persuasion is an attribute successful leaders are encouraged to develop. The question for you is what is it and how can you develop it? The McKinsey report noted that negotiation (a related skill) is a desired skill, in short supply. Consider thinking about persuasion in the following terms, in regard to work-placed learning.

Imagine you start your work placement. You have been given an activity or set of activities to undertake, and you will be asked to present your findings at the end to a group of stakeholders. They could be the team you are working with, another group or perhaps your work is to be presented to senior colleagues. Whoever the recipient of your findings is, bear in mind that your communication needs to be persuasive in order for your work to inform, convince and possibly change minds. Good applied research should always consider this need at the outset. The presentation could take a number of forms: verbal (a briefing in a meeting), written (a report or article) or it could be a visual output (an infographic, a poster or a presentation). Whichever mode of communication is required, the important point to take into consideration is how you are going to *be persuasive.*

Case study 8.3

Anna: How her placement persuaded the organisation to create a new role

Anna is a good example for developing persuasion in the workplace. She so impressed her host organisation, a private data consultancy, that they offered her a position within a year of graduating, actually creating a role for her that had not existed previously. She was the first Social and Political Research Officer they appointed, and rose quickly to become a Senior Research Consultant.

It's hard to remember now, seeing her as a successful professional, how she was at the start of her placement. I recall speaking to Anna during the early days when she was a little nervous and unsure of her ability to direct her placement. They were doing very little by way of political research, which is what she was most interested in, but she used her time there, encouraged by them, to undertake an interesting project. Her passion for political social research persuaded the CEO to develop a new role that has helped them since grow an area of their business.

PS6: Adaptability

Adaptability, and how it can be measured, creates an interesting challenge. An entire chapter is devoted to 'the adaptable graduate' in Normand and Anderson's edited volume *Graduate Attributes in Higher Education* (O'Donnell et al., 2017). Through research-based case studies the authors identified the following criteria for defining an adaptable and flexible graduate:

> Have resilience, resourcefulness and agility in a range of working contexts/ environments. To draw on the existing and evolving stock of knowledge to be able to deal with unexpected circumstances, circumventing problematic issues while finding effective solutions.

> O'Donnell et al. (2017: 27)

Who would not want this set of skills in their team? How though do you demonstrate you have acquired these skills? This is one of the most difficult professional skills to evidence, but let me try to help you deconstruct this 'definition' in order to be able to show that you have, or at least have the potential to develop, this valuable set of characteristics. The ability to handle change proactively is a highly desirable skill (many senior roles demand 'change management' experience).

Dealing with change and being adaptable does not always come easily but is a skill that can be acquired. A good example of how a graduate and former intern needed to develop an adaptable approach is presented in Case study 8.4. This illustrates how Zvi needed to be flexible, adaptable and resilient to acquire the graduate position that most suited him. Although his experience caused some discomfort he persevered to gain a new and prestigious role. He now has evidence of his adaptability to enhance his CV and speak about in his future career.

Case study 8.4

Zvi: How my internship helped me become adaptable

Here Zvi discusses how his personal development through his internship helped him develop the confidence and skills to face up to and deal with challenging situations, appreciate the need for professional skills, and become an adaptable graduate.

After deciding that my first graduate job wasn't for me, I decided to pursue a career in research elsewhere. I had found a Data Analyst role and the job specification looked just what I had been looking for, although it asked for a lot of analytical skills, which I was just meeting the minimum requirements for. I knew I was probably the least well-qualified applicant. However, I still applied.

I know that both 'soft' skills and 'hard' skills are important and how vital it is to present both of these well in an interview. Thinking about how to convey your 'soft' skills, I argue is even more important than your 'hard' skills.

I did not get the post I applied for, but my interview went well, and they offered me another role. I was able to show that I had the soft skills they were looking for in a candidate, and especially that I am adaptable and resilient. Having been willing to move from a position that was not working out for me, to find work elsewhere that aligned with my interests and direction of travel went down really well. I am very happy I turned this around and was able to show how dealing with change is an experience I embraced and learned from.

Zvi had to confront what had, for him, been a difficult decision – to give up his first graduate position in a profession that was highly sought after. He took decisive action though, and then used this to his advantage when he was interviewed for a new position, using the experience to show his resilience and adaptability, He was appointed to a position where he is now doing very well. His adaptability to change the course of his future, and to use this as a positive experience, paid dividends. And the relationships he developed whilst on placement were so good that he used them as a network to support him through this time of change, including gaining supportive references from people he had worked with previously.

PS7: Networking

I include networking in the top seven as it is such a critical professional skill to develop. In previous chapters I make much of developing your support networks, and your work experience will help you do that as you become an early career professional. Rather than provide a case study here I suggest you consider how you will develop your professional identity online. Until now you may have developed an online identity, through various social media platforms, that has not been focused on the impression you give to potential future recruiters. Now is absolutely the time to address this. Not all students, however, feel comfortable doing this so early in their transition from education to the workplace, and some may prefer to connect with individuals privately or through social media or other means. Students may also want to create their own support networks whilst on placement, as this can be an effective way of mutually supporting one another (e.g. through a closed Facebook, or WhatsApp group). Regardless of how the networking is operationalised, as an intern you are encouraged to do this.

I have spoken throughout this book about LinkedIn as a professional networking platform. If you have never seen it take a look at it and use this as an opportunity to develop your LinkedIn profile. This is the beginning of you developing your future networks, and what better place than to do that during a work placement. There is more information covered on networking in the remainder of this chapter, and in the next one.

Here is a fact. All of the case study students in this book are connected to me on LinkedIn. Some of them I lost touch with for a few years, but I have been able to reconnect through this platform. Many have already been mentioned in my LinkedIn posts and articles. The ability to stay in touch has been mutually beneficial and without this professional networking platform I doubt I would have been able to include some in the book. More than that, the pleasure of witnessing the early development of their careers has helped guide my writing and decisions for what to include in this book.

This section has covered a lot. It's now time to help you put all of this into practice by showing you how you can start to develop your own personal development plan – this time for professional skills.

Develop a personal development plan (PDP)

In Chapter 7 I showed you how to develop a personal development plan for your analytical and research skills. That required slightly more work as first you were instructed to focus in on the skill group you wanted to develop whilst on placement, then select the individual skills within that group that you planned to develop. Whilst the aim of this section is the same, although this time for your professional skills to be baselined, developed and updated on your CV, the process of doing this is a little more straightforward.

My Professional Skills (MPS) PDP

Taking the seven top skills PS1–PS7 I introduced above, I now help you develop a My Professional Skills Personal Development Plan (MPS PDP). I said earlier in the chapter that self-assessing these skills and deciding what to focus on is arguably more difficult than analytical and research skills and you will need to decide for yourself what you think you should prioritise. The example below (Table 8.3) shows how two of the professional skills could have been omitted from the MPS PDP as they were not the focus of the placement. You need to use your own judgement here and seek the input of your supervisor(s) to help you decide which professional skills you wish to develop.

Unlike the previous chapter where I provided a mapping between the skills you wanted to focus on, and a framework for doing that, here I simply list the seven selected skills. These professional skills will gain context through jobs that you apply for in the future. In Chapter 3 you were introduced to developing your CV, and letter of application, from the perspective of *applying for* experiential learning. You now need to think about this in the broader context of your future career and aim to develop the professional skills to help you succeed. I have inserted a row to capture your overarching goal, though you could have a sub-goal for each professional skill if that would help.

An example professional skills personal development plan checklist is given in Table 8.2. It will help you self-assess your professional skills to give you a baseline at the start of your placement.

Table 8.2 Checklist for MPS PDP for top seven skills

Date of completion:		
My Goal		
For each row enter the level you feel you are currently at for each professional skill. Use the values from **1** (weak) to **4** (very strong)	**1** (weak and need to work at this) **2** (some evidence, but need more practice) **3** (good at this and can evidence it) **4** (very strong at this and can evidence it)	
My Professional Skills (MPS) PDP	**My score**	**How I will improve my score during the work placement**
PS1: Communication		
PS2: Collaboration and teamwork		
PS3: Time management		

(Continued)

Table 8.2 (Continued)

Date of completion:		
PS4: Creativity		
PS5: Persuasion		
PS6: Adaptability		
PS7: Networking		

One of the difficulties in providing information in this chapter is knowing where your baseline (your starting point) is. Some of you will have experience of having worked in a company before, and some of you will not. In Chapter 3 I used an example from a host organisation which decided to take a student as he had evidence of having supervised some colleagues through his part-time job in a fast-food company. Although that student had not worked in the same environment as the one he was being given a work placement in, he had demonstrated on his CV and at interview that he had transferable skills that they valued. In contrast, earlier in this chapter I showed how a think-tank declined to interview students based on lack of evidence of office work on their CVs. Try not to be put off by this and take comfort from my comments about how you can acquire these skills in the workplace and use your prior experience to show a prospective host that you have the ability and motivation to pick up these skills. Everyone starts from a different baseline.

As in Chapter 7 I have retrospectively produced an example for one of our ten main characters, this time Sarah, one of our two postgraduate students who undertook a short work placement whilst doing her PhD.

Sarah was looking for a work placement to develop skills that she thought would be helpful in her future research career but she had not had opportunity to focus on to date. As she already has prior experience in the workplace, she could decide to focus on the *five skills identified by LinkedIn* as in great demand but short supply. PS1: Communication and PS7: Networking are therefore not completed in this PDP example. Her MPS PDP *could* look something like Table 8.3 (note this is for illustration only based on my completing this tool to show you what it might look like).

Table 8.3 An example MPS PDP

Date of completion: Start of placement		
My Goal: To use the work placement to focus on creative approaches to communicating the results of research		
My Professional Skills (MPS) PDP	My score (1 weak, 4 strong)	How to improve my score during the work placement
PS1: Communication	–	Not focusing on this in my work placement

Date of completion: Start of placement		
PS2: Collaboration and teamwork	2	The research approach taken is quite innovative and as part of my placement I will be able to negotiate to collect data for an academic project as well. The interviews that I will undertake will inform the report for the host organisation (non-academic) and provide data for future academic research. Collaboration across sectors is critical to the success of this project. I also hope to develop my facilitation skills.
PS3: Time management	4	All analysis to be done within the short timescale of the work placement. I have good time management skills but need to stay on target for this project to succeed.
PS4: Creativity	2	I negotiated my own placement with a design consultancy, whose co-founder I had met at a conference during my PhD. The placement will allow me to develop a range of new skills, including some that will strengthen my creativity. I am especially interested in developing my visual presentation skills.
PS5: Persuasion	3	This placement will allow me to develop the ability to write for impact, in clear and concise plain English. It acts as an important and powerful reminder about the distinct difference between writing for an academic and a policy maker audience.
PS6: Adaptability	3	I will need to be agile and open to change as the project progresses especially with regard to PS1 and PS3.
PS7: Networking	–	Not focusing on this in my work placement

You will meet Sarah again in Chapter 9 to find out how she used her work placement in her next steps. Your own MPS PDP will be different to Sarah's, and so think about your own professional skills and how you can use this plan to capture, identify a baseline and develop *what is meaningful and important to you.*

Getting the most out of your supervision

Right, so you have learned what professional skills are, seen the 'most wanted' by companies, and been introduced to a personal development planning tool to use before and during your placement. In this section you will learn how you can be proactive about using your work placement to gain or strengthen these skills by getting the most out of your supervisor. I use the term 'supervisor' broadly here. It could be the person who you report to on a daily basis or the mentor you have or want to find (see Chapter 5). Whoever this is, the purpose is to be proactive about your professional development.

To some of you this might sound a little odd, presumptuous even. However, in the same way that you can be proactive about your learning at university, you can do this in the workplace. Good managers and supervisors want their staff to be successful. Being a work placement student or internship is no different. Your academic instructors want you to succeed, and so too does your host organisation.

Back in Chapter 5 we discussed setting expectations. Getting the most out of your work placement supervision is a natural extension of this. Asking for support whilst on placement is an expectation. However, you need to learn to ask for the right type of support, and getting this right is a little tricky at first. You will most likely be given a colleague at your organisation who is a day-to-day point of contact. This person, by definition, has more experience than you but they also have their own day-job to do. It could be that there is a very clear induction-style process for you to be put through (often public sector organisations have this), but it may be there is a culture of just learning on the job. Whichever scenario you find yourself in you can exert some control over it by being clear what you need to do, and asking what level of support you can expect to be given. Dealing with this is an important part of getting used to the workplace.

In our pre-internship training (I spoke about this back in Chapter 5, in Brushing up your Skills) we allocate each of our interns an academic supervisor. The aim of this, apart from providing a single point of contact back to the university, is to encourage questions on anything related to the work placement. These range from 'What's the dress code?' (every cohort always asks this) to 'What do I do if I'm ill?' or 'What if I can't do it?' If you have this support you are strongly advised to use it before you enter the work placement, as your academic supervisors want you to be a credit to your university.

When you get to the organisation you are placed in, however, you need to use them. After all they are now your colleagues. You may want a few tips though to help you think about the sorts of questions you can ask, and the type of supervision you can expect. As this chapter is about developing your professional skills, I am restricting the questions here to those that are pertinent to that.

Here is a list of questions, then, that I think are perfectly valid for you to raise whilst on your placement or internship. There are no hard or fast rules about how or when you ask these; maybe keep a few up your sleeve to bring out as the placement develops. There will be a natural unfolding of when it makes sense to ask them, but aim to stagger them so you – and the organisation – are not so overwhelmed at the start, and don't store them all up so they come out in a torrent at the end. I have provided a suggestion for when you might ask each one, at the start, middle or end of the placement, but be flexible about this.

Questions to ask your supervisor

Beginning

- How are emails usually written? Can you show me an example? And are there any email policies or practices I need to be aware of?

- Are there examples of reports that have been produced so I can see how the work is communicated to different audiences?
- Are there regular team/departmental meetings? Will I be able to attend? How are these meetings conducted?
- Is there a template for presentations or reports or slide-sets that I need if I am going to be delivering my work to colleagues?
- Is there a social media policy I need to be aware of?
- Are there any confidentiality issues I need to be aware of?
- There are a lot of acronyms I'm coming across. Is there anything you can point me to, to help me understand and learn these?
- I want to develop my professional skills whilst I am here. Are there any training courses I could attend?

Middle

- I would love to work across the business. I appreciate this might be difficult but is there any chance I could liaise with other teams or shadow someone whilst I am here?
- Might I be able to meet other recent graduates to find out what they do so I can see whether I might like to pursue a future career here?
- I am really enjoying being mentored/supervised by you – would you consider doing this after the placement ends?
- What would your advice be about how I can extend my networks whilst I am here?

End

- Can we stay in touch when I leave? And might you be willing to provide a reference please as I start to apply for graduate positions?
- I would be really grateful if you could give me feedback on what you think has gone well, and where I could improve.
- Would it be OK to have an exit interview at the end of my placement? I have heard these are a good way of documenting learning on both sides.
- Is it alright to link to you on LinkedIn?

The first two categories are rather straightforward, and follow very naturally from everything you have read in this book so far. You might need to pluck up courage to ask some of these questions, but in and of themselves they are not scary. The last category, as you approach the end of your placement, is a little different and for that reason I extend this section to deal with some core attributes I think you might need to develop in order to be able to handle these questions.

Adopt a positive and growth mindset, and develop resilience

Becoming a professional and developing these skills for and in the workplace requires a certain way of thinking. You will discover very quickly on your placement that it is different to studying. Many interns I talk to within a few days of starting their placement talk about how amazed or proud of themselves they are for getting into a routine, and some say how difficult this has been for them and sometimes how tiring it is. I recall myself when doing my teacher training how I needed to be on a bus at 6:00 every morning, didn't get back home until 6:00 in the evening and then had to start preparing lessons for the following day. Most work placements will not require you to work in the evening, and so hopefully you can get some rest at the end of your day, but certainly the daily routine of travelling can be tiring. Add to that the emotional effort you need to exert in the early days and weeks of a work placement, getting to know colleagues, understanding the way the workplace operates, not to mention starting to do the research you are expected to do, and you will quite naturally need to ensure you build in downtime, and look after yourself.

One of the best ways to deal with becoming a professional is to go into it with a positive frame of mind and a willingness to learn and reflect on your experiences. This will come as no surprise to you now, this having been a core theme throughout the book. In this section, on getting the most out of your supervisor, I propose *more than anything else* you adopt a positive and growth mindset. You need to accompany that approach with a willingness to develop a level of resilience too, as discussed in detail in Chapter 6.

Rich Karlgaard, in his book on *Late Bloomers* (2019), provides a compelling reason for why grit matters. For grit, read resilience, perseverance or just sheer determination. He cites the work of Angela Duckworth (2016) to show that the older you get, the more grit you are likely to display. Or, as he says 'our ability to persist, increases as we age' (2019: 214). Why? Duckworth suggests it's because life experiences teach us something we didn't know before. Well, isn't the purpose of us gaining new experiences to teach us something we didn't know previously? And opening ourselves up to these experiences requires some bravery on our part, which in turn requires us to become resilient. And consequently, the quicker you can develop this attribute, resilience, the faster you will learn and grow and become the professional you have it in you to be. And in doing this your confidence will develop, as Michelle Obama testifies in the quote used at the start of this chapter. Resilience and confidence therefore go hand in hand, and present two sides of the same coin. But to achieve success you need a growth mindset to even get started.

Using reflection to ask for feedback

How then can you use your work placement to get your academic or workplace supervisor to help you learn and develop? Not surprisingly I reiterate that this is where your reflective practice will help. As my students submit their beginning, middle and end reflective pieces I respond to them with thoughts and advice based on what they write to me. You may not have the advantage of having this when you do your own work placement, and so I propose that you ask your work supervisor to become that sounding board. You have nothing to lose. They can say no – in which case just take that on the chin, write your reflective pieces anyway and try to become your own coach or find someone else who will read and respond. Your supervisor might very well be willing to look at your reflections and make constructive comments. You might even be placed in an organisation that practises this (many do, and 360 degree feedback is standard in many companies). Be bold, ask for support and you will likely be given it.

Measure your progress

The PDP in Table 8.2 was intended to help you assess your professional skills at the start of your placement or internship. Just as in Chapter 7 though, this tool can be used to help you measure your progress as you progress through your work placement (and again why recording the date is so important). The next part of this section shows how you can capture your professional skills as you develop them.

Document as you go

Just as advised in the previous chapter, document as you go, and grow. No need to wait until the end of your placement to do this. By using the reflective framework introduced in Chapter 6 and drawing on feedback from your work placement or academic supervisor as discussed above, you can capture the new professional skills you learn, the challenges you faced, and how you developed during the placement. Evidence your learning. By documenting your professional skills acquisition as you progress through your work placement you will capture your growth moments, and be able to look back and recall how you developed in the role.

Update your professional skills on your CV

In Chapter 3 you were introduced to how to write a CV, ensuring it captures what you need it to for the position you are applying for. The aim there was to produce a CV that you can use to apply for an experiential learning position.

In this and the previous chapter you have been focusing on developing your skills and experience. You need to make sure that your CV is updated to reflect these newly acquired skills. As you will have gathered throughout this chapter, some of these skills are hard to document, and indeed some (like creativity) are better described as attributes, characteristics or ways of working, or in the context of an activity such as problem solving. Nonetheless, given all I have said about your CV being the first engagement you will possibly have with a potential host organisation, or future employer, you definitely need to think about capturing your new learning on your CV, using the professional skills covered in this chapter.

Try to capture everything you do under categories that map onto your CV. I suggest using the seven skills covered in this chapter, which cover the professional skills most often seen in job adverts. This may capture more than you have space on your CV for, but you can collapse them down under the relevant section on your CV. It is possible you have not been able to talk about these skills before in the context of a work setting, so also feel free to make this clear on your CV by subtitling these as 'Professional skills'. These will make your CV stand out, and remember also to ensure that you include the name of the organisation you interned at on your CV. I cannot emphasise enough how this will demarcate you from others, in a good way.

You might choose to refer back to your My Professional Skills Personal Development Plan (MPS PDP) developed in this section to ensure you have captured the finer detail of the personal skills development you hoped to improve on. It is not important to include the full detail on your CV, but Table 8.4 will help you to document it so you have an aide-memoire of how you acquired the skill and experience. This could provide interview preparation material (many of my ex-students have told me this helped them prepare for job applications) and it gives you a record of what you learned during a particular time in your personal development.

Table 8.4 Checklist of professional skills acquired through the workplace

Professional skills I have acquired	How I acquired this skill	Evidence of this skill
Communication		
Collaboration and teamwork		
Time management		
Creativity		
Persuasion		
Adaptability		
Networking		

Host organisations' reflections on professional skills development

This final section in Chapter 8 on how to use your placement to develop professional skills draws together some of the summary points from the perspectives of the host organisations who have taken students, including the case study students in this book.

This synthesis adds the employers' perspectives to complement those of the students that are already included throughout.

Taking the seven professional skills categories developed in this chapter here are some reflections on what organisations say they are looking for, and how experiential learning can help in developing these skills. Importantly, the feedback loop created through developing a reflective framework and a positive and growth mindset creates an ideal opportunity for host organisations to flourish through both giving, and in some cases receiving through their supervision, professional skills training. Keeping in touch with the host organisations helps me better understand how I can appreciate these professional skills in the workplace, and bring them to the attention of my students. Hopefully this benefits you as the reader of this book too.

Table 8.5 Examples of host organisations' comments on professional skills

Employer perspective

Professional skills	Comments from host organisations
Communication	• We expect good written and verbal skills. • We can help students develop their communication skills. • Students can write blogs, emails, industry reports, develop presentations and this really helps us and them. • Junior staff have the chance to develop their own communication skills through supervising students. • Having to explain to someone how we do what we do helped my own personal development. • It's refreshing to be challenged. • It's so important for us to be able to explain complex research more simply – having interns helps me do this.
Collaboration and teamwork	• Team working is a given in our business. Students need to learn this skill quickly to succeed. • The best interns are those who can work independently and in a team. • We expect students to collaborate and recognise this is a skill we can teach them. • No one works alone here – we all collaborate and take responsibility for our part in our shared outputs. • It is vital that there is an ongoing programme linking academia, government and charities – it's one of the ways the UK can remain competitive in the global economy.
Time management	• Time management is key, though this is not simply about being on time, but rather about developing a systematic approach to doing research. • This is such an important attribute. • We have a flexible approach to time management but high standards of work. Our interns learn this quickly.

(Continued)

Table 8.5 (Continued)

Professional skills	Comments from host organisations
Networking	• Sometimes our interns apply to us upon graduating and are recruited. Those who network across the organisation are using their internship wisely. • We try to stay in touch with our interns, it helps us and them and keeps us connected to new talent. • We're happy to give references and testimonials to good students. • I'm still in touch with an intern from five years ago. • We love being involved with the university and learning what they teach; we're happy to come to speak about our work too.

Whilst not all seven skills are included in Table 8.5 it is clear that the host organisations are positive about the experiential learning that they are able to support. Once again it is refreshing to see the benefits to these work placement providers, and the satisfaction that they take from developing early career social researchers.

Summary

I hope you have found this chapter helpful. It was a challenge to condense professional skills down to just seven, but these skills, based on high-profile industry reports, will give you the foundations for a professional skillset you can develop whilst on placement. By creating a baseline and monitoring your professional skills development throughout the work-placed experience you can start to see how your classroom learning has real-world relevance, and how by combining your professional skills development with your analytical and research skills development you are becoming a pre-early career professional. Remember the aim of this is to enable you to capture your new skills on your CV.

The case study examples used in this chapter evidence the professional skills the interns were all able to develop in their work placements, and subsequently. Between them the five case studies included demonstrated the entire range of seven professional skills that I introduced. I built on earlier work covering a positive and growth mindset and the need to develop resilience, showing that this is an approach that if developed early can be tremendously useful to you.

Finally, I introduced some quotes and findings from the host organisations' perspectives. These reveal how the professional skills covered in this chapter can be nurtured and encouraged through good supervision, and I urged you to proactively seek this.

Many self-help, personal development and coaching books focus on how if you want to have a different future you need to change what you do. They all essentially say that to grow, we need to learn, and to learn we need to push ourselves out of our comfort zone. Education, too, is about learning, and being open to growth. Using the tools introduced in this chapter I want yours to be a supported experience, and one that will set you on your way to your future career. Your ongoing professional development will take courage and persistence and I hope you can use this chapter to help you develop resilience and confidence. Chapter 9 will reflect the experiences of some former students who are now in the early stages of their careers.

Three things you can do next

1   Create your own My Professional Skills Personal Development Plan and fill it in. Think about where you are now (self-assess your professional skills) and how you would hope to use a work placement to advance your professional skills. Whilst doing this also check your CV is up to date.

2   Create a LinkedIn profile. Don't let having limited experience discourage you. Take a look at mine if it helps to get you started but ideally find someone who may be in their early career. Ensure you keep this updated as you go through your placement.

3   Take one of the following references from this chapter and find out more about an area you are interested in:

a   Duckworth, A. (2017) *Grit: Why Passion and Resilience Are the Secrets to Success*. Read 'Part II: Growing grit from the inside out', Chapter 7: 'Practice', pp. 141–72.

b   Payne, J. (2017) 'The changing meaning of skill: Still contested, still important', in Warhurst et al. (eds), *The Oxford Handbook of Skills and Training*, pp. 54–71.

c   Karlgaard, R. (2019) *Late Bloomers: The Power of Patience in a World Obsessed with Early Achievement*. Read Chapter 8: 'Slow to grow? Repot yourself in a better garden', pp. 189–203.

HOW TO USE THE WORK PLACEMENT TO FOCUS ON YOUR FUTURE

Learning objectives

In this chapter you will:

- Learn to think about what makes a fulfilling career
- Learn about skills, competencies and capabilities for social research careers
- Be given examples of applied social research careers that value experiential learning
- Evaluate examples of skills and attributes that are sought by employers
- Learn from early career professionals in social research careers what their roles entail
- Hear how work placements inform career choices and further study
- Consider how developing a growth mindset will help with your future career

'*Evolution in our careers is one of the most important things to learn and apply simultaneously as we earn. Without that, there is no door for growth.*'

Goitsemang Mvula (quoted by Edmondson, 2019)

Overview

The quote at the start of this chapter is from a woman who describes herself as a story-teller and problem solver, an entrepreneur and digital content creator. Her profile, and her quote, demonstrates just how versatile a person has to be in order to start a career in the twenty-first century. It also reflects many of the skills, attributes and experiences included in this book. Her quote sets the context for this chapter, which is on how you can use your workplace learning to think about your future career and further study.

This chapter brings together all the preceding ones by focusing both on potential careers you might consider, and on further study that might support you. Until now you have been given the building blocks, to enable you to put your classroom learning into practice. The ultimate goal of this book is to help you to use this new-found knowledge and experience to progress to a satisfying and rewarding role, and career. Career entry requirements differ, and whilst most of the examples included are based on having a first degree, some ask for a higher qualification. Note that whilst non-graduate careers are not included here, entry routes to some careers, for example in data science, are set to open up with apprenticeship schemes growing in numbers.

Building on what I have covered in previous chapters, this one will incorporate the wisdom of professionals, including some who are former interns, to help you navigate towards your career choice. By including industry examples you will start to see how your skills acquired through experiential learning can be used to build a stepping-stone to your future. Previous students' examples will show you how their studies, coupled with workplace experience, helped them get to where they are now, either in their careers or their continuing study. Finally, the reflective approach you have developed through reading this book will be used to help you understand how valuable this can be, and how looking back can help you to look forward.

This chapter completes the 'How to' chapters in the book. You can read it alone to get a sense of what types of careers you could apply for, or further study you might contemplate, before or after a work placement. Or read it alongside the other chapters, so that your learning builds in an incremental way and you can see the relevance of previous examples and advice. Either way I hope you find it helpful.

Three case studies are included in this chapter: Marcus, Sarah and Ella – the latter two being PhD students when they did their work placements. Five vignettes are also included from three organisations to provide examples of some typical early career social researcher roles and activities. The undergraduate disciplines of those in this chapter include sociology, psychology, international relations, politics, philosophy and economics.

What makes a fulfilling career?

This section was challenging but fun to write. My aim here is, rather than help you find a specific career, to use this chapter to help you do two things. First, I want you to think about a career in a broad way, and contemplate what makes work fulfilling, and to do this I will draw on the work of Krznaric (2012). Second, I aim to help you better understand how your analytical and professional skills can be combined, so that you can start to identify the sorts of roles you can apply for or consider undertaking. These, naturally, will vary according to your subject of study, as well as your interests. I hope this chapter will include a broad enough set of examples that at least one, and hopefully more than one, appeals to you. In keeping with the main theme of the book, I focus on applied social research careers.

In his book *How to Find Fulfilling Work* (2012) Krznaric presents some big questions to help the reader find a job that satisfies them. It's a really good read, and I highly recommend it. He draws on experiences of people he has interviewed to show the sheer variety of approaches and roles that are undertaken in pursuit of a meaningful career or work. The essence of his findings is that we all need to discover three things to be satisfied in our work – meaning, flow and freedom – and that we need not to fixate on a single role offering us the ideal career, but be prepared to identify our 'multiple selves' so that we can trial different careers and see which suits us best.

A word on flow, Krznaric explains this as a state that 'commonly occurs when we are using our skills to do a task that is challenging but not so hard that we fear failing. Flow is also enhanced when we are being creative and learning new skills' (2012: 88).

At the start of your career this is wise advice, and note that changing careers and making good decisions along the way is also a smart approach. In Chapter 8 we heard from Zvi who did this almost immediately upon graduating, relocating from a role he was not gaining satisfaction from to a more suitable one in a location and sector he wanted to be in. And I have shared with you my own work-placed experience in government which opened my eyes to new career paths for humanities and social science graduates.

Krznaric talks about experiential learning:

> We must enter a more playful and experimental way of being, where *we do then think*, not *think then do*. … successful change requires a substantial dose of experiential learning. Just like we can't learn carpentry from a book, we can't shift careers without taking practical action. First we should identify a range of 'possible selves' – careers that we believe might offer us purpose and meaning. Then … we have to trial them in reality by undertaking experimental projects.
>
> Krznaric (2012: 77–8)

He goes on to give three approaches to this practice, naming them radical sabbaticals, branching projects and conversational research. Branching projects are the closest to what has been covered in this book through work placements and internships, and although his work is focused on changing careers, and how to do this, the notion of a branching project aligns well with experiential learning.

> Branching projects ... are designed as short experiments pursued around the edge of our existing career, through which we test out our possible selves. We could do a training course that gives us a taste of a different career, or try out an initial scaled-down version of a prospective job.
>
> Krznaric (2012: 79)

One of the valuable sections he includes is called 'Imagining Your Many Lives'. In this he invites you to undertake three exercises to help you reflect on and think about what you consider to be meaningful and important to you for your career. The exercises are 'The Map of Choices', 'Imaginary Lives' and 'Personal Job Advertisement' (pp. 64–8).

Isn't this just exactly what I have been encouraging you to do throughout this book? I have included his work here as it aligns so well with my own thinking and sets up the rest of the chapter nicely. I want you to consider holistically what type of career you would want to be in, what gives you meaning, the types of activities you experience flow whilst doing, and how important freedom or autonomy is to you, before focusing in on the more prosaic issues I cover next. Jump to number 3 of Three Things You Can Do Next at the end of this chapter if you want to do this exercise before reading on.

Skills, competencies and capabilities

Visualising your future career choice is a great place to start but you also need to ensure you have the right skills and attributes to act on this. Much of this book has focused on developing your *skills*, in an applied social research setting. Skills were introduced in Chapter 2, to describe the benefits of experiential learning, featured large in Chapters 3 and 4, helping you create a baseline for your skills, and again in Chapters 7 and 8 to support you in monitoring your analytical and research and professional skills development. Chapter 3 introduced you to *competency-based frameworks*, which are often used by employers, and Chapter 4 extended this by providing examples to help you prepare for competency-based interviews. I have talked much less about *capabilities* as a way of measuring potential to achieve competency in skills development, and so will introduce them in this section.

This chapter is written largely from the perspective of employers and so it helps to know what they are looking for. It also captures the experiences of early career professionals, and so it helps you to know what they do in their day-to-day activities.

First let me present some recent research and findings to set the broader context. *The Oxford Handbook of Skills and Training* (Warhurst et al., 2017) provides a compendium of papers which I draw on here.

Skills

In the handbook's introduction to all the contributions, in a discussion about who pays for skills development the editors note:

> Individuals are finding themselves bearing more of the burden as employers and the state shift the costs and risks of skills development onto workers. ... it is occurring because more workers are finding themselves in labour markets with increasing numbers of highly skilled competitors, both domestically and internationally.
>
> Buchanan et al. (2017: 12)

And as we saw in Chapters 7 and 8 it is not always easy to separate out skills: they often overlap and are specific to the role.

> Employers often require a particular combination of specific and general skills, a combination which may be unique to their workplaces, rather than the two being mutually exclusive.
>
> Gambin and Hogarth (2017: 661)

In her chapter, Bryson (2017) introduces a multi-disciplinary perspective to the term 'skill', showing that depending on your background, your definition of skill can differ. She provides interpretations of skill acquisition and development, showing who gains and how, from various subject domains, including political economy, economics, sociology, industrial relations, organisation studies, and psychology and education. In concluding she notes that:

> ... each disciplinary perspective reveals and explores only part of the full picture of skill.
>
> Bryson (2017: 31)

Collectively these authors set the scene for the world of work that you will enter, and how skills feature in the minds of employers. The student case studies and vignettes featured throughout this book reflect different disciplinary perspectives. As you read through this chapter therefore, think about how the content applies to your own subject or discipline.

Competencies

Competency frameworks abound in careers and educational literature and appear in terms such as competency-based assessment (CBA), competency-based training (CBT) and competency-based interviews. The term is generally used during discussions of how to measure the acquisition and performance of work-based skills, employers seeking evidence that these have been achieved. Although competency frameworks have dominated the literature and discourse around employment for at least two decades, there is some movement away from this approach, as I will show. Nonetheless, it is a term you are likely to encounter as you look for work, and it is helpful for you to understand how you can evidence competencies if required to do so. Chapter 3 already showed you how to do this using the STAR (Situation, Task, Action, Result) method.

Here is an example. Prior to 2020 the UK government Civil Service used a competency-based framework for recruitment and promotion. They then moved to a framework which they call *Success Profiles*, which they define as follows:

What are Success Profiles?

The Civil Service recruits using Success Profiles. This means for each role we advertise, we consider what you will need to demonstrate in order to be successful. This gives us the best possible chance of finding the right person for the job, drives up performance and improves diversity and inclusivity.

https://assets.publishing.service.gov.uk/government/uploads/system/uploads/attachment_data/file/744219/Success-Profiles-Candidate-Overview.pdf

I include both frameworks here so that you can see each one and to illustrate that *things change*. Employers can and do adapt their practices.

The Civil Service is a top recruiter for social science graduates, and many pursue social research careers within government. Victoria, one of the interns featured in this book, is one such graduate, with a first and Master's degree in Criminology, who secured employment in government as a research analyst.

An example competencies framework

The UK government Civil Service used to (until the early 2020s) deploy a competency framework, which can be found online at www.gov.uk/government/publications/civil-service-competency-framework. This describes an outline of the skills and behaviours that were expected and required of civil servants. It links to a 46-page competency framework, which lists ten competencies in three groupings, called clusters. Not all roles required all competencies, and different jobs, at different levels, would require different sets of competencies. It's quite complicated, especially if you are new to understanding what is required of a public sector employee in government. Nevertheless, it provides an example of the competencies that exist across many government departments, from the lowest to the highest grades, and how these were previously described and assessed.

They moved away from this competency framework to one they term Success Profiles (see Figure 9.1), as noted above. The Success Profiles Candidate Overview document is a user-friendly guide that appears far more accessible than the competency framework documents. Information is available on the government webpages: www.gov.uk/government/publications/success-profiles. Figure 9.1 shows the elements covered by this framework.

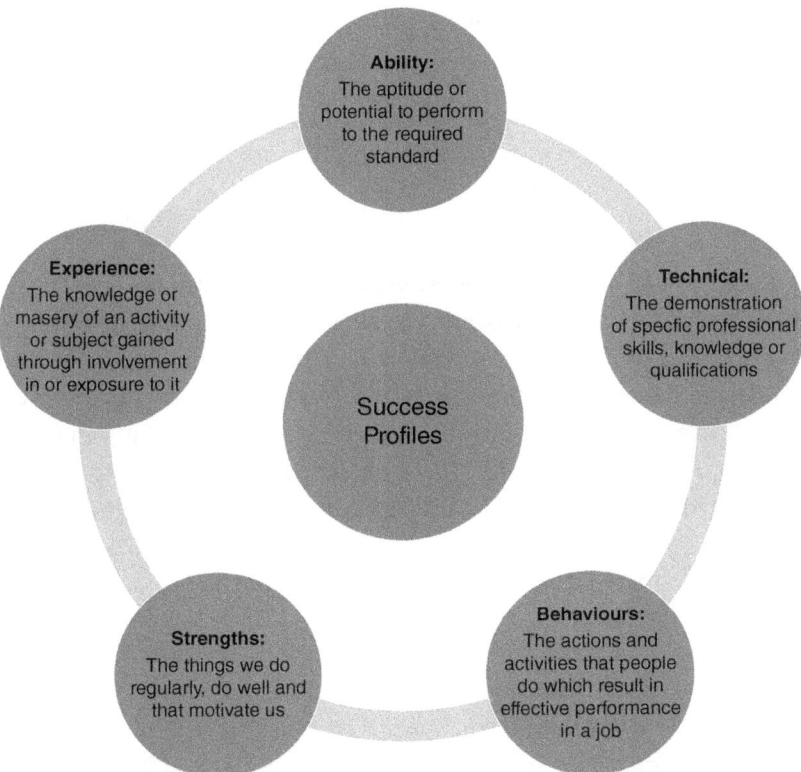

Figure 9.1   Success Profiles for UK government roles

Source: https://assets.publishing.service.gov.uk/government/uploads/system/uploads/attachment_data/file/717279/Success_Profiles_Overview_2018.pdf

The Candidate Overview (and each of the other documents related to it) provides a 'Success Profiles' graphic to indicate what the employer is seeking.

Each of the areas identified in the Success Profiles – experience, ability, technical, behaviours and strengths – combine to make up a collection of skills, attributes and behaviours that the organisation values. Your task in applying for a role with UK central government would be to work out how you can use your experiences to convince them you meet these requirements. To do this you would need to refer to the job description and the material relating to the specific role to work out how and whether you satisfy and can evidence skills required for the role. Chapters 7 and 8 in this book have shown you how to do this.

Capabilities

Although competency-based frameworks in the workplace still exist, some employers are moving towards developing ways of measuring and assessing capabilities as well as, or instead of, competencies. The UK government Success Profiles outlined above are an example. This more holistic view of recruitment is a welcome move. Wheelahan (2017) advocates for capabilities, in contrast to a competency-based framework, at least in terms of training, stating that:

> Education for the professions focuses on the development of the person in the context of their occupation and the knowledge, skills and attributes they need.
>
> Wheelahan (2017: 642)

Her work describes the tension between generic and specific training, and how the difficulties and challenges can be overcome by getting the mix right mix.

As this chapter aims to help you think about your future career aspirations, and how to apply your experiential learning to that, it is helpful for you to know about the different terminology used both in the academic literature on skills and training and in industry. It will help you identify the types of knowledge, skills and attributes that you have acquired, which in turn will help you understand the types of careers that would suit you.

Wheelahan goes on to say:

> The capabilities approach ... focuses on the development of the person and the knowledge, skills and attributes they need for a broad range of occupations. It is designed to support students to engage in occupational progression through a career, link occupational and educational progression, and help them to meet new and emerging needs. ... the capabilities approach starts with the person and not the specific skills. It asks about the capabilities that people need in order to achieve a range of outcomes, and about the social, economic and cultural conditions that are required to realize capability.
>
> Wheelahan (2017: 644)

Wheelahan's summary of a capabilities framework captures perfectly what this book has covered. Separating out one group of skills, or a range of methods, as you have done by following previous chapters, is an approach for helping you understand your strengths and development needs. But thinking about the bigger picture, in terms of a set of capabilities – or your own potential to achieve different outcomes – is where you need to reflect on your experiences to think about your future career. By thinking holistically, you will be able to better understand how you can start to focus in on a career, and see this as a starting, not an end, point. The skills and attributes need to go hand-in-hand with your interests and passions if you are to find a career that is right for and fulfils you, and reflecting is a key part of helping you do this.

Social research careers

Most of this chapter provides information about careers in social research. I will again use examples to illustrate what employers look for when appointing to these roles, and the first part of this section is dedicated to employers' perspectives, focusing on what they look for in their recruitment of social researchers. The second part then provides examples through a series of longer vignettes taken from interviewing early career social researchers from three organisations: NatCen, Ipsos MORI and The Future Society.

Employers' perspectives

What do those recruiting to roles in social research organisations look for? The website https://target.co.uk has a useful section on social research careers. I have adapted and added to it here, to reflect the types of organisations that employ social researchers. You might also like to refer back to Table 1.2 which listed a range of careers and organisations that employ social researchers. The list provided here is indicative and simply intended to help you think about your own future career and where you might find a position.

Typical employers of social researchers

- Local authorities and central government
- Universities
- Health authorities
- Non-governmental organisations (NGOs)
- Commercial market research organisations
- Statistical research organisations
- Independent research institutes
- Data consultancies
- Polling companies
- Data science companies
- Media organisations
- Charities and voluntary organisations

Social researchers design, manage and undertake research projects to investigate social issues such as employment, unemployment, gender, health, education and social policy. Graduates typically enter the profession at research officer level, progressing to senior research officer level after several years' relevant experience. Roles can focus on different aspects of social research, from collecting data to undertaking in-depth analysis, to presenting findings and insights drawn from the analysis.

What does a social researcher do?

Social researchers undertake research projects to investigate social issues and then report their findings. A social researcher will use a variety of research methods to gather their information: these can include questionnaires, focus groups and interviews, and secondary analysis of survey and other data sources. Their findings can be used to change social policies or to test the effectiveness of a current one.

Key responsibilities of the job

- Preparing tenders and project briefs for research contracts
- Receiving instructions and project briefs from clients
- Directing and undertaking pilot studies and fieldwork
- Collecting, analysing and interpreting qualitative and/or quantitative data, from primary and secondary sources
- Writing reports
- Identifying and advising on possible strategies and policies
- Managing budgets
- Managing staff

Qualifications and training sought

A good degree (usually). Employers often require or look for relevant qualifications in social research, business studies, marketing, maths or statistics. Social science degrees in politics, international relations, sociology, economics and philosophy are also welcomed. A postgraduate qualification and/or specialist subject knowledge may be required for some positions, especially more senior roles. Practical and applied research experience is advantageous.

Key skills for social researchers

- Analytical techniques
- Qualitative and/or quantitative research skills

- Numerical skills
- Communications skills, written and spoken
- Presentation skills
- Excellent organisational skills
- Attention to detail
- Ability to persuade, through evidence
- IT skills

Key attributes for social researchers

- Emotional intelligence
- Creativity
- Awareness of the environment (commercial or civic)
- Resilience
- Open-mindedness

It will not surprise you that most of the skills and attributes listed above appear throughout this book. Undertaking work-placed learning gives you an opportunity to acquire all of them, and following the guidance in the chapters (especially 7 and 8) will assist you to evidence them in applications for future roles. The next section provides a little more information on the types of roles social research organisations recruit to, and the skills and attributes they ask for.

Example careers from three organisations

In Chapter 1 I introduced a list of applied social research careers. It is timely to revisit them here. Most of the organisations and sectors listed there have appeared in our student and employer examples. Below, I introduce three organisations that recruit applied social researchers. For each of these organisations I include one or more examples of job adverts for social research positions, and follow this with a vignette, or several, of early career researchers. These vignettes, told in their own words, are collected from people who I asked to tell me about a typical day in their role, or the types of research they are involved in. A little longer than previous vignettes in this book, they are valuable as they give you the chance to find out what social researchers do. By reading on you can start to see what employers look for, and what early career researchers work on. This way you can start to consider how the work placement can help you acquire skills, attributes and behaviours that you can go on to evidence, and you can see whether these social researcher roles provide the types of work you would be motivated to apply for.

Example 9.1 NatCen

The first two examples of job adverts come from a national research centre in the UK called NatCen. The roles are for a Research Assistant, and a Researcher in the Policy Research Centre. Take a look and see the sorts of criteria they are asking for. And then have a look at the three 'day-in-the-life' vignettes from researchers to see the sorts of work they undertake in their roles.

NatCen is one of the most prestigious independent, non-profit social research organisations in Britain. It is an ideal example to include here as they appoint researchers to undertake qualitative and quantitative research, and therefore look for different skills and attributes when they advertise positions. NatCen was founded in 1969 and is perhaps best known for its annual British Social Attitudes Survey. Research undertaken by NatCen informs the government and charities to make decisions on social issues. Positions exist across a number of areas including survey methodologies, policy sector specialisms, data analysis and mixed methods research. NatCen also deliver training courses and have as their mission 'to boost the quality of research in the UK' (https://natcen.ac.uk).

What does a NatCen social researcher job advert look like? Here are two extracts from job adverts to show the skills and attributes they look for. Note the differences and the similarities. Essential and desirable skills for the two posts are summarised in Tables 9.1 and 9.2.

Role: Research Assistant

* Support the Surveys, Data and Analysis (SDA) teams to design and deliver high quality surveys that use a range of methodologies.
* Work across a range of policy areas and support data collection, analysis and reporting to customers and other stakeholders.
* Develop research skills and experience, through formal training and informal learning.

Table 9.1 Compulsory/desirable skills and attributes (Research Assistant)

Compulsory or Desirable	Skills and attributes
Compulsory	A degree in a relevant subject (minimum 2:1)
	Excellent numeracy and verbal communication skills
	The ability to analyse and synthesise complex information
	An aptitude for producing written materials that are clear and accessible to non-technical audiences
	The ability to apply new knowledge and skills effectively
	A flexible approach alongside excellent organisational skills
Desirable	Experience of carrying out, or contributing to, an applied social research project
	Experience of using statistical analysis software

Role: Researcher, Policy Research Centre

- Working collaboratively as part of a team to deliver high quality mixed method research and evaluations across a wide range of projects.
- Designing research, collecting data, analysis and reporting to clients and other stakeholders.
- Developing research skills and experience, through formal and informal learning.
- Building policy knowledge in one or more key areas of the team.

Table 9.2 Compulsory/desirable skills and attributes (Researcher)

Compulsory or Desirable	Skills and attributes
Compulsory	Undergraduate degree
	Experience of qualitative or quantitative research methods
	Evidence of excellent writing skills
	Skills in communication and team working
	Commitment to developing research skills
Desirable	Postgraduate experience in social research
	Experience of using software for statistical analysis

These two examples illustrate nicely the difference between a role as a research assistant and that of a policy researcher, across two different teams at NatCen. They ask for slightly different skills and attributes, both requiring a first degree and evidence of having undertaken social research. I include both here, as it is helpful for you to make the connection back to your work placement, or to think about these requirements in advance of doing a work placement to see how you can try to acquire the skills they ask for, and consider which type of role appeals to you more.

Three vignettes

Two social researchers and a senior social researcher provided the three vignettes here. It is interesting to see the types of tasks they are involved with through their roles.

Katie and Claire are research assistants, both in the health and biomedical team at NatCen but working on different surveys. Katie has a first degree in Psychology and a Master's in Health Psychology whilst Claire's first degree was in Sociology, and her Master's in Social Research Methods. I asked them both if they could describe a day-in-the-life of their roles. Sophie has been a senior social researcher with NatCen for two years, and prior to that was a junior social researcher for four years.

Vignette

Katie – Research Assistant

Since starting, I have developed new skills through the training workshops provided, as well as through guidance and mentoring from senior staff. I work closely with my team, liaise with other teams across the organisation, and with our university collaborators and external clients, including the NHS and Public Health England.

I predominantly work on the Health Survey for England (HSE), a large survey that has run for thirty years. My day-to-day work varies, depending on the stage HSE is at, and the project I am working on. I am involved with all stages for the HSE which means I help get the survey questionnaire together, test it in the Computer Assisted Personal Interview (CAPI) program, develop survey documents, brief interviewers and nurses, create response rates to give to our client, create SPSS tables from secondary data analysis and write sections of the report.

Aside from my HSE work I also work on other projects, usually more short term. These enable me to gain insight and skills into different topics and areas of research. For example, I have anonymised transcripts from qualitative interviews, for use within reports, worked on rapid evidence reviews, requiring me to screen abstracts and papers based on inclusion criteria, and extracted relevant data from selected papers to be included in a report.

I really like the work I am doing – it offers variety and some challenges that keep me on my toes and need me to think outside the box. I especially value that the work I am involved with is used to help deepen society's understanding of health behaviours, and positively impact people's lives.

Vignette

Claire – Research Assistant

I am usually working on several projects at any time – the main one being Natsal, the National Survey of Sexual Attitudes and Lifestyles, a national survey which runs once every ten years. I work on other projects, and undertake ad-hoc tasks, sometimes for other teams, so I get experience of working on multiple things. The tasks I do vary depending on the project and the stage it is at. For instance, I set up team meetings and liaise with the project team and with external collaborators.

For Natsal, I have worked on developing survey questions, adapting existing ones by seeing what has worked well on other studies. I have also done some cognitive interviews on new questions to check whether they are fit for purpose. I attend training, such as on questionnaire design and cognitive testing, which provides me with the skills needed to carry out these tasks. I also update participant-facing documents, such as advance letters and survey leaflets, and work with the designer to get these ready for fieldwork. Updating and checking documents is done using guidance of good practice. I help get the survey ready to go out for fieldwork, for example checking wording for errors or mistakes and working with the programmer to create and test a computerised questionnaire.

As well as working on a national survey, I have also written a report using secondary analysis of national survey data. This primarily involved running the tables using SPSS syntax and populating the report with the tables and analysis.

I am constantly learning new things. The work I do, and the work NatCen does, impacts on national programmes and can advise health policies. Working on research that makes a difference is exciting.

Vignette

Sophie – Senior Social Researcher

Social research might sound boring, or ill-defined, but it's incredible how interesting it can be. Here's one example. I mostly work on qualitative research methods here as part of the Questionnaire Development Testing Hub. There is a survey that asks people about their consumption habits of peel, like peel from fruit, not pears or apples but fruits like mangos, bananas and oranges. If these fruits are treated with chemicals then we need to know if people are consuming the peels. The survey response to this particular question made us wonder if people were answering it 'correctly' to give the information needed. We were able to use a follow up sample, getting back in touch with people who had answered this question originally, to explore this. We found that people's answers reflected that the question was not actually well-understood, and indeed needed to be redesigned.

My work involved contacting participants to see if they were eligible and willing to take part in a cognitive interview, rewording the survey questions, creating interview topic guides and briefing the interviewers on the project. Once the interviews had been completed I charted the interviewer notes and carried out analysis. A report was written up with the findings on how participants understood the questions and the types of things they were thinking about when answering. Recommendations were

(Continued)

made on the final question wording after a debriefing meeting was held to discuss the findings.

This is just one example. Another is developing a screening questionnaire of homeless people who gamble, for hostels to use. They may screen for other addictions but this is an area often overlooked and one that we can help investigate.

Finally – if I have some advice it would be to use your work placement and/ or your lecturers to reach out to organisations that you have contact with. Many will know people who run surveys or undertake research and it's a good idea to learn from their connections. As a sociology undergraduate I had no idea about the sorts of places that do social research, but one of my lecturers told me about NatCen. I now try to bridge the gap between NatCen and my university by giving talks to students there.

Between them these three researchers cover several large-scale, national surveys, and a host of tasks from pre-survey questionnaire checking through to analysis and presentation of results. You can see the diversity of their roles, and the different policy areas they are involved in, as well as the different methods they have a need to be acquainted with. As the Senior Researcher, Sophie describes the more advanced work she has done on improving survey questions, through better understanding how respondents had answered existing questions. Her description of the follow-up sample, using cognitive interviewing techniques, is enlightening, but note that Claire has also used cognitive interviewing techniques to test the suitability of new survey questions. Expertise in survey questions and design is clearly a much in-demand skill from NatCen, and many social science courses teach this. Finally, all three researchers are enthusiastic about the training they have been given on the job – reassuring you hopefully that you do not have to enter a career fully able to perform in the role. Indeed continuing to learn, as I have shown, is at the heart of a growth mindset, and captured in the quote at the start of this chapter.

Example 9.2 Ipsos MORI

Ipsos MORI is a UK-based market research company, formed in 2005. The company conducts surveys and market research for a wide range of clients. Their Social Research Institute undertakes research on attitudes to public services. The company is a member of the Market Research Society (MRS) and the British Polling Council and regarded as a prestigious company where many young researchers gain valuable experience of market research.

They have a different approach to NatCen in advertising their junior roles, and I include them here to show how their website will get you to think about how you can evidence your experience and skills should you wish to apply for a role with them, or with an organisation that takes a similar approach to theirs.

Here is an online advert for a Graduate Research Executive, one of the junior roles Ipsos MORI recruit for.

Role: Graduate Research Executive

We are seeking a Graduate Research Executive role within our Global Healthcare team, within our Therapy Monitor team. Each of our Therapy Monitor teams specialises in a particular medical condition and continuously conducts research with physicians in that area throughout the year. This position will focus on the Autoimmune disease area.

As a Graduate Research Executive, you will:

- Be encouraged to take responsibility from the outset – thrown straight into working on live projects
- Get fascinating insights into diseases, treatments and how the healthcare industry really works
- Analyse large data sets to draw out key stories and recommendations for our pharmaceutical clients within the Automimmune disease area
- Have the opportunity to work with different members of your team who, together with a strong in-team support network (your Line Manager, Grad Rep and Buddy), will help guide your learning and development

About you:

- A natural curiosity about the world we live in and an intrigue for human behaviour
- A passion for inspiring better healthcare (a science/medical/healthcare background is not essential)

Along with:

- The ability to work creatively and think commercially
- Exceptional attention to detail and a meticulous approach to analysing data
- Strong interpersonal skills – the ability to communicate clearly and persuasively

In contrast to the NatCen adverts, this one is more open ended. The application process requires you to complete a web form to say how you have the skills and motivation to apply. The following questions require you to respond in *up to 250 words each*.

- What has attracted you to a career in Research? Why do you think you would be well suited for this career path?
- What makes you want to work for Ipsos MORI? What makes you passionate about the Healthcare team's area of research?
- What challenges and opportunities will there be for this team's area of research in the next two years?

These are great questions. Note how they are not, like NatCen, directed so much at specific technical and professional skills, but are rather looking for applications from people passionate about social research, in the context of healthcare (autoimmune disease). This also sends a strong message about the type of person they are looking for, and gives you an indication of whether this is a role that you would be interested in. With that in mind it would be important to show your commitment to this area of work if you decide to apply. For instance, you might have studied inequalities in healthcare, be interested in the politics or sociology or economics of health provision, or be passionate about virus and contagion (e.g. coronavirus outbreak) and this position could then very well appeal to you. This is a very straightforward application process, but yours will need to stand out; so if you have undertaken a placement make this abundantly clear in your responses. I spoke to the talent partner for early careers at Ipsos and was very pleased to see that they deploy a blind recruitment practice, to eliminate bias from the start.

Note that unlike the NatCen advert, this one does not specify compulsory and desirable criteria; rather it describes more broadly the type of person they are seeking, and places emphasis on curiosity, attention to detail and interpersonal skills. This illustrates what Wheelahan (2017) talked about, in that roles are often looking for a mix of skills matched with the ability to traverse these areas. This job advert encourages applications from those who can bring an innovative perspective, and apply their passion for research to healthcare without demanding expertise in that area.

Vignette

Madalina – Research Executive

Madalina completed a BA in Sociology with Applied Quantitative Methods, then an MSc in Survey Methods for Social Research. She then secured a role at Ipsos MORI as a research executive.

Madalina told me that in her three years at Ipsos MORI she has had multiple opportunities to develop her career. She undertook training for the Market Research Society (MRS) qualification, and for conducting qualitative research and analysis, report writing and ethics. She has attended research methods conferences and seminars, and presented a paper at the European Social Research Association (ESRA), on behalf of Ipsos MORI, in 2019.

I am a research executive in the Probability Survey Unit (PSU), in the Social Research Institute. My role on each project varies, usually being determined by the methodology used, and the size of the study and the research team.

I previously worked on a mixed-mode longitudinal study known as the Millennium Cohort Study (MCS). I was primarily responsible for updating the sample pre- and throughout fieldwork, managing respondent communications, and materials (liaising with the client and suppliers). I was also involved in script testing, interviewer briefings, fieldwork monitoring, client progress updates, and reporting.

I am the main research executive on two surveys. First, the Childcare and Out of School Activities for Children Survey, a face-to-face survey for the Department for Education. For this survey I set up and go through the agenda for the weekly team and field meetings, update materials and liaise with the print and dispatch teams, do script testing and liaise with the scripting team, carry out raw data quality checks, and also do interviewer level data checks using SPSS syntax, and flag any outliers, monitor respondent communications, and more generally fieldwork. Second, for the NHS Maternity Pilot Survey, carried out on behalf of the Care Quality Commission, which is testing the feasibility of a push-to-web methodology on the NHS Maternity Survey, which has traditionally been paper only. On this survey I have been involved in the materials development and testing, liaised with the trusts for sample and survey documentation, sent regular update correspondence to the trusts, and liaised internally with the scripting and data progressing teams.

I have been the lead researcher on three experiments with panel members: an incentive experiment, a telephone reminder survey and an SMS reminder experiment (both aimed at preventing panel attrition). Last but not least, on an ad-hoc basis, I have worked on smaller projects from carrying out telephone and face-to-face interviews on a wide range of topics, to conducting the analysis (whether qualitative or quantitative data), and writing up the report.

As with the examples from NatCen, Madalina has worked across a number of surveys and studies, undertaking multiple tasks from organising team meetings to liaising with data processing teams. She too has worked on projects requiring qualitative and quantitative skills, and her organisation fully supported her in providing training to enable her to undertake her role. Madalina had undertaken an internship previously in her university's careers service, which helped her develop whilst still an undergraduate. Her Master's degree in Survey Research then helped her in being recruited for and undertaking the role at Ipsos MORI. Madalina's is a good vignette to show the range of analytical and professional skills that she must deploy on a daily basis. She is currently hoping to apply her skills to a role focused more on data analysis, which she has found she really enjoys.

Example 9.3 The Future Society

This example is somewhat different to the other two. I include it to highlight how more companies and organisations are recruiting researchers from the social sciences for data science roles. The Future Society provides an example of this.

According to their website (http://thefuturesociety.org), The Future Society is an independent non-profit think-and-do-tank that advances the global governance of Artificial Intelligence (AI) and other emerging technologies. They help society govern AI, seizing opportunities while mitigating risks.

The job ad for this role was long, four sections with 25 bullet points in total. I include verbatim those which are relevant but have collapsed some of the bullet points where the information requested was optional. I maintain it is important for this section so you can appreciate the variety in social researcher roles as well as how they are advertised.

What is interesting about this role is the emphasis on what you will get from the role. It is clearly aimed at someone who wants to work in the exciting area of policy research for emerging technologies. As many social scientists will have undertaken courses that directly relate to policy development and implementation, and ethics of research (if not new technologies), this provides an example of a new type of role that is evolving in data science. The desirables (what they call bonus skills and traits) are chiefly in the technical areas; so what this role is seeking is a person who ideally has those skills, but perhaps more realistically someone who is willing to acquire them.

Role: AI Policy Researcher

The role will involve AI policy research and may also include helping to organize major global AI policy conferences and events.

Our research addresses a range of AI policy and governance topics, including AI for UN Sustainable Development Goals (SDGs), policy & governance for ethics (e.g. fairness, transparency, inclusion) and safety risks (including long-term and existential risks), AI in the law, policy frameworks for AI adoption in developing countries, mapping national AI strategies, global governance of AI, geopolitics of AI, and more. We work with international organizations, development banks, national governments, companies, and more. Our partners include The World Bank, UNESCO, OECD, EY, Microsoft, the Future of Life Institute, leading academic institutions (e.g. Sciences Po Paris, Harvard Kennedy School), and many more.

1.   *Tasks*

    •   AI policy research, analysis and writing reports (drafting, editing)

- Event organization and participation (e.g. AI in the Rule of Law Roundtable, Global Governance of AI Roundtable, OECD AI Policy Observatory, AI for Good)
- Network outreach and community management
- Project proposal drafting
- Internal operations and/or fundraising

2. *Required skills & traits*

- Masters or PhD in social sciences (e.g. public policy, political science, international affairs, economics, law) or a related field
- 2+ years of professional experience in government, think-tanks, business, consulting, law or academia (or PhD)
- Experience in policy analysis and writing
- Passion and knowledge of AI policy and governance topics
- Excellent research, analysis and writing skills
- Mastery of written English
- Ability to work independently
- Detail-oriented, organized, conscientious, diligent

3. *Bonus skills & traits (not required)*

- Five bullet points which refer to expertise in Machine Learning and AI
- Diverse international background and experiences
- Great team spirit

4. *What you can get from this role*

- An ability to directly shape AI policy, ethics and governance with high-level global stakeholders
- Interacting with a high-level global network of experts in AI and leaders in AI policy, including with international organizations such as the World Bank and UNESCO
- Skills in research, analysis, writing, project management, public speaking
- An ability to work with geographic flexibility
- Professional development, networking, and recruitment opportunities
- Experience working in a dynamic, diverse, growing and international think-tank that participates in leading AI policy events around the world

The application process for this role is through completion of a Google form. If selected through this you will be required to undertake three interviews. The form requires you to enter personal details and upload a CV, then fill in the sections as shown in Table 9.3.

Table 9.3 Application form example

Education	Outline and tell us about your education. Max. 1000 characters. Bullet points are preferred
Research and work experience	Outline and tell us about your research and work experience. Max. 1000 characters. Bullet points are preferred
Skills	Outline and tell us about your skills. Max. 1000 characters. Bullet points are preferred
Why are you interested in this role?	Max 1000 characters
Exercise	The European Commission has recently published its white paper titled 'Artificial Intelligence: A European approach to excellence and trust' (https://ec.europa.eu/info/sites/info/files/commission-white-paper-artificial-intelligence-feb2020_en.pdf). This white paper includes policies and strategies to help the EU harness the benefits of AI while mitigating its risks. The white paper is currently open for public consultation and feedback. In 4000 characters or less, please prepare feedback to the European commission on this white paper. You can include critical analysis of their proposals, additional policy and governance suggestions where missing, suggestions to support policy implementation or AI development in EU Member States, or other.
Writing sample	Please upload a writing sample for your application. This can be a published or unpublished piece, so long as you think it best demonstrates your abilities for the role. Your file must be <10 MB.
Other comments (optional)	If you have any comments, feel free to share them with us here. Max. 500 characters.

This is somewhat different to the recruitment processes discussed for NatCen and Ipsos MORI, and is aimed at a higher-qualified candidate (requiring two years' experience and a Master's or PhD). However, many of the skills remain similar, such as attention to detail, report writing and excellent communication skills, and research and networking skills. The big difference is the area of research, AI.

Adriana, who provides the vignette in this section, brought The Future Society and this role to my attention (we connected on LinkedIn). First a little about her background. Adriana undertook a Bachelor's degree in International Relations and Quantitative Methods. She became substantively interested in modern slavery and in her final year undertook an ambitious dissertation on how transparency in supply chains can accelerate the eradication of modern slavery. Data were scarce, although some existed for just four countries through the Global Slavery Index (GSI) and her challenge was to build a model, based on these data, that could simulate results for others countries to learn from, with a view to their adopting similar legislation. The university vice-president praised Adriana's research during her cohort's graduation as an example of piloting innovative research to solve global problems.

She went on to study for a Master's, extending her passion for finding solutions to the complex issues contributing to modern slavery. More data and reports were being made available, and Adriana, although not trained in analysis of unstructured data, found an opportunity to study Machine Learning (ML) to 'unlock the contents of those reports'. She had to train herself in ML and coding. Here is what she said, to illustrate how tenacious she was in pushing herself outside of her comfort zone:

Vignette

Adriana – AI Policy Researcher

As I was not fully satisfied with my undergraduate level of understanding of the question in my dissertation, during my Master's I undertook further training on research methods and continued investigating the developments of modern slavery research. By that time, as a response to the Modern Slavery Act, UK companies started to publish thousands of documents presenting their supply chains and the steps they are taking to assure that slavery is not taking place. I asked my school, SciencesPo, to allow me to write a thesis and waive my requirement of an internship during my 3rd semester of my Master's. My thesis was called: 'Using Augmented Intelligence in Accelerating the Eradication of Modern Slavery. Applied Machine Learning in Analysing and Benchmarking the Modern Slavery Businesses' Reports'. During this period, I also went to Australia to volunteer for the Minderoo Foundation and there I got the chance to challenge my preliminary results with modern slavery researchers. They encouraged me to try to develop something more sophisticated, a state-of-the-art tool that researchers could use to advance current methods in understanding modern slavery. I did just that and built a prototype, which allows me to benchmark all available reports. My thesis was very well received and after sharing it with the Foundation, they offered to explore further collaboration for the development of this prototype into a more advanced tool. If this moves forwards I will soon be able to build my team and manage this research.

Speaking about this work and my quantitative journey at a conference we organised in September 2019, a researcher from the Deep Tech Dispute Resolution Lab of the University of Oxford, proposed that I apply and join them assisting doing the data analysis for collaborative research projects.

The support from my undergraduate degree, coupled with that from my teachers and amazing leaders I have met, have made this possible.

Adriana's vignette illustrates how interesting social science roles exist at the intersection of data science and social research. Her substantive interest in modern slavery, which she developed at undergraduate level, motivated her to learn new skills after graduating, and she has taken these Machine Learning and programming skills into her graduate career. I'm so pleased to include this example as it shows firstly how social science graduates can apply their subject knowledge and expertise to global complex social issues and secondly how they can also learn technical skills to develop solutions to these problems. It's not just science graduates who can enter data science careers, you can too. All of that said, Adriana applied herself diligently and strategically to pursue her interests, and as she says in the final section, used the opportunities available to her through her support networks.

What can you learn from this?

The above examples and social researcher vignettes are included to help you gain an improved understanding of what a career in applied social research might look like, from the perspective of the organisations that recruit social researchers and the early career professionals who work there. The NatCen and Ipsos MORI examples are quite similar; although there is a difference in approach regarding recruitment practices, the roles described by the researchers were not terribly different, and all used existing surveys or studies to undertake their research. The Future Society example, on the other hand, is markedly different, and Adriana's vignette talks about the scarcity of data to undertake international research on modern slavery, and how she had to learn new methods and techniques to analyse unstructured forms of data as various reports became available. Next I will draw out the common threads across the roles that you can use when you are thinking about the types of roles you might apply for whilst you are undertaking your study or placement. You can use these common threads alongside the tools in Chapters 7 and 8 to help you chart your skills development.

Skills and attributes required for early career social research roles

The case studies, job roles and vignettes included in this chapter describe various analyst roles. This is deliberate, as the focus of this book is on doing *applied social research*. It is also helpful to frame your thinking about a future career choice. That said, these examples are included to help you understand how a work placement can help you think through your career options. It would need a whole other book to do justice to the complete spectrum of career pathways available to social science and humanities graduates, or science graduates interested in careers in social research. In the UK some publications collate information about social science careers: for example *Positive Prospects* (CfSS 2018) illustrates the careers undertaken by social scientists with number and data skills, and *The Right Skills: Celebrating the Skills in the Arts, Humanities and Social Sciences* concludes that 'HSS graduates are well placed both to shape the future and to take advantage of the opportunities the future will present' (British Academy, 2017: 12).

For now though, let this section be illustrative of how you can take the learning from your workplace and use it to help you make an informed decision about your next step. And be reminded that your next step is only that; it does not define the rest of your life.

Table 9.4 Checklist of skills and attributes required for early career social research roles

Type of skill	Skill	Skills and attributes for a social researcher role
Research and analytical	A1–A6	Numerical and verbal communication skills
	R2, R5, A2, A3	Ability to analyse and synthesise complex information
	A5, A6	Clear writing, accessible to non-technical audiences
	A1–A6	Experience of applied social research
	A1, A2	Experience of using statistical software
	A2	Experience of qualitative and/or quantitative research methods
	R5, A3	Attention to detail
Professional skills	PS6	Flexible approach
	PS3	Excellent organisational skills
	PS1, PS2	Team working and communication
		Curiosity
		A passion for inspiring change for a better world
	PS4	Ability to work creatively
		Ability to think commercially
	PS1, PS5	Strong interpersonal skills and the ability to communicate persuasively
	PS7	Professional development, networking, and recruitment opportunities

Skills R1–R5 and A1–A6 appear in Chapter 7 (Table 7.2)

Skills PS–PS7 appear in Chapter 8 (top seven professional skills)

Table 9.4 – which is a consolidated list of many of the skills included in the job adverts in this chapter – confirms that all the skills introduced and developed in this book have relevance in social research careers. The analytical and research skills A1–A6 and R1–R5 and professional skills PS1–PS7 are all transferable. These skills can be used in a wide range of jobs, not just in social research, and everything that has been covered in this book can be applied to other careers and roles too. Note that some rows do not have a skill or attribute assigned. Curiosity, passion for inspiring change, and ability to think commercially are skills and attributes that you can make evident on your applications, and now that you have seen them here (extracted from the job adverts) you could add them to your list of skills and attributes to acquire in the workplace.

Experiential learning and reflection

Earlier chapters have stressed the importance and usefulness of a reflective approach, and I have introduced personal development plan (PDP) frameworks and checklists to support you in creating a baseline and documenting your analytical and research and professional skills learning. Looking back over your reflections can assist you in understanding your preferences. It can enable you to be self-aware, and challenge your own beliefs about your strengths as well as hold a mirror up to your own development needs. This is also helpful when considering your future career path, which may require further study. Understanding yourself is important if you are going to make wise decisions about finding a fulfilling career.

In Beverly Barker's paper on employability skills in a marketing education, she notes that:

> ... experiential learning combined with reflective techniques is a positive way to bring out required business skills and professional competencies.

> Barker (2014: 17)

Pool and Sewell (2007) highlight the importance of reflection, evaluation and work experience to help students become more self-aware of their career interests and research the job market:

> Personal development planning (PDP) is a highly appropriate vehicle for reflection and evaluation ... [it] can help students to
>
> • plan, record and reflect upon their experiences in a way that develops their employment related skills and self-awareness;
> • understand how their transferable skills might be applied in new settings;
> • make realistic and suitable career plans based upon their heightened self-knowledge;
> • demonstrate both their employment potential and their ability to manage their future professional development to employers.

> Pool and Sewell (2007: 285)

I hope you can see how, by following the advice in this book, you can start to take charge of your own future and career choices.

To illustrate the value of reflection carried out during a period of experiential learning I provide an example from Marcus. Marcus provided case studies in Chapters 2 and 8. First he spoke about the value of doing an internship in helping him to acquire skills, and confidence and office know-how, then to illustrate his creative approach to a fairly open-ended research task he was given.

Case study 9.1

Marcus: How my placement helped me decide what next

Here is what Marcus reflected on at the end of his internship:

> One of the things that angered me most was researching inequalities across the country in Early Years education. Early Learning Goals are a benchmark used to assess children coming into school in the Early Years Foundation Stage (between 24 to 36 months) and the end of their reception year in primary school. They are assessed against a variety of key goals. They are then judged satisfactory or not. In the North, 50% of children lie on or below the level of the poorest decile in London. These regional inequalities are colossal and worsening.

And here is what he said when I asked him how his internship had informed his continuing study (on returning from the work placement) and future career choice.

> I based my 3rd-year dissertation on a key fact that I had uncovered in my placement – that less than half of deprived children in the North of England had reached a good stage of early years development and this was lagging behind London and the South East. This had consequences for a child's whole life ahead. I wanted to reflect on this and … I focused on assessing equality of opportunity in education policy. Because I had enjoyed in my placement applying things that I had studied in practice, I applied the same assessment framework to a famous early years programme: Sure Start. Overall, it felt quite like a think tank project doing my dissertation!
>
> The key thing is I realised [after graduating] was I wanted to carry on doing what I did during my placement! I wanted to work in a progressive think tank. I enjoyed my placement and … felt that I was actually quite good at applying the assessment framework. I knew that I wanted to do research that had an impact on policy – and now had something in my bank of experience to show that I could do that when applying for jobs.
>
> After university, I had a job as an Economic Consultant in the private sector, doing economic research and writing reports for two and a half years. This

(Continued)